The Art of
Giving and Receiving
Criticism

2801 3

The *Art* of
Giving and Receiving
Criticism

DR. JOHN L. LUND

The Communication Company
Salt Lake City, Utah

Dedication

To my Native American Grandmother, Emma Simmons Lund, a woman who loved much and criticized no one.

To my Gamy, Lela Avis Pollan Schroeder, my Grandmother whose prayers brought Divine Intervention and of whom it may be said, "She was an angel who walked among us unaware."

Acknowledgments

Ruby and Louis Fife of Seattle, Washington. Thank you, Ruby, for typing the original manuscript. Thank you, Louis, for setting an example of a great teacher and a good friend.

Bonnie, my wife. She sacrificed sleepless nights to help meet impossible deadlines. Her capacity to work is only exceeded by her love.

Pam Jannard. It was Pam's financial support which made this book possible. More than the monetary commitment, I acknowledge Pam's faith and trust in me. It is easier to believe in yourself when others believe in you. Thanks, Pam.

For friends like Mike Zundel and Bob and Sharon Carlin, I will be ever grateful.

The Lord raised up Elen McConnell, an editing angel, who appeared and worked her magic in the moment of need. Thanks, Elen.

For the entire team at the Church's Copyrights and Permissions Office. Thank you. The information staff were especially helpful.

In a humble and sincere way, I am grateful to the Lord. This, however, is not an official Church publication. The views herein expressed are my responsibility. I alone bear the burden of what has been written. Every effort has been made to modify the names, places, and circumstances to avoid identifying the true characters of these real life stories. The exceptions are my Native American Grandmother and my friend, Sekeli Sale Manu.

CONTENTS

Chapter   Page

CHAPTER ONE

THE BEGINNING

Judge not unrighteously, that ye be not judged; but judge righteous judgment. (Matthew 7:2 JST.)

There is a beautiful hymn by Eliza R. Snow entitled, "Truth Reflects Upon Our Senses." In the second verse are the words, "Jesus said, 'Be meek and lowly,' For 'tis high to be a judge." Her poem was based upon Matthew 7:1-5. These words were spoken to the disciples. In the Church of Jesus Christ, there are only two job descriptions. One is to "Love and Judge," the other is to "Love." Judgment keys are strictly regulated. Jesus is the "Judge of [the] quick and [of the] dead." (Acts 10:42, brackets mine.) John testified that Heavenly Father judges no man but has "committed all judgment unto the Son (John 5:22)." Those judgment keys belong to anyone who can excommunicate a member of the Church. This means the keys are given to General Authorities, Stake Presidents, and Bishops. The Bishop is referred to as a "judge in Israel." These are they who are called to "Love **AND** Judge." All other members of the Church are called upon to "Love." They are not called upon to pluck the mote from another's eye, but to give loving service.

CALLED TO LOVE, NOT CALLED TO JUDGE

One of the great regrets of my life is not being able to go back and love my "Native American" Grandmother. She was a perfect example of one who loved and never criticized. She ignored racial slurs. She simply didn't allow people to offend her. Her name was Emma. She was born on the Chehalis Indian Reservation and spoke English with a broken accent.

I was eleven months old when Pearl Harbor was attacked on December 7, 1941. With many others, my father joined the Navy to redress the wrong of the "day that will live in infamy." My mother joined the work force as many women did, to support the troops and to run the factories. She became a telephone operator all during the war. Many days she would work twelve hours.

As an only child I was cared for by my Indian grandmother. It was this wonderful woman who changed my diapers, washed me, fed me, and sang Indian lullabies to me when I cried. It was her golden brown and oval face I would see all day long until my mother came home. She called me "Jon-né." With myself, my father, and my grandfather named John, each was given a slightly different version of the name. I was "Jon-né" to her, the rest of the family called me "Lou." She would say, "O Jon-né, it good to see [you]" Her words were choppy, her love was not. She was always glad to see her grandson. I was her first.

The war finally came to a close. Hitler was dead and the Japanese signed an unconditional surrender on board the USS Missouri, the "Mighty Mo." All during those war years I remember my mother and grandmother saying, "When the war is over, your father will come home." I was six when I remember seeing my father for the first time. He was dressed in his Navy Blues with bell bottom trousers and a collar with three white lines that went over his shoulders. He was wearing a white cap and spit-polished black shoes. Because there was a shortage of houses for all the returning servicemen, my father, mother, and I lived in my Indian grandmother's house. It took my father a year to remodel our future home before I left my Grandma Em's place in Tumwater, Washington.

Something else happened. I became aware that everyone didn't have an Indian Grandma. I became judgmental and unloving. People made fun of the way she talked. My schoolmates would mock me and call me "Tonto." To top it off my grandmother had divorced my grandfather and drank "firewater." (I told my children in later years that to be kissed by Grandma was an "intoxicating experience.")

My Indian Grandmother really was a wonderful person. My mother said she never heard her speak ill nor criticize anyone, not ever. Frequently my father would say, "Your grandmother misses you, son, she asks for you all the time. Let's go over and see her." But, I was embarrassed by her. I judged her unworthy of my love. The five mile trips became fewer and fewer between our place in Lacey and Grandma's in Tumwater. I stayed away. I was always "too busy" with my friends. I made excuses and finally Dad stopped asking.

*When I was nineteen, I was called on a mission to Mexico. I remember my father saying something about Grandma Em's heart. Under duress, I went to see this loving and caring woman. When she saw me her whole countenance changed. "O, Jon-né, come, give hug." After a forever hug and an "intoxicating kiss," we sat and talked about my life. "Before [you] go, I give [you a] blessing." She took hold of both my hands and looked deep into my soul. Then she said ten things which I should have written down, but didn't. I remember they all started with "May [you] always. . ." They had to do with the wind, the fire, the water and the earth. I only recall the first one: **"May [you] always walk with love in [your] heart."***

I left for my mission and received word she had died of a heart attack a couple of weeks after I was in Mexico. After the mission, I returned home, went to college, married, and became interested in doing research in family history. I wasn't sure if grandpa, who was a full blooded Swede, wanted to be sealed to her or not. I determined they could work it out with God. My wife, Bonnie, acted as proxy for my Grandmother and I for my "name sake" grandfather. What followed was a sacred experience wherein I knew they had accepted this work. I was dumbfounded. How could it be? She drank, she had a child out of wedlock, her life was not exemplary. A scripture came to my mind. It was Mosiah 3:11, "And also his blood atoneth for the sins of those who have fallen by the transgression of Adam, who have died not knowing the will of God concerning them, or who have ignorantly sinned." I wept that I had been so judgmental of a Grandmother who always loved her Jon-né.

By this time, my father had died in an auto accident and Grandma Em was survived only by her younger sister, Aunt Mildred. Everyone called her Millie. I traveled half way across the State of Washington to talk to Millie. She was old and very wrinkled. Her eyes were bad. When she saw me she thought I was my father who was called "Johnnie Jump Up" after a local flower. When I explained who I was she said, "O Jon-né!" It was as if I heard the voice of my Grandmother again. We talked for hours. Finally, I took both of her hands in mine, just like my grandmother did with me when I was nineteen. I said, "Millie, you have to tell the truth about my Grandmother." She paused a long time and finally told me the whole story.

My Indian Grandmother had been violated on the reservation when she was fourteen years old. It was a traumatic experience in itself. However, the consequences were overwhelming to a child-woman. She was rejected by both her people on the Reservation and those who lived outside. She was very young, pregnant, rejected, and alone. She kept the baby. She started to drink and never fully recovered.

I could hardly see through my tears as I drove to the cemetery. At her grave I knelt and asked her to forgive me for having been so critical and judgmental of her. "For 'tis high to be a judge." This wonderful Indian Grandmother's only crime was loving a judgmental grandson. I have prayed many times for God to forgive me for the greater sin. She was guilty of drinking alcohol; I was guilty of denying her an association with a grandson who should have been loving and appreciative. I also denied myself the association with a loving, nonjudgmental Indian Grandmother. Her every deed and act was loving. The words of her Indian Blessing haunt me to this day, "May [you] always walk with love in [your] heart."

If I could go back, I would stop by her house once a week and give her a big hug and a kiss. I would ask her if I could run an errand for her or take her somewhere. If her lawn needed to be mowed, I would just do it. But, I can't. I can't go back even though I stand on the same quiet earth. I'm confident she and the Lord have forgiven me. It is still difficult to forgive myself for being judgmental, critical, and non-loving. As a grandson I was never called to judge. I was called to love and I failed.

This experience has engraved itself upon my heart. I have tried to value all my relationships with family and friends and leave judgment with Jesus and with those who are called to "love and judge." As for me, I am simply called "to love."

CHAPTER TWO

"THE GREATEST REVELATION
THAT GOD HAS EVER GIVEN TO MAN"

Once a person masters the **ART of giving and receiving criticism in the Lord's own way,** he or she becomes endowed with a new power. It is the power to love, to nurture, and to inspire. Imagine children, friends, and loved ones feeling confident in one's love. They come seeking counsel because there is trust. They truly believe their eternal best interest is vouchsafed in the one who has mastered the ART of giving and receiving criticism. They receive counsel and follow it. They feel inspired, grateful and appreciative. This is not a "pipe dream." It is the reality of those who learn self-mastery over the tongue.

This power to love, to nurture, and inspire must be experienced in order to be fully appreciated. Otherwise it is like trying to describe the taste of salt to someone who has never tasted it.

"Does it taste bitter?"

"No."

"Does it taste sweet?"

"No, it tastes salty."

How does anyone describe the exhilaration one feels when a life long goal is achieved, or the beauty of a sunset at sea, or the miracle of childbirth to one who has never experienced it? The view from the top of the mountain is made sweeter by the difficulty of the climb. It is not easy to climb the mountain nor to control the tongue.

Mastering the ART of giving and receiving criticism is learning to be in control of the words one speaks. Controlling the tongue may be the single greatest step towards self-mastery and discipleship to Christ. The rewards include a greater love for all and love will be returned. It will come without compulsory means.

Giving criticism is not about finding fault. It is about loving. The focus is not on controlling a behavior. It is about changing the heart. The fundamental desire of the messenger of reproof is to guide the precious soul of a kindred spirit back to God. When Jesus said, "I Am the Way," (John 14:6) He was speaking about more than a road. He

5

was teaching His disciples the manner in which they were to journey to their Eternal Home. The way had more to do with motive than it did with magnificent scenery. The vision was not about surviving the mortal experience, it was about preparing for an immortal one.

There is a God. He has a Plan. There is a purpose to this existence. Birth and death are God's constant reminders of a mortal journey that has a beginning and an end. The mission of Jesus Christ was to mark the path, lead the way, and every point define. These inspired words of Eliza R. Snow do not describe an ethereal journey. They speak of living in a world of dirty diapers, of relationships, of betrayal, of loved ones who lie to you and about you. Jesus came to show us how. How to "hold on thy way." (D&C 122:9) Joseph Smith cried unto the Lord from Liberty Jail and reviewed the many trials he and the Saints were going through. The Lord reminded Joseph, "The Son of Man hath descended below them all. Art thou greater than he?" (D&C 122:8).

While in Liberty Jail, Joseph Smith received a revelation from God on how relationships were to be governed. The characteristics of a noble person were set forth. The revelation Joseph received is called Section 121 of the Doctrine and Covenants.

Elder Alvin R. Dyer quoted President David O. McKay as referring specifically to these verses of D&C 121:34-46:

PRESIDENT DAVID O. McKAY
This is . . . the greatest revelation that God has ever given to
man. (Stand Up And Be Counted, Alvin R. Dyer, BYU Speeches,
March 20, 1963, p. 9).

There are many great revelations. However, there can be only one that is **the** greatest. When one ponders the magnitude of that statement, it is breathtaking. Consider The Bible, The Book of Mormon, The Pearl of Great Price, The Doctrine and Covenants. What of the untold and unrecorded revelations from the time of Adam? What about the Temple? What about Joseph Smith's First Vision?

President Stephen L. Richards referred to D&C 121:34-46 as the "New Constitution of the Priesthood."

PRESIDENT STEPHEN L. RICHARDS
But even more important in its novelty do I regard the new
constitution of the priesthood as revealed through Joseph Smith.
To my thinking there is nothing more beautiful or truly
Christ-like in all scripture than this lovely exposition of the
divine commission to men to act in the name of God.
(Stephen L. Richards, Contributions of Joseph Smith, Handbook
of the Restoration, p. 44.)

PRESIDENT HEBER J. GRANT
I am thankful that even when the Prophet Joseph and others were in Liberty Jail one of the greatest of all the great revelations that have come to this people was given to him. (James R.. Clark, <u>Messages of the First Presidency</u>, 5:302.)

President McKay's statement was that D&C 121:34-36 was "the **greatest** revelation." President Grant referred to it and "one of the **greatest of all the great revelations**." President Richard's observation was "there is nothing more beautiful or truly Christ-like in all scripture." These superlative expressions cause one to ponder the meaning of what these men of God saw in this revelation. This part of Section 121 of the Doctrine and Covenants is less than four hundred words in length. Yet, a Prophet of God considered it the "greatest revelation of all time." May, just maybe, it deserves a very thorough examination. In it are hidden keys of knowledge which unlock the doors of discipleship. It teaches one how to love as Jesus loved.

"THE GREATEST REVELATION
THAT GOD HAS EVER GIVEN TO MAN"
Behold, there are many called, but few are chosen. And why are they not chosen?

Because their hearts are set so much upon the things of this world, and aspire to the honors of men, that they do not learn this one lesson—

That the rights of the priesthood are inseparably connected with the powers of heaven, and that the powers of heaven cannot be controlled nor handled only upon the principles of righteousness.

That they may be conferred upon us, it is true; but when we undertake to cover our sins, or to gratify our pride, our vain ambition, or to exercise control or dominion or compulsion upon the souls of the children of men, in any degree of unrighteousness, behold, the heavens withdraw themselves; the Spirit of the Lord is grieved; and when it is withdrawn, Amen to the priesthood or the authority of that man.

Behold, ere he is aware, he is left unto himself, to kick against the pricks, to persecute the saints, and to fight against God.

We have learned by sad experience that it is the nature and disposition of almost all men, as soon as they get a little authority, as they suppose, they will immediately begin to exercise unrighteous dominion.

Hence many are called, but few are chosen.

No power or influence can or ought to be maintained by virtue of the priesthood, only by <u>persuasion</u>, by <u>long-suffering</u>, by <u>gentleness</u> and <u>meekness</u>, and by <u>love unfeigned</u>;

By <u>kindness</u>, and <u>pure knowledge</u>, which shall greatly enlarge the soul <u>without hypocrisy</u>, and <u>without guile</u>—

Reproving betimes with sharpness, when moved upon by the Holy Ghost; and then showing forth afterwards an increase of love toward him whom thou hast reproved, lest he esteem thee to be his enemy;

That he may know that thy faithfulness is stronger than the cords of death.

Let thy bowels also be full of charity towards all men, and to the household of faith, and let virtue garnish thy thoughts unceasingly; then shall thy confidence wax strong in the presence of God; and the doctrine of the priesthood shall distil upon thy soul as the dews from heaven.

The Holy Ghost shall be thy constant companion, and thy scepter an unchanging scepter of righteousness and truth; and thy dominion shall be an everlasting dominion, and without compulsory means it shall flow unto thee forever and ever (D&C 121:34-46, underlining mine).

There are so many great and wonderful principles in this revelation. The focus of this writing is **empowering love** by reproving in a Christ-like way. One of the most Christ-like men that ever walked the earth was President David O. McKay. His insights into this revelation are precious.

PRESIDENT DAVID O. McKAY

"Reproving betimes with sharpness when moved upon by the Holy Ghost,..."—that limiting clause is very significant ["Reproving betimes with sharpness," not because of selfishness, not because of any personal antipathy not because of personality, but "when moved upon by the Holy Ghost] and then showing forth afterwards an increase of love toward him whom thou hast reproved, lest he esteem thee to be his enemy"; (D&C 121:43.) You search through pedagogies, theories of teachings in vain, and find no passage that will compare with that in governing people. (David O. McKAY, Conference Report, April 1962, p. 93.)

Is it possible the reason President David O. McKAY so appreciated these verses is because they are a Divine Blueprint for loving? Hidden within this "greatest revelation" that God has ever given to man is the way to become Christ-like and a partaker of the "Divine Nature." It is a way, maybe the only way, to escape the corruption of the world and overcome the "natural man."

ELDER NEAL A. MAXWELL

Thus at the very time he [Joseph Smith] was suffering telestial abuse and oppression from secular authorities ranging from judges to jailers, Joseph was instructed on the completely opposite manner, the celestial way, in which the Lord's priesthood leaders are to lead!

"No power or influence can or ought to be maintained by virtue of the priesthood, only by persuasion, by long-suffering, by gentleness and meekness, and by love unfeigned; By kindness, and pure knowledge, which shall greatly enlarge the soul without hypocrisy, and without guile—Reproving betimes with sharpness, when moved upon by the Holy Ghost (D&C 121:41-43)."
Obviously this supernal spiritual style of leadership as thus set forth could not be sustained for long by anyone who was casual in his commitment or who was not making significant spiritual strides in developing the attributes of Jesus. (Neal A. Maxwell, But for a Small Moment, p. 10.)

Elder Maxwell calls these principles the "attributes of Jesus." Peter refers to them as the "Divine Nature" (2 Peter 1:4-11). President Richards identifies them as "truly Christ-like." A serious disciple would seek to become like the Master. Regarding "the power to love and reprove in righteousness" the follower of Jesus would want to learn:

- The skill of **persuasion** (Moroni 7:13-18, Ether 8:26, 2 Nephi 33:4).
- The trait of **long-suffering** (I Peter 2:19-21, Alma 42:30, Mormon 2:12).
- The characteristics of **gentleness** and **meekness** (2 Corinthians 10:1, Galatians 5:22).
- The mystery of **love unfeigned** [not pretended nor faked] (1 Nephi 11:22).
- The strength in **kindness** (Joel 2:13-14, JST; Jonah 4:2; 2 Corinthians 6:6).
- The power of **pure knowledge** (Hosea 6:6, Luke 11:52, Alma 32:28).
- The art of **reproving while maintaining the Spirit** (D&C 11:21, D&C 19:38, D&C 20:54, D&C 42:14, D&C 46:7).

The challenge is to apply each of these without compulsory means, without hypocrisy, and without dishonesty.

The "needful thing" is to live these principles of righteousness. (Luke 10:40-42, James 1:22) It is the ability to "Reprove Betimes With Sharpness" and do it so as not to offend the Holy Ghost. A great mystery is revealed in the fact that "reproving betimes with sharpness when moved upon by the Holy Ghost" requires all seven aforementioned traits. The "showing forth afterwards an increase of love" is founded in love unfeigned [not faked nor pretended].

There are two mothers. One seems to have the confidence of her family; the other does not. There are two men. One has power in his Priesthood and the other does not. The power is in the Principles of

Righteousness. When men and women, fathers and mothers, husbands and wives, brothers and sisters act in harmony with these principles they enjoy a greater outpouring of the Holy Spirit. When men and women operate with the principles of righteousness, love will flow without compulsory means. Kingdoms built by force can only be maintained by force. Relationships that are built upon love can be sustained by love.

PRINCIPLES OF RIGHTEOUSNESS	PRINCIPLES OF UNRIGHTEOUSNESS
1. *Persuasion* is a Latin word, (persuadere) "per" = thoroughly; "suadere" = advise. Persuasion is to thoroughly advise. It is to invite and to entice (Moroni 7:13-17.)	1. The opposite of persuasion is compulsion, force, coercion, nagging, intimidation, including yelling, cursing, swearing, and name calling. It is to belittle or to humiliate. These are all forms of "unrighteous dominion."
2. *Long-suffering* requires restraint. It means to be patient and wait for the right opportunity to teach or share. The focus is on the loved one and their preparation to receive it.	2. Impatient, quick tempered, and short-fused are characteristics of the impetuous. The focus of critics is on their frustration. They act before they consider the consequences.
3. *Gentleness* means sensitive of disposition, easy, slow, refined in manner. It means treating people with respect, being "soft-tongued," well spoken, amiable, and courteous.	3. The opposite of gentleness is harshness. It is acting in an autocratic, domineering, oppressive, and heavy-handed manner. It is to bully, demand, and override. It is to be "sharp-tongued," and inflexible.
4. *Meekness* reflects a submissive, humble and mild attitude. It means to remain well composed, tranquil and peaceful, and not easily offended.	4. An attitude opposite of meekness is to be prideful, haughty, arrogant, puffed up, disdaining, high-handed, stiff-necked, egocentric, self-righteous and unapproachable.
5. *Love Unfeigned* means an unpretended love, not faked, nor phony, nor counterfeit. It is genuine, sincere, heart-felt, honest, and true. It is forthright and reflective of love which focuses on the best interest of the loved one. It is a love which "is stronger than the cords of death" (D&C 121:44). It is real, candid, and unvarnished. It is a love to be trusted.	5. Feigned love is a lie. It is counter-feit, manipulative, dishonest, untrue, false and faked for selfish purposes. It is deceptive, hypocritical, a ruse, and a hoax. It is a delusion and make believe. There are grave spiritual consequences. D&C 76:103 says "whosoever loves and makes a lie" will go to Hell.

6. Kindness speaks of benevolence. It means to treat people with respect, consideration, tolerance, generosity. The focus is on "how" one treats another. It is sympathy and tenderness. It is friendly, comforting, and gracious.

6. The opposite of kind is to be inconsiderate of the feelings of others. It is to be hurtful, insensitive, harmful, brash, discounting, denigrating, and imprudent.

7. Pure Knowledge is spiritual knowledge. It means truth which is a knowledge of things as they were, are now, and are to come. (D&C 93:24). This is spirit-discerned information that gives one confidence to act. It is intelligence, light and truth.

7. The opposite of pure knowledge is "no" knowledge, ignorance, or incomplete knowledge. It is acting without the facts, failing to see the big picture, flying off the handle, or over reacting. It is assuming, presumptive, and extremely judgmental. Ignorance, pigheadedness, and foolish traditions replace truth.

8. Reproving Betimes With Sharpness when moved upon by the Holy Ghost means to deliver the message early on, being very precise and exact. It is to preserve the self esteem and separate the issue or behavior from the worth of the soul. It is to conduct oneself in such a way that the Holy Ghost abides with one the entire time.

8. Inappropriate reproving includes uninvited, unauthorized, improperly given criticism. It disregards the ability and preparation of the recipient to receive criticism. It is an unrighteous dominion without respect for the criticized. It is the packaging of any message with unrighteous means. It is based more on the frustration of the critic than it is on what is edifying to the one being criticized.

When an individual is able to reprove or criticize without losing the Spirit, he or she is partaking of the Divine Nature, the attributes of Jesus, and becoming truly Christ-like.

The natural man is a selfish man. Being selfish is opposed to being considerate of others. The selfish, natural man has been described as an enemy to God (Mosiah 3:19). He seeks not the best interest of others. The Lord's Plan requires all to act in the eternal best interest of others. This is His work and glory (Moses 1:39). Those who work against the eternal best interest of others are working against God (Luke 16:13).

Looking back to D&C 121:34-35, many are called and few are chosen. Their hearts are set upon riches, honors of men, and the selfish things of a perishing world. They do not learn this one, overwhelming lesson: The powers of heaven are completely bound and inseparably connected with these eight principles of righteousness, i.e., persuasion, long-suffering, gentleness, meekness, love unfeigned, kindness, pure knowledge, and reproof given with the Spirit. To attempt to call upon the powers of heaven in any degree of unrighteousness will find the

Holy Ghost withdrawing and the person left to himself. [Pride, vain ambition, desire for control, dominion or any attempt to compel, force, or dominate another will result in the person acting without the powers of heaven] A grieved Holy Ghost will stand away from the person and watch them fight against God's ways of doing things. The withdrawn Spirit (D&C 19:20) will stand as a silent witness as he or she makes their destruction sure.

THE PROPHECY OF SAMUEL
. . .your days of probation are past; ye have procrastinated the day of your salvation until it is everlastingly too late, and your destruction is made sure, yea, for ye have sought all the days of your lives for that which ye could not obtain; and ye have sought for happiness in doing iniquity, which thing is contrary to the nature of that righteousness which is in our great and Eternal Head (Helaman 13:38, underlining mine).

Until they repent, they will experience what Mormon called *"the sorrowing of the damned"* because God will not allow them to find *"happiness in sin* (Mormon 2:13)." Try as they might to make it otherwise they will find in the end *"wickedness never was happiness* (Alma 41:10)." Unrighteous dominion is sin and a wicked way of trying to do the Lord's work.

It has always been Satan's plan to disrespect the Agency of men and women. [Compulsion, coercion, physical and emotional intimidation are Satan's tools] (Moses 4:1-4, D&C 29:36-37, Isaiah 14:12-15, Abraham 3:27-28, Revelation 12:3-9).

The irony for those who want to use an unrighteous means to justify a righteous intent, is they fought a "war in heaven" for the right of self determination. They fought Lucifer himself for the privilege of maintaining their freedom of choice. Now they are consciously or unconsciously using Satan's approach (D&C 46:7). As soon as they receive a little power or a little authority they resort to force. Sooner or later they will learn the futility of this pathway. Maybe it will take the loss of a runaway child, a divorce, the loss of earthly possessions, the loss of church membership, the loss of personal dignity and friends before they learn by the things they suffer. (D&C 105:6, Hebrew 5:8, D&C 19:15).

HOLMGANGA, A VIKING FIGHT TO THE DEATH
In days of old, Vikings entered the field of battle to win their freedom. The field was, however, a blanket placed on the ground. It was approximately ten feet by ten feet. Some were smaller. The battle was called a "Holmganga." It was a fight to the death. If

either Viking left the blanket, a judge with an axe would take the coward's life. All of their worldly plunder and possessions were stacked in piles. The "Jarls" were the ruling class. The "Bondis" were the farmers and freemen. The "Thralls" were the slaves. All could be Viking warriors, including the women. Many a "Thrall" fought on the "Holmganga," not for love and not for money. They fought for the right to buy their freedom. Life as a slave was worse than death. Valhalla, the heavenly hall of immortality was waiting to receive the souls of heroes slain in battle. If they could not enjoy freedom on earth, they could do so in heaven. Odin sent one of the nine Valkyrie, warrior maidens, to guide the free soul to Valhalla.

The human spirit and the souls of the children of God yearn for freedom. No price is too great to flee oppression. Today oppression from unrighteous dominion unravels many relationships. Husbands cower at the nagging sounds of a toxic wife. Women flee the hearth and home to escape verbal, physical, emotional and spiritual abuse. Children run into the night for the lack of love at home.

ENOCH
And he beheld Satan; and he had a great chain in his hand, and it veiled the whole face of the earth with darkness; and he looked up and laughed, and his angels rejoiced (Moses 7:26).

It need not be so. There is a clearly lit pathway. It is marked by Jesus and revealed through the scriptures and living prophets. Truly the Lord marked the path, led the way, and every point defined. The "summum bonum" of the entire matter requires that one acting in power or influence act in a loving manner.

God has endowed every human heart to respond to love. It is not hard to love. It only becomes hard as one tries to control another and the loved one resists change. Love turns quickly to frustration. Frustration turns into anger and criticism. The real issue seems to be dealing with the frustration of unmet expectations. Love becomes lost in frustration. The question is how does one empower love and give needed reproof without driving the wounded soul into the wilderness? How does one live in harmony with the Greatest Revelation that God has ever given to man?

To empower is to enable, to authorize, or make possible. How does one make it possible for love to be given and received? There are barriers to giving and receiving love. To empower love means to remove the obstacles that prevent love from being successfully given and received. What are those barriers and obstacles which prevent love from being communicated?

THE GREATEST BARRIERS TO LOVE AND SELF ACCEPTANCE ARE UNINVITED, UNAUTHORIZED AND IMPROPERLY GIVEN REPROOFS

PRESIDENT HUGH B. BROWN

. . . (Doctrine and Covenants 121:43.) Let us be very careful about this matter of reproving. . . let us be careful how we trample on the feelings of our brothers and sisters. Let us lift them and bless them and benefit them as we go forward and never be guilty of humiliating them or causing them to think that we do not appreciate their work. (Hugh B. Brown, The Abundant Life, p. 146).

"Oh, the unkind things we say to those we love.
We have kind words for the stranger
And smiles for the sometime guest,
While oft to our own
The bitter tone,
Though we love our own the best!"
(Hugh B. Brown, Conference Report, Oct. 1965, p. 16.)

ELDER NEAL A. MAXWELL

Practical and spiritual meekness also provides a helpful context for giving and receiving correcting candor when such candor is needed. Graciousness makes easier the following of the injunction of the Lord: "Reproving betimes with sharpness, when moved upon by the Holy Ghost; and then showing forth afterwards an increase of love toward him whom thou hast reproved." (D&C 121:43.) Graciousness facilitates providing the increase in love. President Brigham Young counseled the Saints, "Never chasten beyond the balm you have within you to bind up." Gracious individuals will heed Brigham's counsel. Paul spoke similarly: "Brethren, if a man be overtaken in a fault, ye which are spiritual, restore such an one in the spirit of meekness; . . (Galatians 6:1)." (Neal A. Maxwell, Meek and Lowly, p. 94.)

In listing the qualities of a Zion person the Lord said, ". . . cease to find fault, one with another . . . (D&C 88:124)."

President David O. McKay quoted D&C 121:43 and shared a great insight:

PRESIDENT DAVID O. McKAY
"Reproving betimes with sharpness, . . . and then showing forth afterwards an increase of love toward him whom thou hast reproved, lest he esteem thee to be his enemy." Why, it is a wonderful admonition and lesson in regard to the government, not only in quorums of the priesthood, . . . but also in our home life and in all phases of association in society! Consider, again, the suggestion in regard to the worth of souls (Gospel Ideals, p. 150).

EMPOWERING LOVE

To empower love is to learn how to value the worth of a soul. Empowering love opens the way for love to enter the human heart. The Parables of The Lost Sheep, The Lost Coin, and The Lost Son in Luke 15 confirm the Love of God for each individual soul.

THE SAVIOR'S WORDS
Remember the worth of souls is great in the sight of God; . . .
And if it so be that you should labor all your days in crying repentance unto this people, and bring, save it be one soul unto me, how great shall be your joy with him in the kingdom of my Father!
And now, if your joy will be great with one soul that you have brought unto me into the kingdom of my Father, how great will be your joy if you should bring many souls unto me! (D&C 18:10, 15-16.)

REVELATION FOR JOHN WHITMER
And now, behold, I say unto you, that the thing which will be of the most worth unto you will be to declare repentance unto this people, that you may bring souls unto me, that you may rest with them in the kingdom of my Father. Amen. (D&C 15:6).

Who would attack the worth of a soul? How does anyone denigrate another's value? The opposite of enabling love is to disable love. When one is giving uninvited, unauthorized, and inappropriate criticism he is disabling himself as a purveyor of love. He is also denigrating the recipient of his criticism. Any form of abuse disables love. Even the truth, when inappropriately given is harmful meat, "they cannot bear" (D&C 19:22). To physically, emotionally, or spiritually abuse a child of God is to risk destroying his self esteem. It is to send a message he is not worthwhile. With unkind and critical words one attacks the very core, the spiritual essence of a person. A constant bombardment of criticism will convince even the noblest they are worthless.

PRESIDENT GORDON B. HINCKLEY
There is not a man or woman in this vast assembly who
cannot be depressed on the one hand, or lifted on the other, by
the remarks of his or her associates. (BYU Marriot Center,
March 6, 1994.)

It is difficult to remain in any relationship where even a significant minority of the words are tipped with the poison of criticism.

PRESIDENT GORDON B. HINCKLEY
[*Criticism is the forerunner of divorce,*]*. . . [Speaking of a*
young married couple] They had thrown away with careless and
sour words the hopes and dreams of eternity. With criticism and
shouting, they had violated the sacred promises that might have
taken them on to exaltation (Fireside, BYU Marriot Center,
March 6, 1994).

ALMA TO THE PEOPLE OF AMMONIHAH
For our words will condemn us . . . and in this awful state we
shall not dare to look up to our God (Alma 12:14).

Words matter! Consider the following adaptation of Matthew 25:40:
Whatsoever ye [say] unto one of the least of these my [children],
ye have [said] unto me. (Bracketed words changed from
original).

PRESIDENT J. REUBEN CLARK, Jr.
Brethren, be careful, be prayerful, be wise, when you
undertake to make your reproof, when you undertake to
direct. . . .Be careful of their feelings. Speak kindly and in such
a way that there never will be any question as to your love for
them and your desire merely to be helpful. (J. Reuben Clark, Jr.,
Conference Report, October 1958, p. 83.)

PRESIDENT BRIGHAM YOUNG TO PARENTS
[*Parents should never drive their children, but lead them*
along,] *giving them knowledge as their minds are prepared to*
receive it. Chastening may be necessary betimes, but parents
should govern their children by faith rather than by the rod,
leading them kindly by good example into all truth and holiness.
(Discourses of Brigham Young, p. 208.)

ELDER ARCHIBALD OF THE SEVENTY
SPOKE IN GENERAL CONFERENCE
[It is impossible to emphasize the good in others if negative
words or phrases are readily available on the tips of our tongues
or expressed through our gestures. . . when correction is
necessary, it must take place "betimes" —meaning early
on—under the direction of the Holy Ghost and not in anger.]
The instructions on how to correct are clear and simple: early
on, with the peace of the Holy Ghost, with enough of the healing
power within us to make sure that self esteem is never wounded,
ensuring always that the individual feels important and
capable. . . enlarge the soul. (Church News, The Conference
Issue, October 10, 1992, p. 11.)

ROBERT L. SIMPSON
Let us place first things first and mention love as the prime
ingredient. I rather think that Heavenly Father would like the
idea of love heading our list, for his Only Begotten, the Savior of
the world, had unlimited capacity for love. This single trait of
love was most typical of his brief mortal ministry. (Robert L.
Simpson, Conference Report, April 1964, p. 68.)

LIVING TOGETHER IN LOVE

Is it possible to live in a "love-centered home"? Is this not a utopian fantasy? There have been several groups of people who have lived the law of love. Enoch and his city, the people who were all converted unto the Lord in 4th Nephi, and various individuals and groups have lived together in love. The more pertinent question may be, "Does the critic possess enough love to exercise the necessary patience?" Is the critic willing to subdue his frustrations for a higher cause? It may require a perspective as wide as all eternity and yet grounded in the reality of here and now. Before the critic vents his potentially damaging message is he willing to humble himself in mighty prayer and call upon the Lord for spiritual guidance?

SUMMARY

D&C 121:34-46 has been identified as the "Greatest Revelation God has ever given to man. It is a Divine Blueprint to love as Jesus loved. There is appropriate criticism. There is an appropriate way to share it without offending the Holy Spirit. That way includes persuasion, long-suffering, gentleness and meekness. It involves love unfeigned, kindness, and operating with pure knowledge. The crowning achievement is being able to reprove in such a manner as to not offend the Spirit and to confirm one's love to the one reproved.

The natural man will not yield to the enticings of the Holy Ghost. Instead he will continue to offer uninvited, unauthorized, and improperly given criticism. These become the thieves of self acceptance. Like the Unjust Judge in Luke 18, the critic has little or no regard for "God or man." He is a law unto himself. He is verbally and spiritually abusive. He fails to value the worth of a soul. His end will be bitter.

Contrast improper criticisms with empowering love. Imagine a person or a family where respect for others was manifested by restraint of the tongue. Consider the standard where love of others and concern for their eternal best interest would take precedence over words that do not edify.

CHAPTER THREE

THE SPIRITUAL GIFT OF CRITICISM

Reproving betimes with sharpness, when moved upon by the Holy Ghost: and then showing forth afterwards an increase of love toward him whom thou hast reproved ... (D&C 121:43).

CRITICISM DEFINED

To criticize is to censure, to find fault, to focus on a weakness or a shortcoming. It is to criticize and to reflect disapproval, denunciation, and nonacceptance. Inherent in most criticism is blame-fixing and condemnation. Criticism implies failure *not All* to act appropriately and communicates a sense of inadequacy. Criticism is reproof. It is a negative reaction to an issue or behavior created by self or another. Frequently it is born out of frustration because of expectations for better performance. The objective of those who give criticism is to change the one being criticized. Often the critic is hopeful of a change of heart or an improved behavior. Criticism is extremely toxic to the human spirit. It is more likely to kill the desire for change than it is to inspire it. This is especially true of criticism which is uninvited, unauthorized, or inappropriate. Even when criticism is invited, required, and appropriate the damage to the worth of the soul can be irreparable.

Developing the art and skill of giving and receiving criticism in the Lord's own way is a Spiritual Gift. It has more to do with having a positive attitude then being a perfect person. Criticizing with the Spirit requires self control, patience, and love. When these ingredients are present, the Spirit can bear witnesses to "the truth of all things." (Moroni 10:5.) One of the truths to which the Holy Ghost can bear witness is appropriate criticism.

REVELATION TO JOSEPH SMITH
Wherefore, he that preacheth and he that receiveth, understand one another, and both are edified and rejoice together (D&C 50:22).

If criticism is to be effective, the critic must be in control of his emotions. Under ideal circumstances the critic will ask for the permission of the one being criticized to meet at a time and place which will allow them to be alone. When such kindness and respect are present, they enhance the opportunity for the person being criticized to reflect upon the content of the criticism. The receiver of criticism need not be distracted by the "packaging" of the messenger's manner of delivery.

It is important to remember the mission of the Holy Ghost. He is God's messenger to each of Heavenly Father's children. Among his several functions are to guide, to comfort, and to carry the message of truth to the hearts of men and women everywhere. It is a major part of the mission of the Holy Ghost to bear witness to the truth of all things. This includes changing the hearts of the children of God.

NEPHI'S FINAL DISCOURSE

And now I, Nephi, cannot write all the things which were taught among my people; neither am I mighty in writing, like unto speaking; for when a man speaketh by the power of the Holy Ghost the power of the Holy Ghost carrieth it unto the hearts of the children of men (2 Nephi 33:1).

TWO ELDERS IN GERMANY

A version of this story was told by Antoine R.. Ivins, years ago. It appears that two missionaries were tracting. They knocked on the door and were greeted by a hostile German. The man asked if they were Mormons. Immediately after the Elders answered in the affirmative, he slugged one of the missionaries in the nose and knocked him to the ground. The Elder stood up amidst the curses of this man and managed to make a single statement. He said, "This day you have struck a servant of the Lord who came to bring you a message."

A year and half later two more Elders knocked on this man's door. They were obviously unaware of the greeting given to their predecessors. This time, however, the Elders were invited in. The man was humble and contrite. He related his striking of one of the missionaries. He went on to add, "For more than a year and a half I have awakened every night in a cold sweat to the words, 'This day you have struck a servant of the Lord who came to bring you a message.'"

"Please, please," he begged, "tell me your message." He was baptized and confirmed a member of the Church, and after another year and a half traveled to the Salt Lake Temple to do his temple work. After a few inquiries he found out the missionary he had struck was married and attending the University of Utah.

This time it was the Elder who opened the door. Not recognizing the man, he invited him in. When he spoke English with a distinct German accent, the entire event returned to the Elder's mind. At first he feared for his life. He believed the man had tracked him down. Indeed he had. Through his tears he asked the former missionary to forgive him. The German thanked the young man for telling him, "This day you have struck a servant of the Lord who came to bring you a message." They parted more than friends. They were brothers in the Gospel. [This is the essence of the story to the best of the Author's memory.]

The moral to the story is that the Elder did what he was supposed to do in bearing a witness. It was the Holy Ghost who afflicted the man's mind for more than a year and a half and softened his heart. It is the mission of the Holy Spirit to change men's hearts. Change is hard. True change, which leads a person to a better self, always comes from within. It is a conversion experience. It requires the vision of a better self and belief in one's own worth to make the change.

Like the Elder, a critic who is filled with patience, love, and self control can become a conduit for the Holy Ghost. It is the Spirit that will carry the critical message of change to the heart. The messenger becomes a conduit of love through which the Holy Spirit works. Inappropriate criticism has no chance of success because it offends the Spirit. It is an exercise in frustration. Even if proper criticism is given, it may take years for the receiver to respond to the influence of the Holy Ghost. Hence the need for patience.

The most patient, loving, and self-controlled person in the world was Jesus. Even after the Holy Ghost bore witness to many, there were those who rejected the message and the messenger. (John 6:66). In ancient times runners were sent from the front lines of the battle to the safe retreat of the kings. They bore tidings of the success and failure of the battle. It was common to kill the bearer of bad news even though his message was true.

If change is the objective, uninvited, unauthorized and inappropriate criticism will not do it. If one is not possessed of self control, patience, and love, the giving or receiving of criticism will have to wait until he is in control, in order to be effective. When criticism is given or received by someone who is out of control, impatient, and resentful, poor reactions are predictable. So are the hostile outcomes. Even appropriate criticism runs a high risk of rejection. It may be that Spirit-directed criticism is not just "another way" of approaching criticism. It may be the **ONLY** way that has a real chance of succeeding. Giving and receiving criticism in the Lord's own way requires preparation. If there is a possibility for change, the difference between acceptance or rejection of a critical message may be the demeanor of the message bearer.

GORDON B. HINCKLEY
The snide remark, the sarcastic jibe, the cutting down of associates—these too often are the essence of our conversation. In our homes, wives weep and children finally give up under the

*barrage of criticism. . . Criticism is the forerunner of divorce, the
cultivator of rebellion, sometimes a catalyst that leads to failure
(BYU, March 6, 1994).*

The warning voice of a Prophet of God is sufficient to give serious
attention to the issue of how criticism is given and received. History
records the foolishness of ignoring the warning voice of Prophets. If
patience, self control, and love are requisite principles, then sincere
disciples of Jesus will seek for these things. With Mighty Prayer and a
genuine concern for the one to be criticized, the follower of the Lord
will humble himself. In order to be an instrument in God's hands as an
Agent of Change he will yield to meekness. He will allow the Holy
Ghost to carry the message to the heart of the receiver. The Spirit has
always been associated with true conversion.

REVELATION TO JOSEPH SMITH
*And again, I will give unto you a pattern in all things, that ye
may not be deceived; for Satan is abroad in the land, and he
goeth forth deceiving the nations . . .*

*He that speaketh, whose spirit is contrite, whose language is
meek and edifieth, the same is of God if he obey mine
ordinances. . . .*

*And again, he that is overcome and bringeth not forth fruits,
even according to this pattern, is not of me (D&C 52:14-19).*

THE PEOPLE OF KING BENJAMIN
*And they all cried with one voice, saying: Yea, we believe all
the words which thou hast spoken unto us; and also, we know of
their surety and truth, because of the Spirit of the Lord
Omnipotent, which has wrought a mighty change in us, or in our
hearts, that we have no more disposition to do evil, but to do
good continually.*

*And we, ourselves, also, through the infinite goodness of God,
and the manifestations of his Spirit, have great views of that
which is to come; and were it expedient, we could prophesy of all
things (Mosiah 5:2-3).*

THE TEACHINGS OF ALMA THE YOUNGER
*And according to his faith there was a mighty change wrought
in his heart. Behold I say unto you that this is all true.*

*And behold, he preached the word unto your fathers, and a
mighty change was also wrought in their hearts, and they
humbled themselves and put their trust in the true and living
God. And behold, they were faithful until the end; therefore, they
were saved.*

*And now behold, I ask of you, my brethren of the church, have
ye spiritually been born of God? Have ye received his image in
your countenances? Have ye experienced this mighty change in
your hearts? (Alma 5:4-15.)*

⌈Men are not called to change the hearts of men. Men are called to
love God and to love their fellow man⌉ They are called to be examples
of True Believers in Christ. They are to model Christian ideals and pray
for their loved ones and even their enemies. They are to invite, entice,
encourage, inspire and righteously persuade others to improve. They
are to teach one another. However, one can only teach if the pupil is
willing in his heart to receive the teaching.

⌈On occasion one is justified in "reproving betimes with sharpness."
The qualification is that the critic is prompted by the Holy Ghost and
not his own frustration. ⌉When the Spirit is present and truly dwells in
the heart of the critic, the greatest opportunity for change exists.
Uninvited, unauthorized, and improper criticism will place the focus on
the critic, not on the critic's message. To criticize in the Lord's own
way requires the messenger to be Spirit-directed and Spirit-guided.
When this occurs, one is possessed of the Spiritual Gift of Criticism.

It is important to note how Noah Webster's 1828 Dictionary defined
the words "Criticise [sic]," Reproof," Betimes," and "Sharpness":

- *CRITICISE [sic]: To notice the beauties and blemishes*
- *CRITICISED [sic]: Examined and judged with regard to
  beauties and faults*
- *CRITICISM: The art of judging with propriety of the beauties
  and faults*
- *REPROOF: Blame expressed to the face; censure for a fault,
  reprehension*
- *BETIMES: Seasonably; in a good season; before it is late [early
  on]*
- *SHARPNESS: Keenness of an edge . . . Acuteness of intellect; the
  power of nice discernment; quickness of understanding*

One hundred and seventy years ago a "critic" was one who could
see the beauty as well as the blemish. Reproof had to be spoken to the
face of the person being criticized and not behind his back. "Betimes"
meant when the time was right, "in a good season, before it was too
late." "Sharpness" meant to be acute of intellect and to demonstrate
"niceness" when discerning another. To "reprove betimes with
sharpness" was to censure another directly to their face at a proper time
and season before it was too late and they were past feeling. It meant to
be precise and exact in focusing on the behavior or issue being

discussed. All of this was to be accomplished only when the Holy Ghost gave permission. The Prophet Isaiah could claim the Spiritual Gift of Criticism.

THE PROPHET ISAIAH
The Lord God hath given me the tongue of the learned, that I
should know how to speak a word in season to him that is weary
. . . (Isaiah 50:4).

Being able to speak a "word in season," even the word of knowledge, or words of wisdom, or "spirit directed criticism" is spiritual gifts (D&C 46:17-18). The following insight about speaking a "word in season" is instructive:

REVELATION FOR HYRUM SMITH
Seek not to declare my word, but first seek to obtain my word,
and then shall your tongue be loosed; Then, if you desire, you
shall have my Spirit and my word, yea, the power of God unto the
convincing of men.
But now hold your peace (D&C 1:21-22).

There are times when criticism is necessary. There are circumstances which require the courage to be critical. There are behaviors and issues that demand attention. There are a time, a place, and a season when criticism may be the forerunner for change and improvement. On those occasions, when the Spirit is present, it is possible for both the person who "giveth" and the person who "receiveth" to be edified.

And whoso receiveth not by the Spirit, cannot be benefited
(D&C 91:6).
And that which doth not edify is not of God, and is darkness
(D&C 50:23).

In the day-to-day world most people are moved upon to criticize by frustration instead of waiting to be moved upon by the Holy Ghost.

REVELATION TO JOSEPH SMITH
Verily, I say unto you, he that is ordained of me and sent forth
to preach the word of truth by the Comforter, in the Spirit of
truth, doth he preach [criticize] it by the Spirit of truth or some
other way?
And if it be by some other way it is not of God.
And again, he that receiveth the word of truth, doth he receive
it by the Spirit of truth of some other way?
If it be some other way, it is not of God (D&C 50:17-20).

Giving and receiving criticism with the Spirit is difficult for both the giver and the receiver. It is hard for the giver of criticism not to be overcome with negative emotion, to become angry, to yell, or to package the criticism in such a way that the focus is on the messenger and not the message. It is equally hard for the receiver of criticism to focus on the content of what is being said and not to be sidetracked by defensive reactions, or the manner in which the critic was inappropriate with their timing, tone of voice, or demeanor.

The more centered in Christ a person is, the easier it is to give and receive criticism, reproof, and chastisement. The more one is "ego" involved and "self" focused, the more difficult it is to give or receive criticism. Ego, self esteem, and self worth makes it difficult to receive criticism without making pride the issue. Because it is difficult does not excuse the disciple of Christ from giving and receiving criticism in the Lord's own way:

> ### THE LORD CHASTENS THOSE HE LOVES
> *Verily, thus saith the Lord unto you whom I love, and whom I love I also chasten that their sins may be forgiven, for with the chastisement I prepare a way for their deliverance in all things out of temptation, and I have loved you (D&C 5:1).*

Criticism is not given as an end in itself but as preparation toward becoming a better self. It should be accompanied with love. "How" criticism is given and received may determine whether or not it is honestly evaluated.

It requires humility, even a "childlike disposition" to benefit from reproof. In order to receive criticism the natural man must yield to the Holy Ghost.

> ### KING BENJAMIN
> *For the natural man is an enemy to God and has been from the fall . . . and will be forever and ever, unless he yields to the enticings of the Holy Spirit, and putteth off the natural man and becometh a saint through the atonement of Christ the Lord, and becometh as a child, submissive, meek, humble, patient, full of love, willing to submit to all things which the Lord seeth fit to inflict upon him, even as a child doth submit to his father (Mosiah 3:19).*

There are stewardships wherein if one does **not** criticize he will be held accountable before God for inaction:

THE PROPHET SAMUEL SPEAKING OF ELI
For I have told him that I will judge his house for ever for the
iniquity which he knoweth; because his sons made themselves
vile, and he restrained them not (I Samuel 3:13).

NEPHI'S BROTHER, JACOB
And we did magnify our office unto the Lord, taking upon us
the responsibility, answering the sins of the people upon our own
heads if we did not teach them the word of God with all diligence;
wherefore, by laboring with our might their blood might not come
upon our garments; otherwise their blood would come upon our
garments, and we would not be found spotless at the last day
(Jacob 1:19).

This places criticism as a great burden upon the shoulders of parents, Priesthood leaders, and authorized critics. It requires fortitude to face someone with kindness and to criticize them with a gentle spirit. As with all Spiritual Gifts;

And the Spirit shall be given unto you by the prayer of faith;
and if ye receive not the Spirit ye shall not teach [criticize]
(D&C 42:14, brackets mine).

Those who have tried to give and receive criticism in the Lord's own way know it is a difficult task. However problematical to manage, those who would profess discipleship to Jesus Christ must continue to accept the responsibility of being a giver and receiver of criticism with the Spirit. But, remember, one is not alone. The very God of Heaven is there to help. This assistance may come by being strengthened or it may occur when one's own heart is softened. A person is not excused nor released from this responsibility because of the "packaging" of another. In other words, a true believer in Christ is obligated to have the Spirit when criticism is being given or received, independent of the action or reaction of the other party. It requires great dependency upon the Lord.

Developing the self-mastery necessary to control the tongue requires years of practice and patience with self and others. A profound spiritual commitment to love as Jesus loved and to speak as Jesus spoke is a life-long adventure. James, the brother of Jesus, declared:

JAMES THE BROTHER OF THE LORD
If any man offend not in word, the same is a perfect man, and
able also to bridle the whole body.

Behold, we put bits in the horses' mouths, that they may obey us; and we turn about their whole body.

Behold also the ships, which though they be so great, and are driven of fierce winds, yet are they turned about with a very small helm, whithersoever the governor listeth.

Even so the tongue is a little member, and boasteth great things. Behold, how great a matter a little fire kindleth!

And the tongue is a fire, a world of iniquity: so is the tongue among our members, that it defileth the whole body, and setteth on fire the course of nature; and it is set on fire of hell.

For every kind of beasts, and of birds, and of serpents, and of things in the sea, is tamed, and hath been tamed of mankind:

But the tongue can no man tame; it is an unruly evil, full of deadly poison.

Therewith bless we God, even the Father; and therewith curse we men, which are made after the similitude of God.

Out of the mouth proceedeth blessing and cursing. My brethren, these things ought not so to be.

Doth a fountain send forth at the same place sweet water and bitter? (James 3:2-11).

It appears that motive, the fountain of the heart, is at the core of whether one controls the tongue or not. The natural man will continue to be a selfish man and to speak without the Holy Ghost. More profoundly the Christian man or woman who does not learn to control his or her tongue will be an enemy to self and an enemy to the mission of Jesus Christ, which is to bring to pass the immortality and eternal life of all God's children.

Discipleship to Jesus has always involved controlling the parts of the human body and elevating them to the highest and best in self and others.

BLASPHEMY

Would it not be considered blasphemy if one spoke to Jesus, or Heavenly Father, the way he or she criticizes a friend or loved one? The LDS Bible Dictionary Defines Blasphemy:

Blasphemy. Generally denotes contemptuous speech concerning God, or concerning <u>something that stands in a sacred relation toward God</u>. (p. 25, underlining mine).

What could be more precious to God than the Soul of one of His little ones? It had been better that millstones were hung around the neck of the verbal abuser and he were cast into the sea rather than offend one of His little ones (Matthew 18:6). What could stand in a more sacred relationship to God than His family? Is it not as blasphemous to curse one of His sons or daughters as it is to curse God? (D&C 76:23-24.) Anciently those who blasphemed were put to death by stoning (Leviticus 24:11-16). At the sound of blasphemy, Hezekiah "rent his clothes" (Isaiah 37:1, Matthew 26:65-66). **Verbal abuse is inflicting spiritual abuse because it attacks the worth of a soul**. It is blasphemy. Uninvited, unauthorized, and improperly given criticism is a sin.

Is there a way to package criticism so that the focus can be on the message and not the messenger? The answer is a resounding, "YES!" However, the messenger bears the burden of delivering an unwanted package. There is an aura of negativism associated with the best of criticisms. Piercing the negative darkness is only possible when the receiver of criticism is confirmed in the worth of his soul. Herein lies a Key of Knowledge. The art and skill of negative feedback requires the ability to **separate self esteem from the issue or behavior in question**. It is a task of great intricacy.

Separating ego from issue may be no more challenging than developing the ability to communicate love. It demands that respect is shown to each child of God, "Let them worship how, where, or what they may." (Articles of Faith, #11) If that child of God happens to be one's own child, will he be accorded respect if he holds a different opinion from the parent?

PRESIDENT HUGH B. BROWN
The Christlike life is always a combination of earnest, personal conviction and generous regard for the other man's opinion. Dedication to and defense of truth never require or justify breaking the second commandment to love our fellow men. (Hugh B. Brown, Conference Report, October 1959, p. 108.)

✗ President Stephen L. Richards spoke to husbands about unrighteous dominion:

PRESIDENT STEPHEN L. RICHARDS
The difficulties that arise usually stem from an attempt on the part of the head of the household to exercise inconsiderate or autocratic authority. There is no position in the Church in which the constitution and doctrine of the priesthood as revealed by the Lord has more direct application than to a husband and father in the home. He must never cease to be guided by the divine direction that:
"No power or influence can or ought to be maintained . . . only by persuasion, by long-suffering, by gentleness and meekness,

*and by love unfeigned . . ." (Stephen L. Richards, Conference
Report, October 1954, p. 81-82).*

*The Lord has told us how to reprove. I should like to remind my
brethren and sisters, and tell my other friends, what he has said about
it. . . . It is a kindness to reprove in the spirit of love. (Stephen L.
Richards, Conference Report, April 1957, p. 96.)*

One cannot expect to possess the peace of Christ which surpasses
all understanding unless one is willing to control the tongue, which can
be either an instrument of peace or a weapon of anger. When the tongue
becomes a weapon it unleashes anger and people say things they later
regret.

JESUS TAUGHT

*And he called the multitude, and said unto them, Hear, and
understand:*

*Not that which goeth into the mouth defileth a man; but that
which cometh out of the mouth, this defileth a man. . . .*

*Do not ye yet understand, that whatsoever entereth in at the
mouth goeth into the belly, and is cast out into the draught?*

*But those things which proceed out of the mouth come forth
from the heart; and they defile the man.*

*For out of the heart proceed evil thoughts, murders,
adulteries, fornications, thefts, false witness, blasphemies:*

*These are the things which defile a man: but to eat with
unwashen hands defileth not a man (Matthew 15:10-11, 17-20).*

ELDER J. GOLDEN KIMBALL

*Experience teaches me that when I have been angry, I am
quite sure I did not have the Holy Ghost, and I was not in any
proper condition to administer reproof. It took me quite a long
while to learn that. When I became excited, fanatical, and over-
zealous, I mistakenly thought it was the Spirit of the Lord, but
have learned better, as the Holy Ghost does not operate that
way. My testimony is that the internal fruits of the Holy Ghost
are joy, peace, patience, longsuffering, and kindness. (J. Golden
Kimball, Conference Report, April 1907, p. 81.)*

Under the guise of "righteous indignation" many justify their anger.
They lack the humility of a J. Golden Kimball. They give themselves
permission to be angry at a spouse, a parent, a child, or any person
because the object of their anger was wrong, sinful, or hurtful. Once
blame is fixed, they join their anger with criticism and feel justified in
being "out of the Spirit" because of the other person's actions. One is
never justified in acting out of the Spirit.

THE SACRAMENTAL PRAYER INCLUDES THE PHRASE
. . . that they may __always__ have his Spirit to be with them
(Moroni 4:3, underlining mine).

Anger is a choice. It is a poor choice, because it transfers the focus from the message to the messenger. The Scriptures do not support anger as a Christlike behavior. There are those who support anger as an appropriate Christian behavior under the title of "righteous indignation." They use Jesus cleansing the Temple to substantiate their view of righteous anger. The assumption that Jesus was angry while driving out the money changers is not reinforced in the scriptures. The one time Jesus is identified with anger is in Mark 3:5. He reacts by healing the man with the withered hand. What a marvelous example to respond to anger by doing a good deed. In the King James version, et. al., of the Bible, two key verses are used by the "righteous indignationist." They are Matthew 5:22 and Ephesians 4:26. The Joseph Smith Translation adds a valuable insight into the issue of anger:

MATTHEW 5:22 (KJV-JST)

But I say unto you, That whosoever is angry with his brother ~~without a cause~~ shall be in danger of ~~the~~ *his* judgment: and whosoever shall say to his brother, Raca, *or Rabcha*, shall be in danger of the council; ~~but~~ *and* whosoever shall say *to his brother*, Thou fool, shall be in danger of hell fire. (Matt 5:22, The King James Version/ The Joseph Smith Translation combined; words crossed out and bolded type represents Joseph Smith's Translation).

In the Matthew JST the words "without a cause" were crossed out. In delivering a similar discourse in the New World, the words "without a cause" are absent.

JESUS TEACHING AT THE TEMPLE IN BOUNTIFUL
But I say, unto you, that whosoever is angry with his brother
shall be in danger of his judgment . . . (3 Nephi 12:22).

In the same discourse the Savior would remind all true disciples to remove anger from their hearts, reconcile if they have aught against another, they are to forgive as a prerequisite to "Come unto Me" (3 Nephi 12:23-30). There is never any justification for anger. There is no permission to excuse the Spirit and journey into the emotion of rage or anger. Paul teaches in Ephesians this same doctrine.

EPHESIANS 4:20-32 (KJV-JST)

22 ~~That ye put off~~ *And now I speak unto you* concerning the former conversation, *by exhortation, that ye put off* the old man, which is corrupt according to the deceitful lusts; 23 And be renewed in the ~~spirit of your mind~~ *mind of the Spirit*; 24 And that ye put on the new man, which after God is created in righteousness and true holiness. 25 Wherefore putting away lying, speak every man truth with his neighbour: for we are members one of another. 26 ~~Be ye angry, and sin not:~~ *Can ye be angry, and not sin?* ~~Let~~ not the sun go down upon your wrath: 27 Neither give place to the devil. 28 Let him that stole steal no more: but rather let him ~~labour~~ *labor,* working with his hands *for* the things which ~~is~~ *are* good, that he may have to give to him that needeth. 29 Let no corrupt communication proceed out of your mouth, but that which is good to the use of edifying, that it may minister grace unto the hearers. 30 And grieve not the holy Spirit of God, whereby ye are sealed unto the day of redemption. 31 Let all bitterness, and wrath, and anger, and clamour, and evil speaking, be put away from you, with all malice: 32 And be ye kind one to another, tenderhearted, forgiving one another, even as God for Christ's sake hath forgiven you. (Ephesians 4:17-32, King James Version/ Joseph Smith Translation, combined; words crossed out and bolded type represent Joseph Smith's Translation).

To be hurt, disappointed, and even frustrated by the behaviors of others is understandable. But choosing to lose the Spirit, to be angry, and to be critical are not justifiable behaviors for a disciple of Jesus.

The Lord's anger is the disappointment and grief of heart He feels when His disciples' behavior requires Him to punish them (see Moses 7:26-40). Disobedience brings a loss of blessings with it. A loving Father in Heaven and His Son, Jesus Christ do only those things which are in the eternal best interest of the children of God.

NEPHI'S TESTIMONY
He doeth not anything save it be for the benefit of the world; for he loveth the world, even that he layeth down his own life that he may draw all men unto him. (2 Nephi 26:24).

The Scriptures frequently use the word "wrath" as well as the word anger. Neither of these words connote a God yelling and screaming in a rage of emotion. God is patient, longsuffering, and merciful, but not

31

indifferent. He cares. There are times when the Lord punishes His children. In everything the Lord does He is preparing a way for His children to improve. Especially in chastisement the Lord prepares a way.

> *I prepare a way for their deliverance in all things (D&C 95:1).*

God knows that his children will make mistakes and yield to temptation until they learn to love as he loves.

PAUL TO THE CORINTHIANS
> *There hath no temptation taken you but such as is common to man: but God is faithful, who will not suffer you to be tempted above that ye are able; but will with the temptation also make a way to escape, that ye may be able to bear it (1 Corinthians 10:13).*

In all that God does in the great "Plan of Deliverance," He is allowing His children to learn and preparing them to return to the Kingdom of God.

THE WISE WOMAN OF TEKOAH TO KING DAVID
> *Yet doth he devise means, that his banished be not expelled from him (2 Samuel 14:14).*

Hell itself is an "alternative high school" wherein the Lord has prepared a way for all, but those who choose perdition over Him (D&C 76:43).

NEPHI'S TESTIMONY
> *O how great the goodness of our God, who prepareth a way for our escape from the grasp of this awful monster; yea, that monster, death and hell, which I call the death of the body, and also the death of the spirit.*
>
> *And because of the way of deliverance of our God, the Holy One of Israel, this death, of which I have spoken, which is the temporal, shall deliver up its dead; which death is the grave.*
>
> *And this death of which I have spoken, which is the spiritual death, shall deliver up its dead; which spiritual death is hell; wherefore, death and hell must deliver up their dead, and hell must deliver up its captive spirits, and the grave must deliver up its captive bodies, and the bodies and the spirits of men will be restored one to the other; and it is by the power of the resurrection of the Holy One of Israel.*
>
> *O how great the plan of our God! . . . (2 Nephi 9:10-13).*

At a General Conference of the Church in April, 1930, celebrating an hundred years since its organization, Elder James E. Talmage testified about the role Hell plays in the Plan of Salvation.

JAMES E. TALMAGE

*During this hundred years, many other great truths not known before, have been declared to the people, and one of the greatest is that **to hell there is an exit as well as an entrance** (D&C 76:81-85, 105-106; Matt 5:25-26, bold mine). Hell is no place to which a vindictive judge sends prisoners to suffer and to be punished principally for his glory; but it is a place prepared for the teaching, the disciplining of those who failed to learn here upon the earth what they should have learned. True, we read of everlasting punishment, unending suffering, eternal damnation. That is a direful expression, but in his mercy the Lord has made plain what those words mean. "Eternal punishment," he say, " is God's punishment, for He is eternal; and that condition or state or possibility will ever exist for the sinner who deserves and really needs such condemnation; but this does not mean that the individual sufferer or sinner is to be kept in hell longer than is necessary to bring him to a fitness for something better. When he reaches that stage the prison doors will open and there will be rejoicing among the host who welcome him into a better state (James E. Talmage, Conference Report, April 1930, bold mine).*

Mercy will not rob Justice. The uttermost farthing will be paid (Matthew 5:26). However, in his disappointment and sorrow the Lord has prepared a way for the deliverance of God's children in all things. Seldom do the purveyors of criticism in this world look towards long term best interest. Even fewer prepare a way for the one being criticized to improve. For most people improper criticism is simply venting, an end in itself.

The anger of man and the anger of God are different. It is easy to misunderstand the Divine Nature of God and to transfer to God feelings, attributes, and thoughts which are common to man, but not a part of His Divine Nature.

THE PROPHET JEREMIAH

For I know the thoughts that I think toward you, saith the Lord, thoughts of peace, and not of evil, to give you an expected end.

Then shall ye call upon me, and ye shall go and pray unto me, and I will hearken unto you.

And ye shall seek me, and find me, when ye shall search for me with all your heart (Jeremiah 29:11-13).

THE PROPHET ISAIAH

For my thoughts are not your thoughts, neither are your ways my ways, saith the Lord.

For as the heavens are higher than the earth, so are my ways higher than your ways, and my thoughts than your thoughts (Isaiah 55:8-9).

If man is to follow God, he will always prepare a way for the criticized to improve and to have "hope." Criticism in the Lord's own way may lead to punishment. However, the punishment will be sufficient to teach the consequence and prepare a way for improvement, yet not deny hope. So much of mortal criticism now given is the punishment. It is a message of rejection with no hope of restored trust, love or acceptance.

The authorized times, places and circumstances for Spirit-directed criticism represent less than one tenth of one percent of current practice. Ninety nine point nine per cent (99.9%) of most criticism is ill-timed, unauthorized, out of stewardship, or out of control even within stewardship, unnecessary, improperly given, represents unrighteous dominion, fosters resentment, contention, anger, and is ill-advised. The focus is seldom the best interest of the one being criticized rather it is the frustration of the critic and the disappointment he feels. Developing the art and the skill and the Spiritual Gift of giving and receiving criticism in the Lord's own way requires restraint.

JAMES THE BROTHER OF THE LORD
If any man among you seem to be religious, and bridleth not his tongue, but decieveth his own heart, this man's religion is vain (James 1:26).

Recognizing that each person is a "work in progress" and that it takes time to develop these abilities will help the struggling disciple to rededicate to living the ideal even if one foot is in the Gospel and the other in the frustrating world.

Assume that the reason well meaning people give uninvited, unauthorized, and inappropriate criticism is ignorance. They are unaware of the damage done to the value a person places upon himself. Maybe it is not just ignorance of the negative side effects of improper criticism. Maybe it is an inability to comprehend the worth of a soul. The value that God places on the individual soul is so great that man's inability to comprehend it may be part of the problem. God does not deal in percentages. He loves all of His children. The Fall of Man is universal, but so is the Resurrection.

God is constantly calling after His children to repent and to love one another. The hurt, heartache, and sorrow that are done unto the least of his little ones are done unto Him (Matthew 25:40). The penalties for abuse are so severe man cannot comprehend them.

JESUS WARNS

Therefore I command you to repent—repent, lest I smite you by the rod of my mouth, and by my wrath, and by my anger, and your sufferings be sore—how sore you know not, how exquisite you know not, yea, how hard to bear you know not.

For behold, I, God, have suffered these things for all, that they might not suffer if they would repent;

But if they would not repent they must suffer even as I;

Which suffering caused myself, even God, the greatest of all, to tremble because of pain, and to bleed at every pore, and to suffer both body and spirit— and would that I might not drink the bitter cup, and shrink— (D&C 19:15-18).

This is a day when men and women are hypersensitive to the word "abuse" or at least pay lip-service to it. Physical abuse, battered women, molested children, these are topics of the times. Verbal abuse is thought of as emotional abuse and many believe it is more damaging than physical abuse. There is recognition by those who have studied abuse of its toll upon self esteem. The term "self esteem" has been over used. People are increasingly desensitized and past feeling. Self esteem has become such a "catch-all" phrase and touted as the prime cause of all problems that the masses tire of hearing about it. This makes it more difficult to discuss the most profound of all abuse which is **spiritual abuse or soul abuse**.

BEWARE OF THOSE WHO ARE ABLE TO KILL THE SOUL

And fear not them which kill the body, but are not able to kill the soul: but rather fear him which is able to destroy both soul and body . . . (Matthew 10:28).

Learning to control one's responses in crises when one does not control the timing, the circumstances, nor the disposition of others is a true measure of discipleship to Christ.

THE APOSTLE PETER
For this is thankworthy, if a man for conscience toward God endure grief, suffering wrongfully.
For what glory is it, if, when ye be buffeted for your faults, ye shall take it patiently? but if, when ye do well, and suffer for it, ye take it patiently, this is acceptable with God.
For even hereunto were ye called: because Christ also suffered for us, leaving us an example, that ye should follow his steps (I Peter 2:19-21).

Because criticism is such a toxic response, it is regulated by strict scriptural standards. The damage done by criticism is so serious that its use is prescribed under very limited circumstances even when authorized. A Christ centered life cannot be maintained by one who cannot learn to control the tongue. A Zion "heart," marriage, family, or community cannot be built when criticism and fault finding go unabated.

JAMES, THE BROTHER OF JESUS
Therefore to him that knoweth to do good, and doeth it not, to him it is sin. (James 4:17).

THE APOSTLE PAUL
For it hath been declared unto me of you, my brethren, by them which are of the house of Chloe, that there are contentions among you (1 Cor. 1:11).

JESUS AT THE TEMPLE IN BOUNTIFUL
For verily, verily I say unto you, he that hath the spirit of contention is not of me, but is of the devil, who is the father of contention, and he stirreth up the hearts of men to contend with anger, one with another (3 Nephi 11:29).

WHO MAY CRITICIZE?

The right to judge is a stewardship given to parents and authorized leaders. Unauthorized criticism is a sin and encourages contention. Authorized criticism can only be handled upon the principles of righteousness (D&C 121:36).

Restraint in giving and receiving criticism marks the true believer in Christ (D&C 50:40). It makes a statement that the worth of the soul is of primary concern, not the frustration of the critic. How does one become empowered with this love which allows him to give and receive criticism properly? How does one obtain the Spiritual Gift of Criticism? Jesus would respond with two invitations, "Come and see," and then "Follow me."

CHAPTER FOUR

WHY SHOULD I CHANGE?

In a class on Relationships and Communication a student asked the question "Why should I change?" It is a legitimate question. She went on to explain that life wasn't all that bad as it was. Her relationships were satisfactory. She didn't particularly appreciate it when people were critical of her. It was obvious that others didn't like it when she was critical of them but "Hey, that's life." This was a sincere young lady who was content with her life and saw no need to change.

The question was thrown out to the entire class. "Why should a person be willing to learn how to give and receive criticism in the Lord's own way?" The answers began to come back:

1. Because it is right.
2. It's a commandment.
3. You are hurting other people by improper criticism.
4. What you are doing now isn't effective.

After a little more pondering and meditation the answers took a different direction:

5. It will make you a more effective communicator.
6. It will make you a more emotionally safe person.
7. It will put you more in control of your life.

Even though the answers resembled "sound bites" and one liners, they began to reveal an awareness of a better way. There was more to life than each was currently experiencing. The picture was not clear. The vision was not complete, but there was more and it was better. Finally, an older married student raised her hand and said,

8. It will enable others to receive your love.

There are many good and valid reasons to change a self-defeating behavior. After all the answers were written on the board, the students were asked to expand upon their answers. It was opened to anyone to comment on any or all of the answers:

1. Because it was right to learn to give and receive criticism in the Lord's own way. This answer was enough for some of the students. They didn't require additional motivation. They were willing to change their behavior on that premise alone. One had to admire the strength of character required to operate on that principle.

2. It's a commandment. It was agreed this ability to give and receive criticism in a righteous way was a Christ–like trait and that discipleship to Jesus required obedience to his command-ments.

3. You are hurting other people by improperly criticizing them. This answer demonstrated a certain kind of empathy and evoked the scripture:

   And the King shall answer and say unto them, Verily I say unto you, Inasmuch as ye have done it unto one of the least of these my brethren, ye have done it unto me (Matt 25:40).

   Compassion for others is a worthwhile motive and reveals a tender and sensitive heart.

4. What you are doing in giving and receiving criticism improperly isn't effective. The ultimate pragmatic question "Is it working?" "If its not broken, don't fix it." If it's not working, find another way. What is needed is a solution. Find some way that works and do it. Some people don't know when to let go, even when things are not working. A fanatic is defined as someone who doubles his speed even if he has lost his way. For some students pragmatism was the only motivation they needed to move them towards criticizing in a proper way.

5. It will make you a more effective communicator. Being a better self by improving effective communication skills seemed to drive this particular point of view. There is too much "hassle" in not being a productive and efficient communicator. It's not worth the misunderstandings, the hurt feelings, the arguments and the host of negative spin-offs that accompany improperly given or received criticism. Inefficiency is a poor way to run a business or a human relationship.

6. It will make you a more emotionally safe person. The focus here is on doing good and being an instrument in the Lord's hands to provide a "safe" place emotionally for those that one loves. A safe emotional harbor from the storms of life is a worthy goal.

7. It will put you more in control of your life. There is great truth in this answer. It deals with self mastery. The conquest of anything that keeps a person from becoming their highest and best self is a noble undertaking. Giving oneself permission to become angry and critical at another's behavior is yielding control of one's life. Choosing to direct the inner self to a higher and greater purpose than criticism is more to be valued that conquering Mr. Everest.

8. It will enable others to receive your love. This is a very important statement which includes one of the keys to God's happiness.

God's work is to help each soul become his very best (Moses 1:39). When people enter into the work of helping others achieve their highest and best selves, they have enlisted in the service of their God (Mosiah 2:16-17). In losing their mortal life in loving service to others they secure for themselves immortality and eternal life.

The glorious news of the Gospel of Jesus Christ is that man has the ability and capacity to love as God loves. It may be embryonic, it may be influenced by time and limited in mortality but the genes to love as God loves are there within man. Men and women are the spirit sons and daughters of God (D&C 76:24). The spark is struck from an Eternal Blaze. The acorn is not far from the tree. Jesus came to teach his mortal kin how to love and how to treat one another. Lust, with all of its selfishness would have to be discarded, but passion was not to be killed in man. It was to be directed toward the highest and best in self and others. This passion was to love as Jesus loved.

> A new commandment I give unto you, That ye love one another; as I have loved you, that ye also love one another.
> By this shall all men know that ye are my disciples, if ye have love one to another (John 13:34-35).

Man has the capacity to develop this Godly attribute of love. However, who would light the way? The answer is Jesus. At some point in each person's journey in life or in death he will have to confront Jesus. Eventually every knee will bow and every tongue confess that Jesus was right (Phil 2:10-11, D&C 76:110). This acknowledgment will be accompanied by the awareness there is no other way or manner in which man can live in harmony with his fellow man on earth or in Heaven than Jesus' way (2 Nephi 9:41, 2 Nephi 25:29, Mosiah 3:17). The sooner this truth is learned the less will be the hurt, heartache and sorrow experienced by those who sought alternatives to Jesus.

PRESIDENT HOWARD W. HUNTER

✓ *The great standard! The only sure way! The light and the life of the world! How grateful we should be that God sent his Only Begotten Son to earth to do at least two things that no other person could have done. The first task Christ did as a perfect, sinless Son was to redeem all mankind from the Fall, providing an atonement for Adam's sin and for our own sins if we will accept and follow him. The second great thing he did was to set a perfect example of right living, of kindness and mercy and compassion, in order that all of the rest of mankind might know how to live, know how to improve, and know how to become more godlike.*

Let us follow the Son of God in all ways and in all walks of life. Let us make him our exemplar and our guide. We should at every opportunity ask ourselves, "What would Jesus do?" and then be more courageous to act upon the answer. We must follow Christ, in the best sense of that word. We must be about his work as he was about his Father's (Ensign, May 1994, p. 64).

How can one celebrate "Thanksgiving" without gratitude, or Christmas without Christ? How does a disciple of Jesus Christ develop the ability to overcome inappropriate criticism except by coming to Jesus? The way to conquer all spiritual weakness is to come unto Jesus. The way to overcome a bad idea, trait, or thought is to replace it with a better one. Criticism given or received the right way, at a right time, and with a right Spirit is a better way. It is the only path that a "true believer in Christ" can follow.

JESUS TO MORONI

And if men come unto me I will show unto them their weakness. I give unto men weakness that they may be humble; and my grace is sufficient for all men that humble themselves before me; for if they humble themselves before me, and have faith in me, then will I make weak things become strong unto them (Ether 12:26-27).

For the baptized, confirmed member of the Church of Jesus Christ of Latter-day Saints, coming unto Jesus means receiving the Holy Ghost. It means to live in such a way that one may enjoy the companionship of the Spirit. (John 14:16-17,26-27). Unauthorized, uninvited, and inappropriate criticism drive the Spirit away. There are four steps one must take in order to give or receive criticism in the right way, "in the Lord's own way," in a way that keeps the Spirit with the disciple.

- *RECOGNITION OF APPROPRIATE AND INAPPROPRIATE CRITICISM.*
- *BECOMING AN AGENT OF CHANGE*
- *MIGHTY PRAYER*
- *ACTING OUT OF LOVE*

Each of the next four chapters will deal with these steps. Experience has taught that all four are necessary in order to maintain the strength required to sustain the giving and receiving of criticism in the Lord's own way. The impatience of many will cause them to experiment with short cuts. Detours and backtracking will only weaken the disciple's resolve. Recognition of the difference between appropriate and inappropriate criticism is essential. Knowledge of what is proper and improper will remove the "blind spots of ignorance," wherein well meaning people give themselves permission to use "constructive criticism" only to find it doesn't work. Understanding the different guises of criticism helps one to clearly recognize what is edifying and what isn't.

Desire to effect change, real change, on the part of the giver of criticism is a key to influencing others. Becoming an Agent of Change requires a conversion of the critic's heart. Caring concern can neither be faked nor feigned. It must be real. It will require patience with self and many failed attempts to overcome the addiction to be improperly critical. Frustration with self compounded with frustration with others makes it difficult to sustain the effort to criticize in a proper way.

Mighty Prayer is honest, heartfelt prayer. One's purpose in Mighty Prayer is to bring one's frustrations to God and one's love to the loved ones. The frustrations' one feels and experiences are real. They must be dealt with and placed somewhere. Inappropriate, uninvited, and unauthorized criticism only exacerbate the feelings of everyone involved. It places more roadblocks in the way than it removes. Mighty Prayer involves God as a problem solver. It enlists the powers of Heaven. It calls forth Divine Intervention. Mighty Prayer deposits at the feet of Jesus the primary responsibilities to affect change. Without Mighty Prayer, frustration will rage in the heart and disembowel the spirit of the would-be Agent of Change.

Acting out of love is a phrase of intentional complexity. Usually one thinks of "acting out" as a negative reaction to an unmet expectation. Children are often referenced as "acting out their anger." Acting out carries with it a certain kind of passion. It is not necessary to lose passion. Acting out of love can be a very passionate nonsexual experience. It requires tremendous self control to channel the passion towards the highest and best in self and others. It is a quest for charity. More valued than gold is the prize of being able to gift unconditional love. Coming to understand the difference between trust and love is vital to acting out of love. Unconditional love is not unconditional trust. Unconditional love is not unconditional tolerance for the inappropriate. Unconditional love is not unconditional support, acceptance, or an enabling mentality. Acting out of unconditional love has as its core value the best interest, the **eternal** best interest of another. It is totally in harmony with God's plan and therein lies its strength. The quintessential mission statement underlying acting out of love is this:

"I LOVE YOU"

I love you to your highest and best self. Accordingly, I will help you in all the positive choices you make to become your best. But I will not help you one inch to Hell. I will not enable you to become your worst self. I will unconditionally love you even if I cannot unconditionally support you in your poor judgment decisions. I will never withdraw my love. You will always find within my embrace a safe place.

I am the steward of my resources and therefore I must account to God for their use. To the extent it is edifying and I am capable I will share with you. But I will not support a life style of self destruction.

The gift of life is yours. Know that my love will always accompany you in your journey through life and beyond death. My course is set. I will always be your soul's true friend. (J. Lewis, Personal Journal, 1989.)

When a person's **goals** for a loved one are the same as God's goals, then the blessings and the Powers of Heaven can be actualized. When the **methods** employed in dealing with an appropriate criticism are also consistent with God's methods, the Holy Ghost will carry the message to the heart of the loved one. The greatest potential for change exists when disciples are consistent in both **goals** and **methods** with the will of the Lord.

Now back to the original question, "Why should I change?" The answer is, "The Lord's way works." Faster and easier only make sense if they are effective. Inappropriate criticism is not effective. Yet, there awaits **a greater reason to change**. In changing one's heart the Lord extends a precious promise to those who are willing to commit to His conditions:

THE LORD'S PROMISE
I, the Lord, am bound when ye do what I say; but when ye do not what I say, ye have no promise (D&C 82:10).

BINDING THE LORD WITH FAITHFULNESS

Parents and spouses need to exercise more faith in God's Plan of Deliverance. Fear for the loss of the souls of one of their children has led to desperate and unrighteous acts on the part of parents. With God's love and the Devil's way of doing things they hope to save their children from eternal damnation. Only with God's love and God's way is there a promise.

Suffice it to say that unrighteous dominion, improper criticism and coercion are not the Lord's way. Faithful parents can bind the Lord with a promise. Even as the goodness of Jesus blesses the lives of those "less good," even so a goodly parent can extract from God a promise for their children and their children's children to the third and fourth generation. It can make of the parents saviors on Mount Zion.

REVELATION TO JOSEPH SMITH
For they were sent to be a light unto the world, and to be the saviors of men (D&C 103:9, underlining mine).

God promised Abraham and his seed an everlasting blessing, if Abraham would be obedient unto God (Genesis 17:1-8). Because Abraham did what God commanded, Jehovah was bound to fulfill his promise. Abraham is known as the Father of the Faithful (D&C 138:41). The Scriptures are filled with many examples of the goodness of parents binding God to a promise. Mosiah bound God to a promise for the safety of his sons among the Lamanites (Mosiah 28:4-9). Enos 1:8,10,12,15,18; D&C 10:46-53 are but a few of many such promises.

THE PROPHET JOSEPH SMITH
When a seal is put upon the father and mother, it secures their posterity so they cannot be lost, but will be saved by virtue of their father and mother (TPJS p. 321).

Imagine for a moment the power of faithful parents, friends, or loved ones who by their commitment bind God to a promise. The key is that "ye do what I say." The Lord said He wanted criticism given and received in the spirit of meekness and gentleness and with love unfeigned (D&C 121:41-44). The Lord's love and the Lord's way will bind God to a promise. Heavenly Father has already prepared a way through the Atonement of Jesus Christ for the salvation of His children.

ELDER ORSON F. WHITNEY

You parents of the wilful and the wayward! Don't give them up. Don't cast them off. They are not utterly lost. The Shepherd will find his sheep. They were his before they were yours—long before he entrusted them to your care; and you cannot begin to love them as he loves them. They have but strayed in ignorance from the Path of Right, and God is merciful to ignorance. Only the fulness of knowledge brings the fulness of accountability. Our Heavenly Father is far more merciful, infinitely more charitable, than even the best of his servants, and the Everlasting Gospel is mightier in power to save than our narrow finite minds can comprehend.

The Prophet Joseph Smith declared—and he never taught more comforting doctrine—that the eternal sealings of faithful parents and the divine promises made to them for valiant service in the Cause of Truth, would save not only themselves, but likewise their posterity. Though some of the sheep may wander, the eye of the Shepherd is upon them, and sooner or later they will feel the tentacles of Divine Providence reaching out after them and drawing them back to the fold. Either in this life or the life to come, they will return. They will have to pay their debt to justice; they will suffer for their sins; and may tread a thorny path; but if it leads them at last, like the penitent Prodigal, to a loving and forgiving father's heart and home, the painful experience will not have been in vain. Pray for your careless and disobedient children; hold on to them with your faith. Hope on, trust on, till you see the salvation of God.

Who are these straying sheep—these wayward sons and daughters? They are children of the Covenant, heirs to the promises, and have received, if baptized , the gift of the Holy Ghost, which makes manifest the things of God. Could all that go for naught? (Orson F. Whitney, Conference Report, April 1929, p. 110-111, underlining mine.)

At this point most parents are afraid to hope this promise could apply to them. They doubt their worthiness. Many feel it is perfection or nothing. They know not the love of God. Endure to the end of one's mortal life being loving and with faith and hope in Christ and this promise **will** be realized. (Mosiah 4:6-7, 2 Nephi 31:15-16, 21-21, bold mine.)

JACOB TESTIFIES
God will be merciful unto many; and our children shall be restored (2 Nephi 10:2).

THE PROPHET BRIGHAM YOUNG
I could say something encouraging to parents, if they would heed. Let the father and mother, who are members of this Church and kingdom, take a righteous course, and strive with all their might <u>never to do a wrong</u>, but to do good all their lives; if they have one child or one hundred children, <u>if they conduct themselves towards them as they should</u>, binding them to the Lord by their faith and prayers, I care not where those children go, they are bound up to their parents by an everlasting tie, and no power of earth or hell can separate them from their parents in eternity; they will return again to the fountain from whence they sprang. . . I am sorry to hear Elders of Israel <u>use words, and manifest anger and impatience that are unbecoming</u>. (Journal of Discourses, Vol. 11, p. 215-216, Brigham Young, April 29, 1866, underlining mine.)

This reference "never to do a wrong" had to do with conducting themselves towards their children "as they should." President Young was sorry to hear of those Elders who "use words, and manifest anger and impatience that are unbecoming." Towards whom? Towards their wives and children. Brigham went on to say that impatience and abuse will cause you to forsake the Holy Spirit of God.

Imagine again, binding the Lord with a promise that would save one's children. What will a man or woman give in exchange for the souls of their children? One person can bind God to a promise as well as a couple, a family, or a nation. Most parents would give their lives but will they restrain their tongues? The Lord's promise is received in the Lord's way:

No power or influence can or ought to be maintained by virtue of the priesthood, only by persuasion, by long-suffering, by gentleness and meekness, and by love unfeigned.
By kindness, and pure knowledge, which shall greatly enlarge the soul without hypocrisy, and without guile—

Reproving betimes with sharpness, when moved upon by the Holy Ghost; and then showing forth afterwards an increase of love towards him whom thou hast reproved, lest he esteem thee to be his enemy (D&C 121:41-43).

God is waiting to be bound by the righteous walk and talk of His children. The question must be asked, "Will one reprove in the Lord's own way in order to save their children?" If not for themselves, will they do it for the children?" Each will answer that question in his or her own hearts. And herein may lie the best answer to the question, "Why should I change?" In discipleship to Jesus, one may not only save his soul but become a "savior," not of a world, but of the soul of a loved one.

CHAPTER FIVE

RECOGNITION OF APPROPRIATE
AND INAPPROPRIATE CRITICISM

THERE IS NO SUCH THING AS CONSTRUCTIVE CRITICISM

There is no such thing as "Constructive Criticism." To construct is to build, to edify, or to put together. To criticize is to tear down, to find fault, to condemn. These two words describe two separate and opposite processes. One word takes away the meaning from the other. They are antonyms. The thought of criticism being constructive is absurd. In certain literary circles this coupling of two words with opposite meanings is referred to as an "oxymoron." It makes as much sense as saying someone is a "wise fool."

BLOODLETTING

Knowledge doesn't seem to interfere with human tradition, however. When people have been taught something loud enough or long enough they tend to believe it even in the face of overwhelming fact and evidence to the contrary (D&C 93:39). For years the medical profession practiced "bleeding" their patients. By strong oral and religious tradition, it was believed that all sickness was in the blood. One could not disabuse an educated person of the idea. After all it was taught at Harvard, Oxford and the Sorbonne. It seemed perfectly logical to the doctors and professors that if the blood of a person were impure and the cause of sickness then one should drain off as much as one could to give the patient more opportunity to survive.

Most of the Judaic, Christian, and Moslem world knew of the Fall of Adam and how blood became a symbol of fallen man. Religious reasons for bloodletting became quite formalized and took many forms of blood sacrifice. Animals have always been sacrificed and in many societies even human beings. It was God's will and who could argue with that? While the scientific world was breaking away from religion and all educated men scoffed at blood sacrifice, they nevertheless continued to practice medical bloodletting until the 1800's for scientific healing. Who knows the untold millions who died of bloodletting? Oh well, maybe if a little more blood had been let, the patient would have lived. Who knows the untold millions whose self esteem died of the critical "bloodletting" of well-meaning others? Oh well, maybe a little more criticism and their self esteem will improve and their behavior change.

Imagine living in a society when most of the educated doctors, teachers, rulers, and the mass populous believed in bloodletting and one discovered they were in error. What happens to people who make statements that run counter to popular folk belief? History records that all of their blood was let. How well was Copernicus received when he announced that the Earth revolved around the sun and not the sun around the earth? He feared for his life. It doesn't matter that he was correct. He went against tradition, religion, and "God." Traditions die hard. For hundreds of years there was a "Flat Earth Society." How could there be a flat earth society even after the earth was proven to be round. Most people would chuckle at this. How could any sane, rational, intelligent human being continue to maintain some obviously ludicrous notion in the light of all the evidence to the contrary? So it is with Constructive Criticism. In the current societal structure the educated, the rulers, and the masses all believe and practice Constructive Criticism. It approximates a religious tenet of faith. It is as difficult in our time to convince someone that there is no such thing as "Constructive Criticism" as it was to convince former societies that the earth was not flat and that bloodletting was ineffective.

Criticism in and of itself **never** builds anything. It **never** has and it **never** will. The process of construction is separate from the process of demolition. There are companies that deal exclusively with demolition of buildings. Other companies specialize in building construction. Imagine what would happen to the building if the demolition contractor arrived. What part of construction would take place? There are companies that do remodeling. Two different processes are involved in a remodeling project. It is a tricky business. The remodeler must insure that the basic integrity of the structure remains intact. The part to be remodeled is carefully dismantled. The wrecking crew is cautious to demolish only that part of the building which is to be replaced. The tearing down requires a different approach than does the construction phase. One is either tearing down or building up. The fallacy is one can do both at the same time. How does one build anything while they are tearing it down? In construction, the consequences of a demolition crew showing up to tear down an existing structure which was scheduled only to be remodeled would wind up in a law suit. When a well meaning person shares "constructive criticism," he is sending in the wrecking crew.

That most people misuse the phrase "constructive criticism" in their vocabulary is a testimony of their misunderstanding of the two processes involved. It is also evidence of the difficulty of changing firmly entrenched traditions. Except for its redundancy, "Destructive Criticism" is a more accurate phrase to describe the tearing down process. The constructive process is an edifying one. Positive reinforcement best describes the construction process. Criticism does not reinforce a positive behavior. It describes a negative one. Constructive criticism is a myth in the worst case and a misnomer at best.

Those who emphatically defend criticism as "constructive" tend to idealize it. They see it as a right, a moral imperative, a positive thing and a responsible behavior. Their legacy is a trail of devastation to self concept. If only they could step back and view the consequences of their acts of destruction. If only they would objectively measure the practical effects of criticism. They would conclude that the cure was worse than the illness. The real tragedy is the damage done in ignorance to the self esteem of a loved one. Before doctors washed and sterilized their hands, many people died of infections carried by the doctor from patient to patient. As well meaning as they might have been, as compassionate and self sacrificing their efforts, the consequences were deadly. Well meaning people continue to kill self esteem believing they are doing a good thing. They have failed to understand. There is no such thing as constructive criticism.

There is a time and a place for criticism. There are issues and behaviors which need to be corrected. The demolition process involves the use of appropriate criticism. If criticism is so toxic, how could its use ever be appropriate? Think of criticism like a tiny vial of smallpox vaccine. Applied as small dose in a specific area it will immunize the person. If too great an amount is administered it will inflict the very illness it was intended to prevent. Toxic substances are controlled and frequently carry warning labels. They are carefully regulated and restricted to specific uses.

Criticism is like an herbicide which kills all plant life that comes into contact with it. Even diluted, it is devastating.

THE WELL-MEANING FARMER

There was a farmer in Idaho who sued his well meaning neighbor for the misuse of a deadly chemical herbicide. It seemed that the well intended neighbor had sprayed both sides of a long private road common to both farms with an herbicide to kill all of the weeds growing there. In his desire to destroy the weeds he failed to consider the side effects of the wind. As a result, thousands and thousands of dollar's worth of damage was done to the cash crops growing in the fields. The wind had carried the deadly herbicide far beyond its intended application. So it is with criticism. The judge disregarded the "good" intentions and focused on the consequences of destruction. The well meaning neighbor paid a great price for his ignorance. (Judge's Records, Moscow, Idaho, 1978.)

Well intended critics need to be very cautious. Criticism intended for a specific application has side effects that frequently outweigh the assumed benefits. In human relationships the attempts to remove the weeds may result in the destruction of the plants of creativity, motivation and a positive outlook on life. In one's desire through criticism to remove the tares he or she must be careful the wheat is not destroyed (Matthew 13:29). People tend to justify the general use of criticism when only its specific use is appropriate. There are those who will argue that a sword, although a weapon of war, could be used for varied purposes such as harvesting grain, chopping wood, or defending one's self. However, like the sword, criticism is used for emotional war. It maims, injures and destroys emotional bonding even in the closest of family relationships. A surgeon would be mocked if he came to the operating room with a sword instead of a scalpel. Criticism is often used as a sword when it ought to be used as a scalpel. Exactness and great care are required by qualified hands if the operation is to be successful.

Criticism is so much a part of current society that it is considered normal. Cannibalism is also accepted as normal in certain headhunting societies in Borneo. As repulsive as cannibalism may be to others, it is quite natural to them. Just because something is normal does not make it right. Criticism is cannibalism. It kills self esteem and devours self worth.

CRITICISM IS A CANCER

Imagine being called into the doctor's office and then being told that a malignant tumor was coexisting in one's body. The x-rays show that it is the size of an orange. The doctor suggests immediate surgery, tomorrow. "Don't eat anything for twelve hours before," he says, "I've scheduled emergency surgery for 10 a.m. tomorrow morning." He continues to talk and to say words and one can see his lips moving and hear his voice in the background. They are words of hope. His voice fades in and out. Is this a sick joke? Like some out-of-body experience, one finds himself watching dispassionately this entire scene. It is as if the spirit left the body and one is standing in the corner of the room watching himself sitting there listening to the doctor. "The lab report came back positive," he pauses, "it is cancer." Late payments on a note co-signed with a son seemed important on the way to the doctor's office. Also, the annual performance review with the boss was coming up. There is a busy calendar scheduled for this week. This is a bad time to have cancer. A lot of people are expecting things. There isn't time for cancer. Disbelief sweeps over one. Something inside cries out, "it's a lie, it's not true". Something deep, deep inside just cries and wants to be held. "I don't want to frighten you, it is just routine common sense to check with a lawyer and make sure your affairs are in order, just in case some unforeseen circumstance prevails." If there were ever a polite way to say death, he just did, "unforeseen circumstances prevail".

"Read the pamphlet, it will tell you all we know about cancer." Numb and void of feeling, one's eyes stare at the words. "Cancer is a change in the normal growth of cells, but the causes have not yet been fully determined. A great many cancers can be cured with surgery and radiation treatment." It all sounds so sterile, so impersonal. "But it must be treated properly before the cancerous cells have begun to spread or colonize in other parts of the body. Carcinoma, sarcoma, leukemia, ad nauseam. Dear Lord, if there is anything I can do, any change I could make, I'll do it. Let this be a bad dream, let me wake up in a cold sweat to find out like Ebenezer Scrooge in Dickens's, A Christmas Carol, that it is not too late for me." Criticism is a cancer, Wake up!

IT MAY NOT BE TOO LATE

It may not be too late if you act now. A normal relationship infected with the cancer of criticism will begin to consume itself. Has the cancer of criticism consumed so much of one's language that one is past the point of a cure? Has the disease robbed the relationship of an ability to survive it or one's power to resist it? Criticism gnaws at the sinews of any relationship with its destructive effects until it leaves the relationship lifeless. It creates deep wounds and makes enemies of one-time friends, co-workers, and family. So many have lived so long with intense criticism they can not imagine a relationship without it. They were seriously criticized as a child; why should marriage be any different? Why should one's own parenting be any different? Why should any relationship one has with friend, co-worker or family be free of what has become a way of life. After all, isn't that what life is all about, speaking one's mind at will?

SYMBIOSIS OR PARASITISM

Relationships, like the human body, have a life of their own, and they can die. They can be wonderfully healthy. A relationship is a connection between two people. The best relationships are those where each helps the other become their highest and best self. If one thinks of a relationship as having a shared existence, a mini-ecosystem of its own, it is instructive. Symbiosis is a term used in Biology to refer to the association of two living organisms which exist for the benefit of the other. Symbiosis is the opposite of "parasitism." A parasite, is one organism that feeds on the body of the other. A true parasite lives on or in another from which it gets its food always selfishly at the expense of the host. It may or may not kill the host, but usually parasites are unable to survive independently. Lice and tapeworms are parasites. Mistletoe is a parasite on oak trees. Some human relationships are composed of one and sometimes two parasites who stay together for fear they will not survive alone and for all the wrong reasons. Where both are parasites, they consume one another. The opposite is true of a symbiotic relationship. Most lichens, which are composed of an alga and a fungus, are examples of symbiosis; the alga provides the food, and the fungus provides the water and protection. In this association or relationship, neither is harmed and both benefit. It is truly a mutual improvement association. Relationships, whether husband-wife, parent-child, employer-employee, brother-sister, friend to friends, have a life of their own. The whole is equal to the sum of its parts. The relationship will never be greater than the part that each contributes to make it successful. When both parties are committed to a mutual benefit that helps each to become their highest and best, a symbiotic relationship exists. This is the ideal. This is the only defensible position a loving person can take to help loved ones become their best. Anything less will ultimately turn one or the other into a parasite.

FRUSTRATION COMES FROM UNMET EXPECTATIONS

All frustration comes from unmet expectations. There is no such thing as a frustration that is not tied to an expectation. Sometimes the relationship between an expectation and a frustration is obvious. One was expecting a raise in pay at work and didn't receive it. Frustration is a first response to an unmet expectation. It is normal and natural to feel frustration. Some people set themselves up for frustration by possessing unrealistic or unreasonable expectations. For example, "If you really love me, you will be able to read my mind and know how I am feeling." This is both unrealistic and unreasonable. However, because the expectation wasn't met the party became frustrated. The issue is what happens to the frustration? There is an entire range of human emotions one can choose from in reacting to frustration, i.e., resentment, hate, anger, disappointment, resignation, despair, depression, determination, mediation, relief, and love. Frustration is a first reaction. Choosing an emotion is a second reaction. Choosing a

~~behavior is a third reaction.~~ Often the time it takes to go from frustration to acting out is a millisecond. Practice and habit entrench a negative behavior as well as positive behaviors.

UNMET EXPECTATION	FIRST REACTION	SECOND REACTION	THIRD REACTION
⇒	⇒	⇒	⇒
	PRIME VALUE	CHOICE OF EMOTION	CHOICE OF BEHAVIOR
	Frustration	Resentment	Silence
	Relief	Hate	Rage
	Love	Anger	Criticism
	Fear	Disappointment	Withdrawal
	Survival	Resignation	Crying
		Despair	Yelling
		Depression	Pouting
		Anxiety	Panic Attacks
		Disbelief	Laughing
		Determination	Work Harder
		Joy	Singing
		Happiness	Smiling

Some unmet expectations are met with relief instead of frustration. A case in point would be having a policeman pull one over for speeding and expect to receive a citation and fine for a traffic violation. Instead, one receives a warning ticket. The first reaction to the unmet expectation is relief. There is another option to unmet expectations. It is to love. It is possible to have love as the motivating first reaction. It is possible to have as a second reaction, empathy and compassion. At the behavioral level it is possible to apply the Christian standard.

THE HIGHER LAW
But I say unto you, Love your enemies, bless them that curse you, do good to them that hate you, and pray for them which despitefully use you, and persecute you;
That ye may be the children of your Father which is in heaven. . . (Matthew 5:44-45).

This higher law cannot be lived without the Holy Ghost. It is based in loving God and loving one's fellow man. A paradigm shift is required to love this way. The world and those who are in the world scoff at the higher law of love. The world deals at the behavioral level. Behavior modification is a popular field of study in psychology. There are numerous programs that focus on everything from addictive behaviors to anger management. One program that is conspicuous by its absence is criticism management.

When critical people are asked why they are criticizing, they frequently respond "Because the person being criticized was wrong, and so I wanted to correct their behavior, answer, issue, or statement". People usually criticize because someone is not measuring up to expectations, and the critic is frustrated. The truth of the matter is that most criticism is based on frustration. People want other people to do what they want them to do, what they think is right and proper. Therefore, when others are not performing to expectations, they lash out, nag, gripe, complain, murmur, cry, swear, and verbally attack them. Another response to unmet expectations is to sulk, pout, withdraw and give them the silent treatment. Neither of these reactions to unmet expectations is as healthy as criticism properly given while being in emotional control and logically explaining one's frustration at a mutually agreeable time and place with the one concerned.

Ironically, while one's lips drip with verbal venom, his heart is hoping that someone will love him, care for him, respect him, accept him, appreciate him, and want to be with him and, yes, even overlook his weaknesses. There are more productive ways of communicating frustration, and they work. Criticism doesn't remove frustration, it describes it. Frequently, criticism feeds its own fire, and what started out to be a contained burn, becomes a massive forest fire burning out of control. It's a description, not a cure. If the critical person does not find appropriate ways of communicating his frustration, he will eventually and invariably increase his critical nature and destroy his own effectiveness as a communicator. Being less effective, his frustration increases until he explodes into anger or tears of resentment. He may implode into sulky silent oblivion, where despair dwells and all travelers nearby give him a wide berth. It need not be. There is a way to properly express one's frustrations and to do so in such a manner that both the giver and receiver are edified. Before pursuing how that is accomplished, there is a need to focus on another myth about criticism.

DOES IMPROPER CRITICISM CHANGE BEHAVIOR?

[If the sheer act of criticism worked in changing behavior, there would already exist a perfect utopian society. The irony of ironies is that many people criticize in order to change behavior.] They truly believe that describing unacceptable behavior will make it go away. Criticism, especially uninvited, unauthorized, improper criticism, only antagonizes, alienates, and creates hostility towards the giver of criticism. Many self-righteous givers of criticism feel divinely appointed and comfort themselves by knowing they and God are on the same side. So they tilt at the windmill as if this critical quest were some holy mission and they must expect rejection from others as the price they must pay for being "right" as the emissary of truth. Tragically, it is self-delusion. There are things that change human behavior. However, describing behavior in critical terms, or rejecting behavior through critical words and deeds does not change it.

Non-verbal criticism such as a frown does not change the behavior. At best, a verbal or non-verbal critical message only describes the behavior in question. Whether the message of rejection comes verbally or non-verbally, the person being criticized will most often reject the one who is doing the criticizing instead of rejecting the unacceptable behavior. Change occurs when the motivation for change comes from within. [Criticism comes most often from the outside. Criticism is a lousy motivator.]

Coaches who exert the most profound positive effects upon their athletes are the ones who believe in their players, who genuinely care about them and accept them and inspire them to greatness. Most outstanding coaches recognize that relationships are like bank accounts. One has to make deposits if one expects to make withdrawals. Those coaches who use fear, intimidation, ridicule, criticism, sarcasm and other belittling ploys, seldom inspire anything but resentment, hostility and poor self-image. Sincere praise and acceptance inspire behavioral change because the motivation for change is coming from the inside.

Criticism is an outside force that may achieve a degree of control, but control is not change. Continued criticism will result in a double standard wherein the criticized party abides a controlled standard in the presence of the critic and abides his own standard when away and on his own. A sponge, for example, can be made to conform to whatever outside pressure is exerted upon it. Yet, as soon as the pressure is released, the sponge will assume its previous shape.) Control is not change. So it is with the pressure of criticism. One may be able to temporarily impose conformity, but conformity isn't change. As soon as he leaves, the person reverts to previous behavior.

Criticism is not only ineffective, it may well be counter-productive because it weakens a person's self esteem as well as his confidence. The net effect of criticism is that some people change in spite of it, not because of it. Criticism, invited or not, lessens the probability for real change. One of the true dangers of listening to criticism day in and day out is that those so treated come to believe they are not worthwhile, they can do nothing right and they may become hyper-self-critical. Soon, there won't be a need for anyone else to criticize them, for they will do it themselves. Self-criticism becomes self-fulfilled prophecy and all of the evidence of being criticized by others now is joined by all the evidence one amasses against himself. In the jury of one's mind there can be only one verdict with so much internal and external evidence, i.e., guilty as charged of not being worthwhile.

For centuries, tyrants have controlled the masses through fear, threats and criticism. What they also created was an underground movement against themselves, adversaries to what was, instead of partners working in a common cause for the good of each. There will always be opposition, even to a benevolent king. But should a man's enemies be those of his own house and heart? Enemies from the outside, yes, but why would anyone want to create enemies of their friends, family or co-workers by being a controller of others through constant criticism? Forced conformity is a shallow victory and a poor substitute for cheerful conformity rendered from a willing heart.

One observer has noted that grandparents get along better with their grandchildren than with their own children. They seem to be more loving and far less critical with their grandchildren. This has lead to a humorous saying: "Grandparents and grandchildren are natural allies, because they share a common enemy." Ironically, most grandparents focus on loving their grandchildren and not on changing them or criticizing them. The result is grandparents are more effective in creating an environment which is more conducive to change in human behavior with their grandchildren than they were with their own children. One wise grandpa observed, "I just love 'em, I don't try to change 'em. There are plenty of folks out there who will try to change 'em but there aren't very many who will just love 'em".

There are two very important questions that need to be answered, first "How do people learn?" and second, "What are my limits in effecting change in another?"

HOW PEOPLE LEARN

I.   People learn by observation, example, role models, and what they see with their eyes.

56

II.   People learn by instruction, an open mind, a listening heart, and what they hear with their ears.

III.   People learn by experience, suffering, school of hard knocks, and by what they feel.

By understanding how people learn, one can save an enormous amount of time and frustration by not expecting people to learn in ways that won't work. Uninvited criticism will not change behavior and is a waste of time. There are many scientific and scholarly ways to describe the reality of how learning takes place. The three ways most learning occurs is by observation, instruction, and experience.

I. <u>Learning from observation, example or role models</u> means that for sighted people their eyes are the instruments of observation. They see their universe respond to natural or man-made laws that interact with their world.

An example of a learned behavior would be the magic bottle.

THE MAGIC BOTTLE

A young baby, too young to crawl, is lying on the carpet in the middle of the front room sucking on a bottle. The baby drops the bottle and it rolls just out of reach. Try as she might, the baby cannot reach the bottle and begins to cry out of frustration. The father happens by and hears the baby's plea and goes over and puts the bottle back into the baby's mouth. This happens a number of times. Soon the baby learns that by crying, she can magically make the bottle come to her.

<u>People learn by observation</u>. By watching the examples of others and by mirroring those behaviors, each repetition brings the skill or behavior into the life experience of the learner. "Monkey see, monkey do," is an old adage which reinforces the importance of proper role models, for it is true that, "what you do speaks so loudly, I cannot hear what you say". Observation, example and role models are primary ways of learning.

II. <u>Learning by Instruction</u> is fundamentally an ear experience. Even more important, learning by instruction requires an open mind and a willing heart. There is a difference between criticism and instruction.

Sometimes people will ask, "Isn't criticism a form of instruction?" The answer depends upon the open mind and listening heart of the receiver. Criticism which does not respect the "space" of the receiver is rarely instructive and mostly counter-productive. Invited criticism, properly given, may be instruction. Uninvited criticism seldom is well received.

The basic truth is, one can only teach to the level of willingness of the listener. If one is unwilling to learn, he may not be instructed and may perceive the two-way communication to not have existed at all, it was only a one-sided lecture. Without the willingness or preparation of the listener to keep his mind open to the information shared, it does not qualify as learning by instruction.

JIM DOESN'T LACK KNOWLEDGE

For twenty years, Jim's wife has nagged him about throwing his dirty clothes in a pile in the bedroom. It's not important to Jim. It doesn't matter. He has heard the same message for twenty years. Jim has not learned to put his dirty clothes in the laundry room. He doesn't lack knowledge, he lacks commitment to the value.

Hearing is only learning if the listener is open to change, and willing to do so because life will be better.

III. Learning by Experience, by trial and error, and by the suffering one endures is difficult. This is learning by feeling, by touching, by bumping into boundaries and learning one's limitations. This is learning at the school of hard knocks. There are those who will not learn by observation, nor by instruction and are left to learn by the tough lessons of life. A young child may be told to watch out for the corner of the table, or else she may hit her head and it will hurt. The child may even watch another bump his head, and only after two or three knots on her own head, does the child learn for herself to watch out for the corner of the table.

THE SPOILED SON

The story is told of a wealthy man who wanted to teach his spoiled son the value of money before the father died and left his estate in the hands of an irresponsible son who would squander his wealth away. One day, the father called the son into his den and told the son to go out and earn $500 and bring it back to the father or he would cut him out of the will. the troubled young man went to his mother with this tale of woe. The mother counseled him to wait for a month, dress up in work clothes, and give the father $500 that the mother would give to her son. The time passed, and the son met his father in the den and had on his work clothes, and gave to his father the $500 his mother had given him. The father promptly took the $500, walked over to the fireplace, which had a cozy fire burning in it, and threw the $500 into the flames and said to the son, "This is not your money. You did not earn it by the sweat of your brow. Now, go out and earn $500 and bring it to me or I will cut you out of my will."

The young man returned to his mother and commiserated with her about the failed ploy. "This time, wait a month, cover your face and clothes with some dirt, and be sure your father sees you leave for work every day. Then sneak back to the house and I will give you another $500 to take to him in a month." The time passed, and the son met the father in the den. Once again, the father took the money and threw it into the fire and said to his son, "You must earn this money yourself." Totally bewildered and frustrated, the young man went out his mother and inquired as to how the father knew that neither the first nor the second time he had earned the $500. They concluded that the father must have spies watching them and therefore there would be no way out except for the son to get an honest job and earn the $500 as the father had directed. So it was that the son went forth and found employment and worked hard in the heat of the day, and after a month he met a third time with his father and gave him the $500 he had earned. The father took the $500 and threw it into the fire. Immediately, the son jumped to the fire and began to pull back his hard-earned money. "Yes", said the father, "this is money you have earned." (Anonymous)

Some people can learn by observation, and some can learn by instruction, but there are some people who will learn certain lessons only by the things they suffer. Most lessons are best learned by natural consequences instead of artificially imposed ones.

WHAT ARE ONE'S LIMITS IN EFFECTING CHANGE IN OTHERS?

There are five things one can do to effect change in others:

1. Set an example of the things one values
2. Share to the level of willingness of the person
3. Love
4. Pray for them
5. Set one's own boundaries

1. THE POWER OF EXAMPLE

People can choose to learn by watching, by observation, example, and role modeling. One way to influence those one wants to see change their behavior is to be an example of the principle, value, or behavior he is trying to teach. The power of personal example is a strong witness and testimony that cannot be denied by the observer.

SOLOMON
Train up a child in the way he should go, and when he is old,
he will not depart from it (Proverbs 22:6).

Impressions received in the eyes of the young leave a marked imprint upon their minds forever. They may walk a thorny path as they learn from the things that they suffer. However, as they progress in age those values will remain with them. Setting a good example is not wasted effort.

NEPHI TEACHES OF JESUS
And again, it showeth unto the children of men the straitness of the path, and the narrowness of the gate, by which they should enter, he having set the example before them.
And he said unto the children of men: Follow thou me. Wherefore, my beloved brethren, can we follow Jesus save we shall be willing . . .? (2 Nephi 31:9-10).

2. SHARE OR PREACH

A second and very profound way to influence another is to share with them verbally. Sharing implies a **willingness** on the part of both to engage in the verbal experience. When only one party is willing, the shared experience becomes a lecture. In a religious context it becomes a sermon. At that point it is no longer a shared experience but a preaching one. The same applies to teaching. The teacher is limited by the **willingness** of the student to listen. The challenge to the teacher, or anyone in the position of authority, may be to figure out inventive and creative ways to entice, encourage, and inspire the listener. Those who want to appeal to their position for authority are frequently disappointed. For example, "You are going to listen, because I'm the boss", "the spouse," "the parent," or "the friend." They are appealing to their position in order to encourage the listener to hear them (D&C 121:36, 41-42). Appeal to authority is one of the weakest approaches. It assumes conformity. How often it is the case that employees perform one way when the boss is present and another when he is absent. Appeal to authority imposes a position but does not assure compliance.

What if no attempt were made to appeal to the power of the position? What if the listener were invited and respected? What if the objective were agreement and not conformity? Obviously there will be times when agreement is not possible. The boss, who has ultimate responsibility, will have to act unilaterally. However, agreement and sharing in a decision are preferable to mandates.

What if the space of a person who was going to be criticized was not violated without their common consent? "I have something critical I would like to say. When would be a good time to share it with you? I would like to talk to you sometime within the next couple of hours." Here, the invitation is made. Respect for others is modeled by the power of personal example. To have unwanted, and unwelcomed criticism received is enhanced by the delivery of the bearer. Since the one with the criticism has the expectation to share it, it devolves upon him a greater responsibility. There are many ways to share the information. Critical information should always focus on the issue or behavior while preserving the self-worth of the one being criticized. Otherwise, the best information falls on deaf ears. Without agreement or sharing, one's words become a lecture or a sermon. The preacher, teacher, parent, or boss's words are tolerated at best, or rejected at worst.

3. LOVE AND TRUST

Maybe the most profound way to effect change in others is to love them, to strengthen them and their self-esteem in such a way they come to believe in themselves. The power of unconditional love has yet to be measured. This much is known. It is difficult to resist forever the unconditional love of another. There is so much to say about the power of love, of acceptance, affection, and appreciation. There are some cautions. Love and trust are two different things. You can love someone and not trust them. Also, you can trust someone and not love them. You can both love and trust or you can both not love and not trust. TRUST is the function of freedom and responsibility. "I will give you as much freedom as you demonstrate responsibility to handle."

Unconditional love, on the other hand, does not mean one has to be stupid or be taken advantage of, or made to feel a fool. Unconditional love is something one does because he is a good person, not because the loved one deserves it. However, the loving thing is almost always the responsible thing. The loving thing is to help a person become their highest and best self. It is not love to enable someone in poor judgment decisions. "I will not help you one inch to hell," is a loving stance. Irresponsible people want to play upon the love others have for them in order to escape responsibility.

SAM'S STORY
Sam was a responsible seventeen year old in everything but driving fast. In a single month he received three speeding tickets. There was an important prom dance coming up. Sam asked his father if he could borrow his Dad's expensive car. The father responded, "No."

Sam was disappointed and naively asked, "Why?

Dad's reply was straightforward, "I love you, son, but I don't trust you once you get behind the steering wheel of a car."

Sam pleaded, "How can I ever prove to you that I can be responsible if you never trust me?"

The father retorted, "When you have paid me back the money I loaned you to pay the speeding tickets, and if you receive no more traffic violations for three months, I'll be willing to extend trust once again and loan you the car."

Sam said, "But Dad, the dance is this Friday night. In three months it will be too late. I promise I'll drive responsibly."

Sam's mother would have let him take the car. In her heart she thought it would be the loving thing to do. She looked at her husband with pleading eyes.

The father stood firm, "I'm sorry son, the answer is no."

Sam stomped off angry and mad and slammed the door to his room. The mother was also upset with the father. She felt that mercy was needed. The dad explained that doing the responsible thing is almost always the truly loving thing to do.

Trust and love are two separate issues. The mother would have caved in to the disappointment she saw in her son. She would have given trust in the name of love. Trust, however is unlike love, respect, and forgiveness which can be gifted. But to forgive doesn't mean one is trusted. A child molester can be forgiven, but never trusted again with children. An alcoholic can be forgiven, but not hired as a bartender. Trust must be earned by responsible behavior. Sam would agree with the statement, "If you love me, trust me." So would his mother. The problem is the mother winds up being an enabler. Sam wanted freedom without responsibility for the past. The father's decision was a correct one, a loving one, and a very unpopular one.

Quickly, a person can see that with each relationship one needs to have two programs. One is an "I Love You" Program, and the other is an "I Trust You" Program. The two programs should be kept separate. When love and trust become mixed up, people begin to act in bizarre ways. They set themselves up to be taken advantage of and then are hurt and wounded. In the name of love they trust the untrustworthy. Unconditional love does not mean unconditional trust.

People have a responsibility to protect themselves from the untrustworthy. To allow another to take advantage of one in the name of love is to be foolish. It is to be an enabler in the worst way. It reinforces manipulation as a reward for the untrustworthy. The wounded party decides to withhold love as a punishment for not being trusted. When the "I Love You" Program is separated from the "I Trust You" Program, clear-headed decisions can be made. Indeed, love and trust need not be related at all. The "I Love You" Program has a simple governing value.

"I LOVE YOU" CREED
Because I love you, I will assist you in doing everything
within my power and limited resources to help you become your
highest and best self. But I will not help you one inch to hell!

There in a nutshell is the affirmative statement which declares one's position of loving. In regards to the "I Trust You" Program, the governing value is a simple declaration.

"I TRUST YOU" CREED
I will trust you as you demonstrate responsible behavior.

There is much that will be left unsaid at this point about trust, or reinvesting trust in one who has demonstrated irresponsible behavior. Offending parties frequently demand trust as a sign of being loved. Only the foolish will be convinced by this faulty reasoning. Those who are unable to separate love and trust often wind up enabling unhealthy behaviors to continue in the name of love.

4. PRAY FOR THEM

The issue of "Mighty Prayer" will be dealt with extensively in chapter seven. Suffice it to say prayer is one of the most productive principles for effecting change in others. Prayer is one of the keys to Divine Intervention. It is also an eternal form of communication.

- Premortal spirit children pray (John Taylor, N.B. Lundwall, comp., The Vision, p. 146).
- Mortals pray.
- Deceased souls, who exist as spirits in the Spirit World, pray (Revelation 6:9-10, Genesis 4:10).
- Resurrected beings pray (3 Nephi 17:15-18, 3 Nephi 19:19-35).

Prayer will always be a medium of communication between God and His children. Prayer is not a prisoner of time, distance, or death. Prayer is an eternal form of communication.

5. SET ONE'S OWN BOUNDARIES

This principle will also be dealt with in several of the later chapters. The essence of "setting one's own boundaries" relates to protecting oneself against a toxic personality, or a physically, emotionally, or spiritually abusive person. It is an issue of tolerance. It sends a message to others as to what one's limits are. For example, using illegal drugs in the home, loaning money, staying in an abusive relationship, all have their limits. Everyone must decide, according to their value system, what they will and will not tolerate. The major problem is that most do not follow through on supporting the boundaries they set. "If I catch you smoking in the home, I'll kick you out that day." It is an artificial boundary, but not a real one. The offended party often winds up eating their own words. They destroy their credibility because they never follow through. Others are so extreme on the "perfectionist" side, their boundaries are unrealistic and unreasonable. Each boundary needs to pass the "third party reasonable test." This means the boundary will be considered reasonable by an objective third party.

There is an eternal principle which is self-evident. It is the reality that every relationship stands on its own merits. No one can have a relationship for someone else. In any given relationship one has a hundred percent control over their half of the relationship.

UNDERSTANDING THE NATURE OF STEWARDSHIPS

Using the paradigm of the family, we could say that all stewardships fall into one of three categories: Father-Mother, Brother-Sister, or Son-Daughter. In other words, one is either a parent, a brother-sister, or a child.

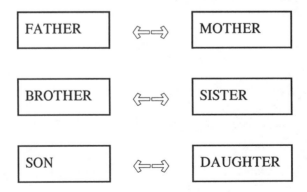

Many times one changes hats and plays all three of these roles in a short period of time.

CHANGING HATS

> *While serving as a Bishop, I was in a meeting with other Bishops discussing regional welfare needs. My relationship to them was Brother to Brother. The Stake President called me out of that meeting for a short consultation. My relationship to him was Son to Father. On the way back to the Bishop's meeting a ward member stopped me to share a concern. My relationship to the ward member was that of Father to Child. In a matter of minutes I had played all three roles, i.e., Brother, Son, and Father (Dr. John L. Lund, Personal Journal, 1975).*

One's relationship as an employee would be Child to Parent. The role of boss would be Parent to Child. Co-workers would be Brother to Sister. All those who are in authority over a person would be in a Parent role. Those for whom one had no responsibility would be at a level of Brother-Sister. Continuing to use this model, pursue the question,"What gives one the right to criticize?" Is there a right, an inherent privilege, a just prerogative for parents to criticize children? Yes, when done properly. Is there a right for children to criticize parents? Under certain conditions the answer is yes. Is there a right for a brother to criticize another brother? There are circumstances when the answer is again yes. However, no one has a blank check to criticize. .

Those in the Father-Mother role probably have the most latitude, but even here it is not unconditional. Those in Brother-Sister or Son-Daughter roles would have even less leeway and more narrowly defined parameters for giving criticism. The question is asked, where does the Husband-Wife relationship fit in?

THE EQUALITY OF MEN AND WOMEN

> *Nevertheless neither is the man without the woman, neither the woman without the man, in the Lord. . . .*
>
> *But if any man seem to be contentious, we have no such custom, neither the churches of God (I Cor 11:11, 16).*

As they relate to each other, it is a brother-sister relationship. There seems to be but few who understand it that way. Many husbands feel they are "Father" to their wives and not co-equals. They treat their spouse as if she were a child and tell them what they "should," "need," and "ought" to do, or say, or be. They feel free to criticize, and somehow feel as though marriage gives them that "right." In all brother-sister relationships, that which gives one a "right" to criticize" is the PERMISSION of the one being criticized.

In all fairness, there are many women who parent their spouses. They assume a "Mother" role over their husband without the slightest regard for co-equality. They tell their mate what he "should," "needs," and "ought" to do, or say, or dress, or be. This is a major mistake when either a husband or wife assume that marriage gives them the right to be disrespectful or to act as a parent to their spouse. It sets a terrible example for the children who grow up to perpetuate it.

Children who tell their parents to "shut up," and who feel free to criticize their parents at will are considered disrespectful. It's not right for children to criticize their elders, to tell the adults what they "should," "need," and "ought" to do. Is respect a demanded right? Is respect something the vassal owes to the suzerain, the serf owes to the king, the child owes to the parent? How does a child treated with disrespect ever learn respect?

> *"FATHERS PROVOKE NOT YOUR CHILDREN"*
> *Children, obey your parents in the Lord: for this is right.*
> *Honour thy father and mother; (which is the first commandment with promise;)*
> *That it may be well with thee, and thou mayest live long on the earth*
> *And, ye fathers, provoke not your children to wrath: but bring them up in the nurture and admonition of the Lord (Eph 6:1-4).*

Maybe children never learn respect and simply grow up and marry and have kids and continue onward in the same pattern. There is a way to criticize and to do it effectively. Appealing to one's position as parent, spouse, or sister is not it. Claiming to be right or to be bigger, or to be smarter, or to be faster, does not qualify one to criticize. Loving someone or caring deeply does not give a right. It may be the motivation and witness to the pure intent of the heart of the giver of criticism. But it must be remembered that only in the most desperate, life-threatening, extreme circumstances, should one offer uninvited criticism without receiving first the permission of the one being criticized.

To daily find one's self criticizing his or her loved ones, employees, and friends is to assume an ego of God-size proportion. Where is the child that needs a constant diet of criticism? Where is the spouse for whom it can honestly be said they need to be daily criticized? Do people marry in order to be criticized? Or do people marry in order to love and be loved? Criticism is a cancer that will kill love or sap its strength as much as any parasite or tapeworm will attack its host body.

When a men or women say they are not being treated right, they almost always mean they do not feel respected, valued, nor equal because of the critical things said to them by their spouse. Choosing to respect all persons and their right to their own opinions, attitudes and space, used to be called courtesy and regard.

It is the opinion of most professionals that a major contributor to the rampant dissolution of marital ties is the inability of one or both spouses to demonstrate courtesy and regard. The lack thereof is demonstrated by the impunity with which they criticize. The ability to respect another is an issue which bespeaks the strength of character of the giver of respect. It sets an example amidst a society out of control with unkind words and behaviors. It calls for order from chaos and is a beacon of light to those sailing the rocky shoals.

Respect is a gift. It says more about the giver than the receiver. Respect is given to others because the "giver" is a good person. To treat each person with respect is a higher law. Those who continue to live the law of an eye-for-an-eye will soon find the blind leading the blind. Those who believe that respect must be "earned" will discover that eventually no one can be respected. The reason for this is the lack of absolute standards for evaluating who deserves to be respected. Ultimately, even self-respect will disappear if the standard is "perfection or nothing."

One of the great messages from the play Pygmalion, and later the movie My Fair Lady, was how people respond to being treated with respect. What is it about that movie that lifts the human heart? Why do tears come into the eyes as someone triumphs over a difficult background? Why does the idealism of Cinderella inspire hope? What is it about the human spirit that calls one to a higher and better self? Why do people cheer when common men act in an uncommon manner and rise to the occasion, and behold, a hero is born?

THE "POSSIBLE" DREAM

In Man of La Mancha, Don Quixote, possesses an impossible dream. He treats people with respect and sees in them a higher and better self. Though surrounded by the mirrors of reality which bespeak of filth and wretchedness and of man's lowest nature, he encounters a bar maid, known by many men. Her name is Aldonsa, literally a "dunce", a slow minded dullard. There was a time when children were humiliated by being required to sit in a corner of a school room upon a dunce stool. Some were required to wear a "dunce cap," a tall cone-shaped cap. Its intent was to punish the child who was slow in learning his lessons in school. Don Quixote refused to call the bar maid the "dumb one." Instead, he called her, "The sweet one," or Dulcinea. A "dulse" in Spanish is a sweet or candy.

"No," she responded. This was a case of mistaken identity. She had been confused with someone else. She was in her own eyes, a dumb one,

a dunce. And as long as self-perception was reinforced by those around her, she continued to act the wench. She concluded he was nothing but a crazy old man, deluded by his impossible dream. He refused to see her in any other light. There, in the darkened heart of Dulcinea, he saw sweetness. Finally she became convinced that in his eyes she was "sweet." His perception became hers.

Don Quixote was much like an obsessed miner panning for gold. He continued to search in the mud of humanity for the gold nugget. He swirled the water about his pan again and again. He washed away the dirt until the precious gold was freed from its earth bound prison. So it was that Don Quixote, undaunted, continued to see the best in Dulcinea. He treated her with respect and was mocked and scorned for it. Even Dulcinea at first mocked the old fool. However, as time passed and with his unrelenting respect he treated her as "a fair lady." She could not resist imagining even for a moment what it felt like to be respected by someone, even a crazy old fool. Her reality rejected all rights to be respected as judged by everyone. Ah, but it was his reality to respect her. He saw the good within, the sweetness of her, and he gifted to her respect. He treated her with respect, because it was his standard. He chose to respect her independent of others, independent of her own self-esteem, and independent of all circumstances. His respect for her was a gift. There seem to be many willing to condemn, but few who love and gift respect because it is their standard.

As the play continues, a marvelous transformation occurs. Aldonsa becomes Dulcinea. Self-respect was born because someone gifted respect. The bar-tending wench, a woman bought for any price, was now offered a new price, i.e., respect, and she liked it. She liked how it made her feel inside. It felt better than anything else.

At the very end of his life, Don Quixote questions for a moment if he has just been a fool after all. His friends assure him that he has not been a fool. He dies firm in the faith of his "possible dream." The wench left the death bed of Don Quixote. A former acquaintance called out to her, "Aldonsa, Aldonsa". Her eyes flashed. She fixed her gaze upon the supplicant and announced with conviction that her name was Dulcinea. And so ends the movie, but not the message. Respect is a gift, and maybe the ultimate gift is self-respect.

JOHNNY LINGO

There is a great story told of one Johnny Lingo, a Polynesian who was considered a wonderful catch by both the island maidens and their fathers. Women were compensated for by paying the father in cows. As totally disgusting as that appears today, and as politically incorrect as it could be as judged by current societal standards, it was nonetheless the accepted practice.

Johnny Lingo was wealthy, he was handsome and owned many cows. The father of Mahana held his daughter in lowest regard and complained to the intermediary he would only be able to bargain one cow for Mahana, as she was ugly and shy and hid in the trees so as not to be seen of others. She let her long hair hang in front of her face, so that others could not see her. However, one day Johnny Lingo saw her face and knew of her true beauty.

As was the custom and tradition, the father of Mahana sat across from Johnny Lingo with the mediator at the side of the father. The women in the village were in the background. They were recalling the days when their husbands met with their fathers and bargained for their hand in marriage. "I was a 'two cow' wife," proudly boasted the one." She was quieted by another who had been a "three cow" wife. Sometimes a cow would be sacrificed and divided as a part of the bargaining. The father whispered to the mediator, "I'll be lucky if I get the ears and a tail for Mahana." Then the father spoke up and told of all of Mahana's virtues, how she is strong, and a good worker, and how much he would miss her. Johnny Lingo listened very carefully and agreed with the father that his loss would be great, and he truly needed to be compensated for such a great sacrifice. All were listening, the other maidens, the one, two and three cow wives; all were waiting for Johnny Lingo to offer a cow for Mahana. Even Mahana, hidden by a tree waited her fate. "I offer you eight cows, but no more," Johnny said. The father was stupefied, the women were agape, the mouths were open, but no one spoke. No one had ever offered eight cows before. It was unheard of, not on this nor any island. Many wondered if Johnny Lingo were a fool, for he could have had her for a cow, but he offered eight cows. Johnny Lingo was no fool. He knew that Mahana's self-esteem would mean more than all of his cows and wealth.

Johnny Lingo treated Mahana with respect and continued to do so. Everyone knew Mahana was an "eight cow" wife. As her confidence grew, her natural beauty began to show forth. Her hair no longer drooped in front of her face. Her self-confident smile radiated an inner worth. After awhile, the father came to see Johnny Lingo and Mahana. He could not believe his eyes. Her beauty was unsurpassed, her grace and charm were abundant. The father left by saying to Johnny Lingo, "You cheated me, Johnny Lingo, she was worth more." Maybe respect, like beauty, lies first in the eye of the beholder. Some have said the eye is the window to the soul and there reflects in the eyes the values of the soul.

Some will discount the entire notion of respect being given as a gift. Nevertheless, one appeals to the Supreme Court of the conscience of each man and woman to find the truth within their own soul, i.e., respect emanates from the giver, and should be gifted to all.

JESUS AND RESPECT

The Savior gifted respect to all people because he was Man's Great Exemplar.

And again, it showeth unto the children of men the straitness of the path, and the narrowness of the gate, by which they should enter, he having set the example before them. . . ,

Wherefore, follow me, and do the things which ye have seen me do (2 Nephi 31:9,12).

A great Bible scholar and commentator is J. R. Dummelow. In his commentary he defines the use of the term "Woman" as follows:

Woman, or rather "Lady" is in Greek a title of respect, used even in addressing queens (Dummelow, One Volume Bible Commentary, p. 778).

On at least two separate occasions the Lord spoke to his mother, Mary, and addressed her as "Woman."

THE MARRIAGE IN CANA
Woman, what wilt thou have me to do for thee? That will I do: for mine hour is not yet come (JST John 2:4).

JESUS ON THE CROSS
When Jesus therefore saw his mother, and the disciple standing by, whom he loved, he saith unto his mother, Woman [My Lady], behold thy son! (John 19:26).

To the Samaritan woman at Jacob's well, Jesus would ask for a drink of water. The Samaritans were hated by the Jews as a mixed race of apostates with a heathen core. The Samaritan woman was surprised that Jesus would even speak to her. She seemed doubly shocked that he would ask her for a favor.

THE SAMARITAN WOMAN AT JACOB'S WELL
Then saith the woman of Samaria unto him, How is it that thou, being a Jew, askest drink of me, which am a woman of Samaria? For the Jews have no dealings with the Samaritans (John 4:9).

Jesus spoke to her with great respect. Later, in the conversation he addressed her as My Lady. This is after he announced that she had been divorced five times and the man with whom she was now living was not her husband. Did such a moral vagrant deserve to be treated with respect? Apparently, the Savior thought so.

> *Jesus saith unto her, [My Lady] Woman, believe me,*
> *the hour cometh, when ye shall neither in this mountain,*
> *nor yet at Jerusalem, worship the Father (John 4:21).*

Remember, respect says more about the giver than it does about the receiver. Jesus gifted respect because He was good, not because she earned it, or deserved it. Jesus followed this pattern of gifting respect to the woman who was taken in adultery. After the scribes and Pharisees dropped the stones they had planned to throw at the woman, Jesus was left alone with her.

> *THE WOMAN TAKEN IN ADULTERY*
> *When Jesus had lifted up himself, and saw none but the*
> *woman, he said unto her, Woman [My Lady], where are those*
> *thine accusers? Hath no man condemned thee?*
> *She said, No man, Lord. And Jesus said unto her, Neither do*
> *I condemn thee: go, and sin no more (John 8:10-11, underlining*
> *mine).*

Immediately after this event Jesus spoke to the people.

> *Then spake Jesus again unto them, saying, I am the light of*
> *the world: he that followeth me shall not walk in darkness, but*
> *shall have the light of life (John 8:12).*

Jesus continued to gift respect even to the hated gentiles. When the Syrophenician woman who was a Greek asked him to heal her daughter, Jesus refused. Following a discussion of "crumbs from the Master's table," Jesus said,

> *THE GENTILE WOMAN*
> *. . . O woman [My Lady], great is thy faith: be it unto thee*
> *even as thou wilt. And her daughter was made whole from that*
> *very hour Matthew 15:28).*

It is a marvelous example to treat people with respect. In all relationships, whether Parent, Sister-Brother, or Child, people deserve to be treated with respect.

Later, each will be instructed to ask for permission before they criticize. Why? Respect is the answer. Because one is modeling the principle of respect. One is setting a standard of excellence in each relationship to which he is a party. One is sending a message that he respects the space, the time, the privacy of another. One is requesting permission out of respect, even if one's role as Mother-Father figure would not require it. But one is not appealing to authority, to being bigger, faster, nor smarter. For what happens when a child, spouse, or friend becomes bigger, smarter, or faster than the critic? Does one then enter the chicken-fighting arena of trying to prove who is most right or least to blame? Respect begets respect, and, even if it didn't, it would produce self-respect, self-control, and foster self-mastery.

It has been a dedicated purpose of the author to study criticism and its effects during more than twenty-five years of post-doctoral research. Most people criticize out of frustration, as previously mentioned. Their objective is frequently to change behavior, which has been discussed as terribly ineffective. Unhealthy people use criticism as a form of emotional intimidation, born out of their own fear of not being loved on their own merits. So they criticize to manipulate, coerce and badger others into doing or being what the critics want. They believe that appearance is substance. Some delude themselves into believing they are productive as critics. Those around them have conformed to the critic's value system. Conformity is not change.

COMMON CONSENT AND CRITICISM

Common consent is a noble principle, and like respect, is a key to a healthy human relationship. Amos, a wonderful Jewish Prophet, posed a question.

AMOS THE PROPHET
Can two walk together except they be agreed? (Amos 3:3).

Will someone be open to criticism unless they agree to hear it? If criticism is imposed upon them at a time and a place contrary to their volition, will it be received? In two different revelations the specific point of the need for common consent was addressed.

REVELATIONS TO THE PROPHET JOSEPH
And all things shall be done by common consent in the church, by much prayer and faith, for all things you shall receive by faith. Amen (D&C 26:2).
For all things must be done in order, and by common consent in the church, by the prayer of faith (D&C 28:13).

> *Behold, this I have given unto you as a parable, and it is even*
> *as I am. I say unto you, be one; and if ye are not one ye are not*
> *mine (D&C 38:27).*

How does this relate to criticism? The answer is, by treating people
with respect and by asking for and receiving permission to criticize one
has achieved common consent. This sense of oneness and agreement is
the unity Jesus prayed for in behalf of his disciples (John 17:20-23).
How does one approach a brother with whom he has to reconcile? How
does one leave his gift at the altar and make amends? (Matthew
5:23-24.) It requires humility to ask for forgiveness. It requires courage
to let go of an issue which destroys unity.

The intent is clearly that two people walk a common path. The
moment one party becomes insecure and fearful, and wants to exercise
any degree of compulsion upon the other, the journey of true common
consent is over. Uninvited criticism is a form of coercion and
intimidation. Just as teaching requires the common consent of the
learner so does criticism require the common consent of the receiver.
Without common consent achieved by asking for permission to criticize,
the criticism will be heard as lecturing, preaching, or nagging. The
principle of unity is a characteristic of a Zion community and of a
"Zion" relationship. Inappropriate criticism does not achieve unity.

RECOGNIZING COMMON FORMS
OF INAPPROPRIATE CRITICISM

Sarcasm: Is the act of making fun of a person in a clever way. It is
an ironical taunt in the guise of humor. The word originally came from
the Greek [sarkazein] meaning literally to strip the flesh. So it is that
sarcasm becomes justified because it is infused with humor. The one
being sarcastic can always claim humor as their objective, while
removing a strip of flesh from the one lashed by the tongue of the critic.

THOMAS CARLYLE
Sarcasm, I now see to be, in general, the language of the
Devil (1846).

"I like your hair, dear. I wonder how it would look if you combed it."
It's a funny line. Everyone laughs. Even the one who is the brunt of the
joke may laugh, but inside, where self-esteem abides, they bleed a little
and feel less worthy as a human being.

Analysis, Appraisal, Evaluation: Because these terms are primarily
logical and not emotionally based, they frequently seem justified.

Things can be evaluated and ideas can be and ought to be subjected to the scientific method. Performance can be measured, productivity can be evaluated and appraised. But when analysis, appraisal, and evaluation become subtle forms of masking criticism, they are no less devastating to the one being judged. Because the criticism has been intellectualized, it appears more "constructive," more palatable and less toxic. Not so. People are human beings with basic emotional needs of acceptance, love, belonging, and appreciation. The most self-actualized person on earth, subjected to a consistent diet of criticism, will eventually retreat to a fantasy world of books, TV, sports, become a hermit or fall apart emotionally. A key in giving criticism when it must be given in job performance or life performance is to separate "the ego", the sense of self-worth from the behavior or issue to be criticized. This will be discussed in greater detail later. For now, the focus is to come to understand the destructive, toxic, and damaging nature of criticism. Many fail to recognize how much criticism impacts upon their daily lives. They are unaware of its many forms and its effects.

Questions: Many people feel that if their criticism is placed in the form of a question, it is not really criticism, it's only a question. But the "didn't you", "haven't you", "aren't you" questions have an implied criticism within the asking and the assumption is they "should have". Does this mean that one can never ask a question? No. It means be aware that many questions are implied criticisms and therefore "destructive". Some questions masquerade as innocence, but are subtle forms of criticism. This blind spot qualifies the giver of criticism as emotionally unsafe and dangerous to the self-esteem of others.

The issue here is quite simple. Is one concerned about building the self-esteem of a loved one, an employee, or a friend? If the answer is no, then proceed full-speed ahead. "Damn the torpedoes" and let the emotional chips fall where they may. However, do not sit there in a rest home a bitter, sour, old person, wondering why no one comes to visit you. Don't expect to be loved for being toxic in the here and now. If one is such a realist, then follow this pragmatic counsel; develop the art and skill of giving and receiving appropriate criticism. These skills will make one more effective, not just well-liked. Frequently, people in positions of authority, such as CEO, production managers, quality control, say, "I don't have time to worry about 'feeling'. I'm responsible for bottom line, production goals, quality product". It's as if all employees are to be devoid of feelings, but they are not. Job satisfaction, approval, appreciation, validation, are work related self-esteem issues. To ignore them is to fail to consider all elements of a problem one is trying to solve. So, does one need to be preoccupied with the nature of the questions asked that are implied criticisms? Yes, unless an employer wants to spend his time dealing with employee "turn over," "retraining costs," and personnel problems above and beyond the normal headaches of management.

Direction Giving: "I wasn't being critical, I was just giving them directions." When someone is always giving directions to a loved one or an employee, especially uninvited opinions or uninvited directions, it is interpreted as a lack of confidence by the one who is receiving the directions. "Do this, do that, don't do it that way, watch out for that car, turn left, pick that up, put that down, . . ." ad nauseam. Be aware that direction giving can be a form of criticism and assumes the person is not capable, without the boss's special knowledge, of performing to an acceptable level. People like to please. Children want to impress their parents with their new-found knowledge and skills. Employees like to impress a boss with new-found ways of improving production performance. Excessive direction giving stifles creativity. It sends a message of incompetence to the receiver. The real problem may be an over-inflated sense of ego on the part of the giver of directions. Some psychologists suggest those who are always giving directions are themselves quite insecure. The constant giver of directions may want to feel needed.

"I declare, I just don't know what goes on here when I'm not around to keep this place together. I don't think you could find your head if it weren't attached to your neck."

In giving directions, the same principle of respect applies when invading the space of any person or relationship. First, ask for permission. Genuinely petition. For example, a small child is just learning how to tie his shoes. "No, no, you are doing it all wrong. Do it this way!" The tone of voice is critical and the directions are saying, "You are incompetent". They may lack the skill, the practice, and some knowledge, but are they really incompetent? Do they deserve the impatient, critical tone of voice? What is the objective? Is one too busy? But if the objective is to assist in the development of an independent personality, then ask for permission before you give directions.

"Honey, would you like me to show you how to tie that shoe? I remember how frustrated I used to get when I was your age when my fingers didn't do what my brain wanted them to do."
"No, I want to do it myself."
"OK, but just in case you need some help, let me know."

If the direction-giver is not careful, they will develop dependency-centered children or employees. They will feel incapable of doing anything, Also they will fear that whatever they do will be wrong to the direction-giver. Therefore, they show no initiative, no creative efforts. Now, the direction-giver has created his own nightmare. More and more of the decisions have to be made by him. People are always coming to him to have him tie their shoes, since he is the only one who really knows how to do it right. Now the direction-giver can complain that nothing gets done unless he is there to tell everybody what to do. Usually, the direction -giver rises to the level of his incompetence and ends up feeling over-burdened with the work of ten. The point being, don't get into this kind of a bind by being one who is always giving directions. If one is in this pickle and wants to get out of it, stop giving uninvited directions. "I'm sure you can figure it out, and by the way, whatever you come up with will be fine." If it's really not fine, then don't offer it, but begin to let go and foster independent behavior. "Come up with a couple of options Dave, and bring them back to me."

Being Contrary: There is a blind spot for some called "being contrary". It is sometimes called contrariness. It is the practice of correcting facts as perceived by the critic. Typically, one person will be telling a story, making a statement, or relating an incident. The one "being contrary" will jump in uninvited to tell the truth of what happened, to correct an error, to set things straight. It is intimidation, a kind of emotional arm-twisting. Being contrary is a compulsion. It is also rude, insensitive, and a violation of the space and relationship of the speaking person. The contrary person feels justified in displaying this lack of respect, because they are "RIGHT". They are "BEING HONEST", or they are "TELLING THE TRUTH." This empowers them in their own mind to butt in. Contrariness is the act of interfering in an ongoing conversation in order to correct a perceived misstatement. It is the act of interruption. It is a form of criticism. It is presumptuous and acts without the permission of the speaking party. It is argumentative, frequently arrogant, imprudent, and distracting.

SALLY, MARY AND JOHN

Sally and Mary are having a conversation about a recent trip to the zoo that Sally and John had taken with their two children. Sally says to Mary, "We really had fun and the kids loved it."

John, who is in the room, but not invited into the conversation, interjects, "No, they didn't. The animals scared them to death. They didn't have fun at all."

"Well, I thought they had fun in spite of being frightened by the bears." "Anyway," Sally proceeds talking to Mary, "the kids were so cute when we got them cotton candy."

John interrupts, "They weren't cute, they made a mess and got it all over their hair. It was terrible."

Sally persists, "As I was saying, Mary, I wish I had a camera and could have taken their picture, it was a precious moment."

"You hate cameras," insists John.

MIKE AND JANE

Mike and Jane are talking to each other. Mike is remembering how they first met. The feelings Mike is experiencing are warm and loving towards Jane.

"I remember when I first saw you after graduating from High School."

"No", said Jane, "you first met me at a dance in High School."

"Anyway", said Mike, "the first time I saw you that summer, you were sitting on the fender of my best friend's car. I thought how lucky he was to have such a pretty girl sitting. . . ;"

"It wasn't your best friend's car, it belonged to his dad, and I wasn't sitting on the fender, I was in the front seat."

Whatever good feelings Mike had for Jane are now gone. He is angry with her. She, on the other hand, feels totally justified, and wonders why he can't be honest in telling the story. She is blinded by contrariness. After all, she was only setting the record straight, telling the truth. He shouldn't be so sensitive. He is only angry because she caught him in a lie. "I wish he would not exaggerate. It is so embarrassing when he tells these stories and gets all the facts mixed up." So goes the reasoning of Jane. However, contrariness is contradiction and an invasion of the right of the speaking party to relate their own first person experience. As such, both John and Jane should have asked for permission to criticize.

Most of the time, it is unwise and inappropriate to be contrary. It is especially rude to interfere between two others involved in an ongoing dialogue, even if one is a part of a conversation. Contrariness is counter-productive to a healthy verbal interaction. Most people afflicted with contrariness have a "debate mentality" and see their interdiction as being intellectually honest, open and forthright. In other words, they see it as a strength and are often puzzled as to why others are sensitive.

Another form of contrariness is taking the "opposite view" or the "opposing side". They see themselves as defending the "under dog" or bringing balance to an issue. It is a way of thinking and an extremely difficult bad habit to break.

TOM AND KATHY

Tom is expressing his frustration at his work, how unappreciated his boss is, when Kathy begins to defend Tom's boss by pointing out the pressure he must feel by having all the responsibility. Kathy is being contrary. She is trying to make the situation better by arguing with Tom about his feelings. "You should be grateful you have a job," says Kathy. "It's worth not being appreciated and maybe he was just having a bad day."

Contrary people defend and try to explain an opposite view when the real issue is the right of someone to express their frustration. The situation of Tom complaining to Kathy calls for understanding and not for solution.

Ideally, contrary thoughts are best written down. They are best shared at another time, or reserved for a later, private moment. Permission to express the contrary thought should be sought for first. Next an appropriate time and place should be agreed upon. Disregard for this counsel will lead to the person who is afflicted with contrariness to stumble blindly through life. They will feel as though they are wonderful communicators. In reality, they are passed over for advancements or promotions because they are perceived as brash and lacking in sensitivity. Many contrary people are gifted, talented, bright, capable, and superior in performance. Therefore, contrariness becomes a liability, not a virtue, not an asset. Although they may be right, and certainly are in their own eyes, they are not as useful to the company, organization or relationship as they might have been. Instead of abandoning the behavior, they abandon the job or the marriage, or the relationship. They move on with the same self-defeating behavior to inflict it upon the next job, the next relationship, until it too crumbles under the weight of contrariness. Once recognized, then acknowledged, and then controlled, the contrary person can again be perceived as emotionally safe and function as a productive partner in a relationship.

TRUTH as criticism: "I'm not being critical. I'm only TELLING THE TRUTH. I'm just being honest," comes in various packages. There are many who are most unkind and lack judgment. In the name of TRUTH they brutalize others. Smugly, the critic hides behind the truth regardless of its consequences. Some people feel that because something is true, they are justified in printing it in the newspapers, or saying it. There is a higher and nobler principle than truth, it is to edify.

REVELATION TO JOSEPH SMITH
And that which does not edify is not of God, and is darkness
(D&C 50:23).

One could yell fire in a crowded theater, and there might be a fire in a waste basket. It is true. You could expose young children to every detail and sexual perversion known. It is true. TRUTH-seekers should not be kept from their quest, but only as they are prepared to receive the truth (Alma 12:9-11).

REVELATION TO JOSEPH SMITH
For they cannot bear meat now, but milk they must receive;
wherefore, they must not know these things, lest they perish
(D&C 19:22).

Criticism is a toxic, destructive substance injected from the outside. It needs to be controlled in its administration or the effects of the cure are worse than the original illness. It is well established that overcoming weaknesses, bad habits, and inappropriate behavior are best accomplished by building up the self esteem and self confidence of the individual. Sincere praise for productive effort and positive reinforcement are the basis of modifying behavior. Blasting someone with their faults, even though true, is non-productive and certainly not edifying. It is true that people say truthful things in order to hurt or make another feel bad, and they are said in the heat of anger or frustration. Wisdom and common sense require that criticism be used sparingly. One should criticize so seldom that when he does he will be heard. The frequently critical person is tuned out before the message is delivered. Nor is it justified to criticize in the name of being honest. The so-called "open" relationship, where both members feel free to express their concerns, often provides a forum for the more critical partner. Maybe the fundamental question that ought to be asked is not, "Is it honest?" but, rather, "Is it edifying?" Will it ultimately be uplifting? Will it be good for the individual and the relationship?" If a criticism does not qualify under the latter, it should not be spoken at all.

Usually at this point in a seminar people begin to feel they can't say or do anything. They imagine they have done just about everything wrong. They feel there is no hope for them. They are convinced they have made a mess out of everything. Many would just as soon take another assignment other than Mother-Father, Boss, Friend, Brother-Sister, etc. It is a bit overwhelming. It is easy to get discouraged and even depressed. However, there is hope.

Most people are unaware that one's chances for increased health begin immediately when one stops smoking? One's health doesn't change when he thinks about not smoking anymore. It doesn't change when one makes a commitment not to smoke. One's health improves when he actually stops and sustains the commitment by abstaining from further smoking. So it is with criticism.

THE TWENTY-FOUR HOUR CHALLENGE

For a period of twenty-four consecutive hours, refrain from criticizing anything, anyone, or even one's self. It isn't as easy as it sounds, nor as difficult. When one "slips" he must start his twenty-four hours over again. One man moaned, "It will be the Millennium before I get this assignment right."

SELF CRITICISM

Many people are their own worst critics. Their self esteem is so low they have a difficult time receiving love from others. Frequently they lack a certain kind of graciousness which causes them to reject sincere complements from others. When one can not find self acceptance it is very hard to believe an acceptance message from outside. However, some people enjoy fishing for compliments by being self critical. The hope is others will come to their emotional rescue. This type of self effacing is a ploy to receive acceptance.

> *"Did you make that dress?"* or *"Did you make that coffee table?"*
> *"Oh, yes, but it's just something I threw together. It's not very good at all."*
> *"No, no, I really like it. I think it's beautiful. I wish I was that creative."*

Most self-criticism is a self-defeating behavior, and a bad habit. Many times it is an effort to protect one's self before someone else has a chance to tear one down. All of these scenarios are emotionally unhealthy. There is appropriate self-criticism which has as its goal to become one's highest and best self. But it is a false humility to deface one's self in front of others. Personal, private soul searching and reflection upon becoming a better self is the kind of self evaluation which may lead to improvement. In an appropriate environment confessing one's faults may be appropriate (James 5:16). Making comments like, "I'm so dumb," "I never do anything right," "I can't believe how stupid I am," are not productive. Likewise an inability to receive a compliment shows disdain for the giver of the compliment. It is rude and lacks graciousness. If someone gives a compliment, an appropriate response is, "Thank you."

CRITICIZING OTHERS

Unless it is a life or death situation, or the job absolutely requires a critical review, abstain from all forms of criticism. This includes sarcasm, uninvited opinions, analysis, appraisals, evaluations, insights, questions, direction giving or contrariness. There are a few people whose employment requires them to be critical, for example, building inspectors, supervisors, quality control, et. al. These special cases are exempt as long as they are on the job, additionally the criticism must relate directly to the work. Lastly, even if the criticism is justified, ask for and receive permission to criticize.

All others will be required to abstain from all criticism for twenty-four hours. The majority of people do not succeed in their first attempt. Do not be too discouraged if one has to start over again thirty or forty times. But the moment one slips and criticizes, the twenty-four hours starts over again. Do not criticize self, spouse, children parents, co-workers, the boss, the government, or dumb drivers.

Warning! There are some traditionally hard times at which one is prone to criticize. These include being tired, hungry, driving, or when one is under a time pressure. Getting the kids to bed may push parents over the line. Notice most of this criticism is frustration. It is not geared to helping self or others become their highest and best selves.

WHAT ABOUT NONVERBAL CRITICISM?

If one thinks it, but doesn't say it, does it count against the twenty-four hours?

If a critical thought enters one's mind and he gets rid of the thought in a moment, then it does not count and one does not have to start his twenty-four hours over. If, on the other hand, one lets that critical thought stay in his mind and he develops it into a full production with quadraphonic sound and vista vision, then the one must start over again.

"IT'S HARDER THAN I THOUGHT"

One lady who asked this question, looked puzzled for a moment, glanced up at her husband who was standing by her side, and said, "OK, I'll try to go for twenty-four hours without criticizing or dwelling upon a critical thought." Then, pointing to her husband, she said, "But, he will never make it!" There was a pause. "Oh dear," she said, " I will have to start my twenty-four hours over again, won't I?"

*Her husband did not verbally respond. However, he frowned
at her and a slight sneer formed at the edge of his mouth. He also
pointed his finger at her in a mocking manner. This, of course,
was nonverbal criticism. It was pointed out to him that nonverbal
criticism was also a reason for him to start his twenty-four hours
over again.*

*The two of them walked off muttering, "This is going to be
harder than we thought."*

"Yes," I said, "Overcoming a lifetime of habit is hard."

In one study involving more than eight hundred people, after three
days only twenty people had been able to go for a period of twenty-four
hours without criticizing. They were permitted to count sleeping time
as a part of the twenty-four hours! The responses from those who made
it were interesting.

*"It was easy," said one woman. "My husband and son were
out of town."*

*Another woman said she had attended a seminar where
everyone wore a rubber band around their wrist and each time
they broke the rules of the seminar they snapped the rubber
band.*

*One man in the group observed, "I was so criticized as a
child that I decided I would not be a critical adult."*

*One man suggested that we form an organization called
"C.A." or Critiholics Anonymous and hold weekly meetings.*

*One mother reported that after she had gone twenty-four
hours, her teenage daughter, who was unaware of her mother's
efforts, asked if she were feeling OK.*

Because of the culture and the accepted mode of communication, it
is difficult to refrain from criticizing. Most have been raised in a critical
environment. Many have been taught to be critical, analytical, and to
subject people and things to the scientific method. Some have difficulty
speaking a single sentence without criticizing. One shouldn't be too
hard on himself if he doesn't succeed in a week. This is a difficult
assignment.

WHY SHOULD ONE TRY ?

These are the results one should experience by abstaining from criticism:
- To be able to go twenty-four hours without criticizing.
- To increase one's awareness of the critical nature of society.
- To become aware of one's own compulsion to criticize.
- To experience the power of self-mastery.

There are several answers to the question, "Why should one try to stop criticizing?" Here are some of the more important ones:

- To lay the foundation for love instead of rejection.
- To be able to increase the number of positive interactions.
- To be more emotionally safe as a person.
- To be more effective in communicating
- To reduce unnecessary conflict.
- To experience greater peace and harmony in all relationships.
- To have the Holy Ghost as a companion.

SHOULD YOU FEEL INCLINED TO CENSURE

Should you feel inclined to censure
Faults you may in others view,
Ask your own heart, ere you venture,
If you have not failings, too.
Let not friendly vows be broken;
Rather strive a friend to gain.
Many words in anger spoken
Find their passage home again.

Do not, the, in idle pleasure
Trifle with a brother's fame;
Guard it as a valued treasure,
Sacred as your own good name.
Do not form opinions blindly;
Hastiness to trouble tends;
Those of whom we though unkindly
Oft become our warmest friends.
(Text: Anon., ca. 1863, LDS Hymn, # 235, 1985.)

The hymns of Zion teach powerful doctrine. The following revelation was given for Emma Smith:

REVELATION FOR EMMA SMITH
For my soul delighteth in the song of the heart; yea, the song
of the righteous is a prayer unto me, and it shall be answered
with a blessing upon their heads (D&C 25:12).

"Should You Feel Inclined To Censure" (Hymn #235), "Let Us Oft Speak Kind Words" (Hymn #232), and "Nay, Speak No Ill" (Hymn #233), are doctrinal messages. They have but one purpose which is to control the tongue in order that the Spirit of the Lord might prevail in the lives of the Saints.

NAY, SPEAK NO ILL
Nay, speak no ill;
a kindly word
Can never leave a sting behind;
And, o, to breathe each tale we've heard
Is far beneath a noble mind.
Full oft a better seed is sown
By choosing thus the kinder plan,
For, if but little good is known,
Still let us speak the best we can.

Give me the heart
that fain would hide,
Would fain another's faults efface.
How can it please the human pride
To prove humanity but base?
No, let us reach a higher mood,
A nobler estimate of man;
Be earnest in the search for good,
And speak of all the best we can.

Then speak no ill,
But lenient be
To other' failings
as your own.
If you're the first a fault to see,
Be not the first to make it know,
For life is but a passing day'
No lip may tell how brief its span.
Then, oh, the little time we stay,
Let's speak of all the best we can.
(Text, Anon., ca 1894, LDS Hymns, #233, 1985.)

CHAPTER SIX

AGENTS OF CHANGE

Know this, that every soul is free
To choose his life and what he'll be;
For this eternal truth is giv'n:
That God will force no man to heav'n.
He'll call, persuade, direct aright,
And bless with wisdom, love, and light,
In nameless ways be good and kind,
But never force the human mind.
(Boston, 1805, Anonymous; "Know This, That Every
Soul Is Free," LDS Hymn # 240, 1985 LDS Hymnal.)

True change comes from within each person. God **will not** force His children back to Him. The other reality is that man **cannot** change a friend or loved one, unless he or she is willing to change. Is it hopeless? Is it vain? It is hopeless and vain if the means for change are not consistent with the laws of heaven. It is vain and hopeless if one's objectives and means include force, coercion, abuse, and uninvited, unauthorized, and improperly given criticism. What hope is there to assist a loved one? Rather than stand by as an idle witness to the self-destruction of a friend, isn't there something one can do to become an Agent of Change?

BECOMING AN AGENT OF CHANGE

Becoming an Agent of Change requires a conversion on the part of the would be catalyst. It is a change of his or of her own heart to doing things in "the Lord's own way." There is a tremendous amount of good one can do in behalf of another to become an Agent of Change. By definition a catalyst is an Agent of Change in chemical reactions which speeds up the process. Parents and loved ones want to speed up the process of change in the life of the one about whom they are concerned. Therefore, they criticize them, hoping the truth of what they have to say will speed up a change. It doesn't. Now, more frustration brings more criticism. The negative downward spiral continues until one, or both, flees the relationship.

For an outside party to become an Agent of Change for a friend or loved one requires a positive interaction and patience. It requires a different approach. The challenge faced by most "want-to-be-change-agents" is patience. What they face is a friend or loved one who doesn't want to change. They may even be belligerent about it. They face loved ones who are out of control with their own lives. Because of frustration, both parties are out of control, but for different reasons. The wayward is out of control because of poor judgment decisions. The catalyst (Agent of Change) is out of control because of frustration. The frustration neutralizes the Agent of Change so that he cannot be effective.

True change comes from within. Control is not change. Conformity is not change. Submission and acquiescence are not change. The frustrated Agents of Change wonder what more they can do. They try to save the wayward from the consequences of the loved one's poor judgment decisions. They want to rescue the wayward from himself. They bail him out of problem after problem, only to find that nothing has changed. The loved one is still on a course of self destruction. They loan him money. They pay for programs to help him. They bring him to counselors. It seems that every solution is defeated by the wayward's unwillingness to accept responsibility for making his life better. Nothing seems to work.

Most do not start out with the Lord's programs. Instead they run the gauntlet of frustration and exhaust all of their personal options. The Agents of Change tried love and understanding. Their impatience and frustration reached the breaking point. They abandoned love and understanding as one more failed attempt. They resorted to improper criticism, force, coercion, punishment and finally abandonment. Hurting and smarting, they gave up. They emotionally withdrew to a safe distance and mourned the lost potential of what might have been.

This pattern is being played out daily in the lives of thousands. What a tragedy. What a waste of energy, finances, and personal effort. The Lord's program requires patience, but at least it works. Those who thought they had tried the Lord's program were too impatient. They did not receive the immediate answer they expected to their sincere prayers. Their frustration with the wayward expanded to include frustration with Heavenly Father. They concluded that if God wasn't going to do what they wanted, when they wanted it, they would do it themselves. So trusting in the "arm of flesh" they pressed forward believing that God had abandoned them. The truth was they abandoned their faith in God's ability to rescue their loved one.

JILL AND HER SIXTEEN YEAR OLD
Jill had a sixteen year old daughter who was out of control. Jill was a single mother of five children and worked full time out of the home.

Brenda was her challenge. The other four children seemed to be on track. They were doing well in school and active in the Church. Brenda was failing school because of her unexcused absences. The mother had become a screaming banshee. There was a physical fight. This is where the counselor was brought in. Punishment only led to more rebellion. What Jill was doing wasn't working. She was doing the best she could but it was not effective. Brenda was lying, uncooperative, immoral, and now violent. A very basic contract was drawn up with minimal requirements.

In a private session with just the mother, the counselor reviewed her alternatives:

- *Things could stay as they were.*
- *Things could get worse and Brenda would be removed from the home.*
- *The mother could become an Agent of Change.*

One of the difficult issues Jill had to face was the feeling she was rewarding Brenda for acting poorly. To show love to an abusive child, a lying, dishonest child, went against Jill's basic values of respect and responsibility. The relationship had degenerated to where neither of them could be civil one to another. Brenda resented her lack of freedom. She just wanted to have fun and be with friends and live in the moment.

It was agreed that perfection or nothing would be unrealistic for either the mother or the daughter. There would be mistakes and setbacks. In order for Brenda to change, the mother would have to change her approach. It began by Jill stopping her constant messages of disapproval. Since Jill thought criticizing and carping were signs of responsible motherhood, it was difficult for her to keep her mouth shut. Only the fear of losing her daughter altogether motivated Jill to follow the counsel. She began by taking her frustrations to God and not to Brenda. Jill was afraid Brenda would think she had won the power struggle. The mother was concerned that Brenda would become more difficult to manage.

The truth was Jill wasn't managing Brenda at all. It was only an illusion. Brenda agreed to five minutes a night where her mother could give her negative feedback. The rest of the day, for twenty-three hours and fifty-five minutes, Brenda would not be criticized. The counselor recommended that Jill write down her criticisms in black and white where Brenda could see them without the mother's facial expression, body language, and tone of voice. This would allow Brenda to focus on the content. With a few major exceptions, it began to be more peaceful in the home. Finding ways to take her love to her daughter and her frustrations to God was getting easier. With absolutely no trust for her daughter, the mother began gifting unconditional acts of love, one each day.

Brenda didn't lack knowledge of values. She lacked commitment to values. Brenda's selfish need for peer approval had caused her to trade away all values except the acceptance of her friends. Her guilty conscience made her angry with God, the Church, and her family. She was the black sheep and she knew it.

This story is not over. Brenda is now seventeen and attending an alternative high school. The mother has let go of nearly every expectation. She continues to do daily deeds of love. Brenda and her mother are talking, not yelling.

In a counseling session, Brenda confessed she is a disappointment to her mother, but now she knows her mother loves her anyway. Brenda has not come back to the Church but she will participate in family prayer and in family activities. The relationship is better, but not perfect. It would not be where it is now except for Jill's willingness to be an Agent of Change.

There would be less hurt, heartache, and sorrow in the world if people went directly into the "Lord's Program" for changing the heart of a loved one.

THE LORD'S PROGRAM FOR CHANGE AGENTS

1. Take One's Frustrations To God In Mighty Prayer.
2. Take One's Love To The Loved One.
3. Set Boundaries To Protect Oneself.
4. Be An Example Of The Values One Desires.
5. Share To The Level Of The Loved One's Willingness.
6. Exercise Faith And Patience In God's Divine Intervention.

1. TAKE ONE'S FRUSTRATIONS TO GOD IN MIGHTY PRAYER

More will be said on "Mighty Prayer" in the next chapter. For now it is sufficient to understand that the "powers of heaven" can be activated for the good of one's loved one by the prayer of faith. By taking one's frustrations to God in Mighty Prayer it spares the relationship from fruitless carping, from emotional alienation, and from having to reinstate lost rapport. The Agent of Change must be willing to change his approach. Often this desire only comes after one has learned by the things he has suffered that the alternatives to Christ are not worth it.

REVELATION AS TO WHY ZION WAS AFFLICTED
And my people must needs be chastened until they learn obedience, if it must needs be, by the things which they suffer (D&C 105:6).

PAUL TO THE HEBREWS
Though he were a Son, yet learned he obedience by the things which he suffered (Hebrews 5:8).

Like the "Prodigal Son," each must come "to himself" (Luke 15:17) and desire a more excellent way. There is no substitute for coming to oneself. The alcoholic, the criminal, the wayward can be led like the proverbial horse to water, but the desire to drink the water cannot be forced upon them. Desire is a seed which must grow in the ground of one's own heart. The wayward are held hostage by self doubt and by the knowledge of their own unworthiness. They know they are in rebellion against God's love and live in fear and anger. If they keep their lives busy enough they can ignore for a time the presence of God in their lives. The fact that God does love them is lost in despair. At the same time they would "curse God and want to die" (Mormon 2:14). In this miserable state they are hypersensitive to any criticism. They want wickedness to be happiness, and it is not (Helaman 13:38). They demand freedom without responsibility, acceptance for noncompliance, and trust in the face of being untrustworthy. Even justified criticism makes it harder for them to believe in self, in God or in anything but escape from reality.

Most wayward are in a desperate search for approval, love, acceptance, and belonging. Freedom, fun, and friends are his or her obsessions. " Live for the moment" is his or her creed. What they **really want** is to be loved. The seed for desired improvement bakes in the sun of their own disappointment. They do not lack for criticism. They are amply supplied with self criticism. What they lack is the water of love which must come from an outside source. For the wayward, accepting God's love is an option they ignore. It is not God who is rejecting the wayward. It is the wayward who are turning from their Heavenly Father. Prayer, study of the scriptures, the words of church leaders, and friends are abandoned. Love must come from the Agent of Change who is not consumed with frustration. The Agent of Change in following the Lord's plan has taken his frustration to the Lord in Mighty Prayer and left all hostility on the altar of God. For now the focus is on converting the Agent of Change to a new way of doing things. Therefore, it is the Agent of Change who must undergo a heart transplant.

DAVID'S PLEA
Create in me a clean heart, O God; and renew a right
spirit within me (Psalms 51:10).

Armed with a desire to change, but filled with trepidation, the disciple of Christ commits to taking his love to his loved one.

2. TAKE ONE'S LOVE TO THE LOVED ONE

The Lord's Program is to focus on the good in a person and build upon it. Truly, in the heart of the most wayward is a spark to be better. However, dim the glow of that spark, it can be fanned into fire by the love of another or the love for a better self. God's longsuffering love for each of His children sets an example for all who believe in His Son. God's love reaches out in loving service.

JESUS TO NICODEMUS
For God so loved the world, that he gave his only begotten
Son, that whosoever believeth in him should not perish, but have
everlasting life.
*For God sent **not** his Son into the world **to condemn** the*
world; but that the world through him might be saved
(John 3:16-17, bold mine).

Jesus did not condemn the woman taken in adultery. Neither did He approve of the sin. He gave her love and respect, not condemnation. (John 8:10-11.)

NEPHI'S COMMENT ON JESUS
He doeth not anything save it be for the benefit of the world;
for he loveth the world, even that he layeth down his own life that
he may draw all men unto him. Wherefore, he commandeth none
that they shall not partake of his salvation (2 Nephi 26:24).

In the Lord's Program He calls others to reach out and fan the flame of His love. He needs Change Agents to become Agents of Love. There is an eternal truth which says uninvited, unauthorized, and improper criticism will not generate love, nor change behavior. Love generates love.

LOVE GENERATES LOVE
We love him, because he first loved us (I John 4:19).

The wayward do not lack knowledge. They do not lack for condemnation. They lack love.

MARTI AND HER WAYWARD SON

As a counselor I asked Marti to go one month without once criticizing her fifteen year old son. I challenged <u>her to go to the Lord every time she felt upset or frustrated with her son.</u> I explained to her that the Lord was anxious to soften his heart.

"Let G<u>od change your son. Let God have the burden.</u> Lay the responsibility for change upon the altar. Become an Agent of Change by becoming a Agent of Love. Every time you are tempted to vent your frustration to your son, go to God in prayer and ask for strength to love him. For one month do at least one loving thing a day for your son, but not one word of condemnation."

Marti asked me what she should do with her resentment. I said she should turn it into a loving behavior.

"For one month, Marti, just thirty days, don't give one criticism. If you fail, start your thirty days over. Think of this as the 'loving thing' to do.

"Imagine you have been called into the office of the Prophet of God. He places his hands upon your head and give you a mission call. For one month you are called to only give love and not one word of criticism. Would you do it, Marti? Would you follow the counsel? I know you would. You are a woman who loves the Lord. Pray about this counsel. Follow your heart, but not your frustration."

We met once a week for the next month. She reported how hard it was at first to break the old habit of criticizing. She did think of it as a mission. Marti found herself praying fifteen or twenty times a day. She said every time she felt frustrated she would go over and put her arms around her son and say, "I love you." He was hostile at first and very defensive. By the end of the third week he began to hug her back. It was during the forth week he came to his mother and cried. He just wanted to be held. Her words were words of love, "It has to be hard for you, son. I'm sorry you're hurting. I know you'll get through this. I love you and I'll always be here for you."

"Mom, I've made such a mess out of my life and I'm only fifteen years old. I've got to stop screwing up."

Marti continued praying and loving. For the first time she saw a ray of hope. She continued with her mission. Several years had passed when one day the phone rang and I was invited to the missionary farewell of her son.

Change Agents must come to recognize that love is the catalyst for change, not inappropriate criticism. Love will bless both the giver and the receiver. It will power the engine that propels the disciple to the necessary patience. The Agent of Change must seek for love, approval, and appreciation from God in Mighty Prayer. In turn, God will strengthen the disciple to give love to the wayward. But from where does the wayward seek love? The answer is "in all the wrong places." The wayward is desperate for acceptance and love. Desperate people accept desperate alternatives to their highest and best self. They set up barriers which block out their ability to receive the love of God. They discount themselves and even hate what they do or what they have allowed themselves to become. Therefore, love from self or for self is eliminated as a source. From where will the love come? If the Agent of Change is in a critical mode and their frustration manifests itself in raging disappointment they cease being an instrument in God's hands. They are neither an Agent of Love nor an Agent of Change. Compounding the problem is that most feel an overwhelming sense of failure. They are as inclined to turn from God as the wayward, but for different reasons. Nevertheless, there is no acceptable alternative except the Lord's Own Way. The Agent of Change must take his or her frustrations to God in Mighty Prayer and seek for the strength to nurture the one who is difficult to love. Charity for all begins with charity for one.

Love is a Spiritual Gift given of God to every man, woman, and child on earth. It is embryonic and needs to be nurtured. Love grows by loving.

WHICH ONE WILL LIVE?

Living inside of me are two ravenous animals. One is an animal of fear and doubt. The other is an animal of love and faith. Which one will live? The answer is, the one I feed (anonymous).

Feeding self with the love from God derived by Mighty Prayer, with meaningful study of the Words of Life found in the Scriptures and The Living Prophets, and with loving service to others gives one the reserves to love another. Without reserves of love, one remains an empty well. Occasionally one is blessed with loved ones and friends who gift love and sustain the Agent of Change so that he in turn can share his love with the wayward. Eventually, however, each will have to tap into the waters of everlasting life, even Christ. Jesus becomes a source of Loving Water, as well as Living Water, that springs up as an eternal fountain of love. The Agent of Change who is connected to that fountain is appreciative of the love of others, but not dependent on that love. Not being dependent, he is available to love and to gift his love. He frees himself in Christ of the expectation of being loved in return. The frustration of unrequited love is removed by unconditional love. This is charity, the pure love of Christ. This is also the ideal. Most live in a reality where the love of others is essential to their own feelings of worth. This is why one can become an Agent of Change by loving. One does not have to be perfect in order to love.

THE PROPHET DAVID O. McKAY
Just think of that use of the word unfeigned. Love pretended
has no influence. Love unfeigned always has the power to reach
the heart (David O. McKay, Gospel Ideals, p. 150).

However, it may require that for a period of time one does not seek the love of the one being criticized. The pain of criticism may inhibit the one being criticized from doing anything but withdrawing. It may be, that short of perfect charity for all people (2 Nephi 33:7-9), the Agent of Change will practice **selective charity**. Remember "charity for all begins with charity for one." Usually, people marry their greatest challenge in life, give birth to it or struggle with love for self. Often one is taught charity by bearing with a difficult-to-love member of the family. This allows one to grow line upon line in developing the spiritual gift of "the pure love of Christ." One cannot be used as an Agent of Love if he does not show forth loving behaviors. Without some semblance of charity or love, how can anyone serve as an instrument for good in the hands of God? "He is nothing" (Moroni 7:46). One must go to source of charity, even Christ, to obtain the needed love. By following the Lord's plan, the Agents of Change are Agents of Love.

3. SET BOUNDARIES TO PROTECT SELF

The principle of protecting oneself from physical, emotional or spiritual abuse seems obvious. However, there are well meaning people who confuse the issues of love and trust. It is as if these two issues were put into a blender and mixed together. The resultant effect is a hodge podge of confusion wherein the victim of abuse is unable to discern between loving behavior and when to trust. Nevertheless, it is the responsibility of individuals to set limits on what they are willing to tolerate.

For example, if someone is yelling, cursing, or giving one uninvited, unauthorized, and inappropriate criticism it would be appropriate to say,

I'm leaving the room, (or the house, or the car), because I do
not give you permission to treat me in this manner. I am not
leaving the relationship. I will be happy to talk about this when
you are in emotional control.
If you cannot handle a calm discussion of your concerns,
please write them down and I will read them tonight.

If someone becomes physically abusive, call the police. To stay in a physically, emotionally, or spiritually abusive situation only gives permission to abusers. It encourages them to continue and to escalate their abusive actions. Not only is it damaging to the relationship, but it fosters coercion, intimidation, and manipulative behaviors. It is understandable that children who are abused have a harder time as adults knowing where to draw the lines and establish boundaries. Once aware, there is no excuse to permit abusive behavior from friend, family, spouse, or child. Sometimes calling the police is the loving thing to do. As hard as it may be, parents may have to remove a toxic child from the home.

DARLA AND HER PARENTS

Darla is a fourteen year old who is verbally abusive to her mother and father. She has learned they have no limits on her abusive behaviors. Darla has found power in abuse. She has found more freedom to be with her friends, to have fun, to enjoy autonomy and to live for the moment by being belligerent, arbitrary, and combative.

The parents, in the mistaken guise of love, have tolerated Darla's abuse. They thought it was the loving thing to do. They were fearful of her running away and being in a worse environment. They were concerned about her losing future opportunities. They were, in fact, being held hostage by fear, doubt, and a confused notion of love.

When the counselor outlined a strategy for dealing with Darla, the parents were horrified. What they failed to recognize was they had already lost Darla. The strategy involved a declining list of options for Darla. They included more freedom for responsibility. What the parents lacked was credibility. Darla did not believe her parents would follow through with their stated intentions. The declining list of options included Darla being placed in a home for troubled girls. There are such places from Florida to California. The counselor explained that this final option was to send the message loud and clear that the parents would not tolerate abusive behavior.

The parents held the power but were not exercising common sense. There was room in the program for Darla to be forgiven and to earn trust by obeying a few simple rules. She was to be where she said she was going to be. Also she would be doing what she said she was doing. Darla was expected to be home at the mutually agreed upon time or, if the agreement was violated, upon the arbitrary time imposed by the parents. Her freedom to function at school, at home, and with her friends was conditioned on her behavior. Each violation would add one week onto the time she would be permitted to obtain a driver's license. The parents were going to enforce the new rules completely. If Darla did not respond to the positive reinforcement program, the parents were to implement the consequences in three stages. The last stage being her exit from the home. By following through with their stated objectives, it was hoped that their credibility with Darla would be established.

The counselor warned the parents that unless their resolve was firm and unwavering Darla would return to her old ways. Because of the past belligerence , the parents were told to expect that Darla would try escalating the conflict. The parents were to exit the room if Darla became verbally abusive or critical. They were to offer her another opportunity to communicate, following the rules of courtesy and respect. Under no conditions were they to allow her to take them out of control of what they would tolerate and not tolerate. The counselor affirmed with the parents they would operate with two separate programs, i.e. an "I Love You" program and an "I Trust You" program. They agreed they would help Darla with all of the positive moves she would make , but they would not "help her one inch to hell." The parents agreed to put her into a Christian girl's school near Orlando, Florida for a minimum of six months if she failed to respond to their few, but reasonable, boundaries. The parents continued to do loving things on a daily basis with Darla. At the same time they held firmly to their stated agenda. As the counselor predicted, Darla increased her belligerence and escalated the conflict. Soon Darla was looking at over a hundred violations. This meant she could not drive until she was eighteen. Quickly, Darla moved through each level of strategic retreats the parents had outlined. One day, unannounced to Darla, two huge Samoan security guards and a lady hired as a companion and driver entered Darla's room and hauled her off to a girl's "reform school." She was kicking and screaming, swearing, and cursing at her parents. " I'll never forgive you," she shouted, "I hate you! I hate you!" She yelled rape and tried to get someone to rescue her. She was no match for the Samoans.

The facility was escape proof. The girls could earn privileges by obedience. There were four levels of freedom. It usually took forty-five to sixty days before the girls realized this was real. Darla was told to make her bed. She refused and found her bed was taken away and she was given a sleeping bag and a pillow. She was informed that if she faithfully rolled up her sleeping bag for a week they would restore her bed. After a month Darla earned her bed back. She could only write to her parents and all mail that arrived for her was sent back to her parents. Darla begged and pleaded with her parents to let her out. She promised obedience. She had learned her lesson and would be a new person. The parents wavered and called the counselor. The father wanted mercy and the mother held firm. The counselor informed the parents that the real issue was their credibility. They had said six months and they needed to stick to it or they would be right back where they started.

The parents agreed and prayed mightily for a true change of heart. They wrote to her and told her of their resolve. If she worked her way up *to at least the third level she would be released at six months. If not, she would be required to stay another six months. Darla was beginning to believe her parents for the first time in her young life. At six months Darla had achieved the fourth level of freedom which permitted her to go with a group to an outside movie. Later she confessed that she thought she would run away while at the movie. What she didn't know was that the Samoans were guarding the exits. Had she run she would have been returned to the first level and a sleeping bag and a six month extension. She finished a year's worth of home study high school in six months.*

Her parents met with her at the end of the six months and informed her that if she returned to her old ways they would send her back. She believed them. A contract was drawn up with very specific behavioral objectives. The past was forgiven and Darla would again be able to obtain her driver's license at sixteen. Violations would add one week beyond her sixteenth birthday for each infraction before she would be able to get her driver's license.

After the honeymoon period of a couple of months, Darla tested her parents again and found them absolutely committed to do what they said they would do. The parents continued to love Darla. Trust was a separate issue. Darla went on to drive at sixteen years and one month because of a few infractions. She graduated from high school and attended a local community college. She married a returned missionary in the Temple, with parents crying the entire time. The parents ended up being instruments in the hands of the Lord. Who better to love her to her highest and best self than her parents?

These parents learned the value of real boundaries. They also recognized the need to be realistic in their expectations. Their "I Trust You" program was based on responsible behavior, not on perfection. These parents learned that the art of parenting was the art of gradually transferring responsibility for life from their shoulders to those of Darla as she demonstrated an ability to handle it. They found the art of parenting is the art of letting go. It was not the skill of hanging on. By protecting themselves, establishing boundaries, and setting reasonable behavioral objectives, they now enjoy a loving daughter.

4. BE AN EXAMPLE OF THE VALUES ONE DESIRES

The key here is to model the behavior one expects of others. This does not mean perfection or nothing. It means striving to do one's best. This adds credibility to the message as well as the messenger. A "false message" would be "Do as I say, not as I do." James advised all disciples to "be ye doers of the word, and not hearers only." (James 1:22). Jesus counseled the multitude and his disciples to beware of the Pharisees.

"DO AS I'M DOING. . ."

All therefore whatsoever they bid you observe, that observe and do; but do not ye after their works: for they say, and do not." (Matthew 23:3.)

ALMA TO HIS SON, HELAMAN

My son, give ear to my words; for I swear unto you, that inasmuch as ye shall keep the commandments of God ye shall prosper in the land. .

I would that ye should <u>do as I have done</u> . . .(Alma 36;1-2, underlining mine).

JESUS TO NEPHI

Wherefore, follow me, and <u>do the things ye have seen me do</u>. (2 Nephi 31:12, underlining mine.)

JESUS AT THE LAST SUPPER

A new commandment I give unto you, That ye love one another; <u>as I have loved you, that ye also love one another</u>.

By this shall all men know that ye are my disciples, if ye have love one to another (John 13:34-35 underlining, mine).

THE SEKELI SALI MANU STORY

This is the true life story about a Samoan boy named Sekeli [Shekel from the Bible] Sali Manu. He was born the tenth of eleven children in Western Samoa on the Island of Savai'i. His father was the Branch President and went through incredible persecution. Twice his father was stoned and left for dead. What the father said and how he lived were one and the same. He said there was always time to read the Scriptures. While fishing in his outrigger canoe with his six brothers, the father would call them to the surface by pounding a rock against the canoe. While bobbing up and down with the undulating waves, seven Samoan boys saw their father take the Scriptures out of a plastic wrapping. They listened to him read to them for twenty minutes a day.

When the father was dying he gave a father's blessing to each of his sons and daughters except for Sekeli. This son was far across the island working. A runner was sent to fetch Sekeli. The father stated to his wife, "I no die [sic] until I give my boy, Sekeli, a blessing." The frightened Sekeli entered the "fale" [oval hut], out of breath and fearful he would be too late.

Sekeli knelt on the mats in front of his standing father. The father gave Sekeli a tremendous blessing and closed with these words: "Sekeli, you be the kind of father that I was [sic]." In a few minutes the father passed away. Sekeli went on to serve almost six years as a building missionary for the Church and two more years as a regular missionary. This was from seventeen to twenty-four years of age. He later served two additional missions for the church. He died in his forties and left eight children with a loving wife, Connie. But he also left his testimony sealed by his personal example.

As a man he was once asked, "Do you ever think of your father, Sekeli?"

He responded, "Every day of my life I hear the voice of my father saying to me, "Sekeli, you be the kind of father that I was."

"When you die and see your father again, what will you say to him Sekeli?"

"I will look him in the eye and say to him, "Father, I was the kind of father that you was."[sic]

The power of personal example seals the truth of one's words (D&C 135:3-5). Even when people repent at a later time in life, it sends a message to the hearts of the children. But it cannot be a **"promised" change**. It must be a change in behavior that can be **seen**. Anger must be exchanged for patience. Respect must replace verbal abuse. Kindness and gentleness must win over harshness and being inconsiderate. Invitation, enticement, and persuasion must emerge in lieu of compulsion, intimidation, and domination.

THE PROPHET MORONI
But behold, that which is of God inviteth and enticeth to do good continually; wherefore, every thing which inviteth and enticeth to do good, and to love God , and to serve him, is inspired of God. . . .

For behold, the Spirit of Christ is given to every man, that he may know good from evil; wherefore, I show unto you the way to judge; for every thing which inviteth to do good, and to persuade to believe in Christ, is sent forth by the power and gift of Christ; wherefore ye may know with a perfect knowledge it is of God (Moroni 7:13, 16, underlining mine).

The key words are invite, entice, and persuade.

THE DILEMMA OF FAMILY PRAYER
Frequently the father would yell and coerce and deny privileges to anyone who missed family prayer. The children came to prayer, but often with resentment and a negative spirit prevailed. The mother observed there was a better spirit in the home without coerced family prayer. The Bishop suggested that the father drop the punishment program and simply invite, entice and persuade his children to come to family prayer. On the first night free from mandatory family prayer only the mother and father showed up. The mother and father left after family prayer and

went to the ice cream parlor. When they returned with their mostly eaten ice cream cones the children asked why there wasn't one for them. The mother replied, "Its an unannounced reward for those who come to family prayer with a good attitude."

A bribe is usually an illegal influence. A reward is an enticement for positive deeds. By the end of the first week, all but one of the children were attending family prayer. There was a better spirit in the home. The love and example of the family eventually brought the last holdout. The power of personal example, the principle of enticement, and a little ice cream brought a new spirit to the home. It required patience, love, and the power of personal example, plus a weekly trip to the ice cream parlor. It became a family tradition.

ELDER STEPHEN L. RICHARDS
Here is the genius of the government of Christ. No compulsion, just persuasion; no unrighteousness or autocracy, just goodness and love. Here is the answer to the religious intolerance and crimes of the centuries (Stephen L. Richards, Conference Report, October 1936, p. 132).

5. SHARE TO THE LEVEL OF THE LOVED ONE'S WILLINGNESS TO SHARE

A basic truth about human relationships is that they can not be forced. Each relationship stands on its own merits. It is a wise person who realizes the level of willingness another possesses. Next, build a bridge from where they are to a better place. This is best accomplished by the principle of common consent. Find a common ground and begin to build a bridge of understanding and shared experiences.

JACK AND HIS WORKAHOLIC FATHER
Jack was eighteen and the only member of the Church in his family. His father was cold and very business-like. Jack desperately wanted a relationship with his father. Jack was a great athlete. His father was always too busy with work to attend any games. Finally, Jack realized that if he were going to have a relationship with his father it would have to be on different terms.

I suggested to Jack that he show up unannounced at his father's place of business. His dad was shocked and wondered if there was an emergency. Jack told his father that he wanted to understand what his father did for a living. The father was too busy then, but set up a time to meet with Jack. The father was excited that Jack would show an interest in the business. Jack invested many hours learning more about the business than he wanted to know. After six weeks Jack looked up into the stands and saw his father for the first time in his life come to a game. Finding a common ground and sharing to the level of the other's willingness to share is always a good place to start.

6. EXERCISE FAITH AND PATIENCE IN GOD'S "DIVINE INTERVENTION."

THE LIGHT OF CHRIST

Each and every person born on this earth is given a conscience. Disobedience, ignorance, and the traditions of the fathers can dim the conscience (D&C 93:39), but cannot extinguish it. The conscience is also known as the Light of Christ (Moroni 7:16, 18-19). Heavenly Father loves His children more than any earthly parent loves those same children (Orson F. Whitney, Conference Reports, April 1929, p. 11). Because of His love, God has placed in each child two internal guidance systems. The first is the Light of Christ. The Scriptures sometimes refer to the Light of Christ as the Light of Truth or Conscience (John 8:9; D&C 88:6-7, 11-13).

Latter-day Saints believe that a veil is placed over the mind when everyone is born on this earth. They have no memory of their premortal life as spirit sons and daughters of God. This also applied to Jesus.

ELDER JAMES E. TALMAGE
Over His mind had fallen the veil of forgetfulness common to all who are born to earth, by which the remembrance of primeval existence is shut off (Talmage, Jesus The Christ, p. 111).

Because of this veil of forgetfulness, God insured that all His children would have an inner light to guide them back to his glorious home, i.e., the light of truth, the conscience, the Light of Christ. In spite of any dysfunctional background or levels of abuse inflicted upon any child of God that Light of Conscience will not leave him. It is interesting to see that the enemies of Jesus in a fallen and apostate condition were still affected by their consciences.

THE WOMAN TAKEN IN ADULTERY
So when they continued asking him, he lifted up himself, and said unto them, He that is without sin among you, let him first cast a stone at her. . . .
And they which heard it, <u>being convicted by their own conscience</u>, went out one by one, beginning at the eldest, even unto the last: and Jesus was left alone, and the woman standing in the midst (John 8:7, 9, underlining mine).

Even the vilest of sinners have burning inside the Light of Christ, the first internal guidance system, to lead them back to God. (Mosiah 4:2-3). It is important for every parent, spouse, and friend to know they are not alone in their concern for a wayward loved one (John 16:32). God is calling to each through the Light of Christ to become a better self. When mortal voices are out of control, when they are screaming or yelling or giving inappropriate criticism, it is hard to hear the inner voice of conscience. Often it is in the quiet and reflective moments that the conscience speaks the loudest.

THE PROPHET ENOS
Behold, I went to hunt beasts in the forests; and the words
which I had often heard my father speak concerning eternal life,
and the joy of the saints, sunk deep into my heart (Enos 1:3).

THE WITNESS OF THE HOLY GHOST

The second internal guidance system which Heavenly Father gives to each soul born on this earth is the ability to respond to a witness of the Holy Ghost. It is different from the **companionship** of the Holy Ghost which is given after baptism by the laying on of hands. It is the mission of the Holy Ghost to bear witness to the truth of all things. Whenever a person comes into contact with the truth wherever it may be, the Holy Ghost will witness to the soul. In a classroom, in the laboratory, when contacted by the missionaries, the witness to truth is given by the Holy Ghost (Moroni 10:5).

Member, nonmember, excommunicated member, heathen gentile, the vilest of sinners are all alike unto God. The Witness of The Holy Ghost is available to all. It is universal. It is also another part of God's "I Love You" program. The Holy Spirit bears witness to the truth of all thing to all people. God "never gives up and never gives in," in the guidance of His children. God is patient and long suffering while others misinterpret Heavenly Father as indifferent and uninvolved (D&C 60:4). Frequently loved ones are unaware of either the Light of Conscience or the Witness of the Holy Ghost in their lives. God's hands are daily involved in the lives of His children. One hand of God is the conscience. The other hand of God is the Holy Ghost. Often God guides His children with His hands while He Himself goes unnoticed. When this life is over each will be overwhelmed at God's participation in his or her life and the lives of their loved ones.

God, who rules the universe, is deeply centered in the life of each child on this earth. This includes the wayward and the faithful. Many are unaware even when they have the Holy Ghost (3 Nephi 9:20). Each can rest assured and exercise faith in God's plan of Divine Intervention. He who directs the Heavens will not abandon His Footstool. Heavenly Father directed Jesus to "save all" except the sons of perdition who choose not to be saved (D&C 76:44). Today is a part of God's eternity and He does Divinely Intervene. What is called for is greater faith in God's love for his children. Remember that Orson F. Whitney bore testimony to this truth in these words, "Heavenly Father loves his children more than any earthly parent loves those same children." (Conference Reports, April 1929, p. 11.) Faith in self is a poor substitute for Divine Intervention.

HOW DOES GOD DIVINELY INTERVENE?

In addition to providing the Light of Christ (the conscience) and the Witness of the Holy Ghost, the Lord will Divinely Intervene. A review of all the Standard Works reveals five principal ways the Lord Divinely Intervenes:

I. **GOD WILL SOFTEN THE HEART:** I Nephi 2:16; I Nephi 7:5; I Nephi 7:19; I Nephi 18:20; Mosiah 19:14; Mosiah 20:26; Alma 24:8; Alma 19:23; 2 Nephi 10:18; Mosiah 21:15; Mosiah 23:29; D&C 104:80; D&C 105:27; D&C 109:56; D&C 124:9; Helaman 12:2; etc.

II. **GOD WILL STRENGTHEN PHYSICALLY, SPIRITUALLY:** Isaiah 12:2; Isaiah 40:29; Luke 22:42; 1 Nephi 17:1-3; Words of Mormon 1:14; Mosiah 9:17; Mosiah 10:10; Mosiah 21:15; Mosiah 24:14; Alma 2:18, 28, 31; Alma 14:26; Alma 20:4; Alma 31:38; Alma 43:49; Alma 45:5; Alma 46:20; etc.

III. **GOD WILL RAISE SOMEONE UP TO HELP:** Gen 12:1-5; Gen 45:7; Exodus 3:10; Judges 6:17-14; Alma 1:8; Mosiah 27:14; Mosiah 3:4; Moroni 7:36-37; 1 Nephi 3:29; Mosiah 29:20; Mosiah 25:16; Alma 15:1; 3 Nephi 20:26; D&C 1:17; etc.

IV. **GOD WILL REMOVE ONE FROM THE PROBLEM, EXODUS:** Exodus 13:16; Jacob 3:4; 1 Nephi 2:2; 1 Nephi 5:20; 2 Nephi 5:5; Omni 1:12; Helaman 12:2; Ether 9:3; D&C 127:1; Mosiah 2:4; Mosiah 7:33; Mosiah 29:20; Mosiah 11:26; Alma 36:27; Alma 38:4; Alma 48:15; Alma 50:22; Alma 56:47; Alma 57:35, etc.

V. **GOD WILL REMOVE THE PROBLEM:** Exodus 14:28; 1 Nephi 4:18; Alma 44:3; Alma 30;50, 60; Alma 12:3, 6-7; Jacob 7:1-3; Jacob 7:14-15, etc.

Because He sees the "big picture" with eternal perspective, God knows "how," "where," and "when" to intervene. Man's vision is blurred as he sojourns in time (I Corinthians 13:9-12). What one thinks is in the best interest of a loved one may not be in their "**Eternal** best interest." Only God knows "how," "where," and "when" to Divinely Intervene. This is a true principle which requires man to have faith in God's love and timing. The hands of God are manifested daily. The face of God will be unveiled to His children only when it would be a blessing for them.

REVELATION TO JOSEPH
. . . for he will unveil his face unto you, and it shall be in his own time, and in his own way, and according to his own will (D&C 88:68).

True believers in Heavenly Father are required to bow the head and bend the knee and say what Jesus said in the Garden of Gethsemane, "...**nevertheless** not my will, but thine, be done." (Luke 22:42.) As much as one may desire and deserve a needed blessing, the word "NEVERTHELESS" must be added to the faith-filled prayer. "Not my will, but thine be done," acknowledges God's eternal perspective and faith in a God who loves His children. It is important to note that Heavenly Father did not remove the cup from Jesus in the Garden. However, Heavenly Father saw fit to Divinely Intervene in "strengthening him." There is no question in Heavenly Father's love for Jesus, or for the wayward, or for the Agent of Love.

There was a greater mission for Jesus in the hours which lay before Him. It was the supernal Atonement. The Mortal Messiah taught His disciples the meaning of a "greater love," through loving service. (John 15:13.) In the "Big Picture," in the eternal best interest of Jesus and all mankind, Heavenly Father allowed Jesus to suffer unto death at the hands of wicked and cruel men. With hindsight each can behold the wisdom of God in allowing Jesus to suffer. In the imperfect lives of those who are self-destructing, the long suffering of God is misinterpreted as disinterest or abandonment. Sins, weaknesses, and lack of worthiness adds to the doubt and fear of not being loved of God.

Suffice it to say that one asks for the blessings of Divine Intervention in the **Name** and **Worthiness** of Jesus. One does not call upon God by virtue of his own worthiness, but in the Name of Jesus, The Great Mediator whose worthiness qualifies the prayer (2 Nephi 2:27, D&C 76:69, D&C 107:19).

WHAT POWER QUALIFIES
THE PRAYERS OF MORTAL MAN?
Listen to him who is the advocate with the Father, who is pleading your cause before him—
Saying: Father, behold the sufferings and death of him who did no sin, in whom thou wast well pleased; behold the blood of him whom thou gavest that thyself might be glorified;
Wherefore, Father, spare these my brethren that believe on my name, that they may come unto me and have everlasting life. (D&C 45:3-5).

HOW DOES ONE QUALIFY TO ACCESS
THE POWERS OF DIVINE INTERVENTION?

Whether it is for one's own life or for a loved one the process is the same. God requires three things:

- **HUMILITY**
- **DILIGENCE**
- **THE PRAYER OF FAITH IN CHRIST**

It matters not what problem one brings to the Lord. The problem could involve finances and debt, moral problems, addictive behaviors of self or a loved one, or a hardened heart. The Lord is concerned that His child is Humble, Diligent, and exercises the Prayer of Faith in Christ to bring about the needed change. Nephi was acceptable to the Lord because of these very traits.

THE LORD SPEAKS TO NEPHI
*The Lord spake unto me, saying: Blessed art thou, Nephi, because of thy faith, for thou has **sought** me **diligently**, with **lowliness of heart** (1 Nephi 2:19, bold mine).*

Lowliness of heart is humility. **Diligence** is "keeping on." "Sought me" represents the **prayer of faith** in Christ. As an Agent of Change, one must become as a child,"submissive, meek, humble, patient, full of love, willing to submit,...to his father (Mosiah 3:19)." When one so appears before the Father, God is free to Divinely Intervene in a manner consistent with the eternal best interest of all his children. This means the righteous, the wicked, and the indifferent. The spoiled child who only wants what **he** wants, lacks the perspective of God's eternal view. The proud, willful child throws a tantrum if he does not get his way. The child's way may not be the best way (Isaiah 55:10-11). In addition, how can the Lord use a proud, lazy, willful child to serve as an instrument in His hands? The child is not open to all the alternatives of Divine Intervention.

Jesus did not tarry as long as Peter, Mary, or any of His disciples wanted Jesus to stay. Joseph Smith left this world as a martyr. Emma and the children and even Brigham Young wanted more time for Joseph. One's parents, spouse, or child may die, leaving one with feelings of abandonment.

Lacking perspective, one may ask for the **problem to be removed** when **softening the heart** may be a better solution. One may ask to be **removed from a difficult circumstance** when the Lord could **raise some one up** to solve the problem another way. Maybe the Lord will choose to **strengthen** one in all cases. It is not unusual for God to use a number of these options in Divine Intervention. Here is a review of the Divine Intervention Principles:

I.   Soften The Heart
II.   Strengthen Both Physically and Spiritually
III. Raise Someone Up To Do What One Cannot Do
IV.   Remove One From The Circumstance (Exodus)
V.   Remove The Problem

Regardless of the nature of the problem, God is more concerned that the person who is offering the prayer for assistance is humble, diligent and exercises the prayer of faith. These requirements of God span all of time and all dispensations of the Gospel. Examples are found everywhere in the Scriptures. Once a person is aware of the requirements and the principles of Divine Intervention, the hand of God is more easily discerned.

I. SOFTENING THE HEART

Notice how the Lord chose to Divinely Intervene in Nephi's life.

GOD'S REVELATION TO NEPHI
I, Nephi having great desires to know of the mysteries of God, wherefore, I did cry unto the Lord; and behold he did visit me, and <u>did soften my heart</u> that I did believe all the words which had been spoken by my father; wherefore, I did not rebel against him like unto my brothers. . . (1 Nephi 2:16, underlining mine).

The first heart to be softened belongs to the Agent of Change. Then the Agent of Change can become an Agent of Love. In this dispensation the Church had a problem with financial indebtedness. The Church had bills and financial obligations it could not pay. The Prophet Joseph

Smith went to the Lord in Mighty Prayer asking for relief. He was told that what he lacked wasn't money. What he lacked was Humility, Diligence, and the Prayer of Faith.

> *THE LORD ANSWERS JOSEPH'S PRAYER*
> *ABOUT THE DEBTS OF THE CHURCH*
> *And again, verily I say unto you, concerning your debts—behold it is my will that you shall pay all your debts.*
>
> *And it is my will that you shall humble yourselves before me, and obtain this blessing by your **diligence** and **humility** and the **prayer of faith**.*
>
> *And inasmuch as you are <u>diligent</u> and <u>humble</u>, and exercise the <u>prayer of faith</u>, behold, I will <u>soften the hearts</u> of those to whom you are in debt, until I shall send means unto you for your deliverance. . . .*
>
> *And inasmuch as ye are <u>humble</u> and <u>faithful</u> and <u>call upon my name</u>, behold, I will give you the victory.*
>
> *<u>I give unto you a promise, that you shall be delivered this once out of your bondage</u> (D&C 104:78-80, 82-83, underlining and enhancement mine).*

On this occasion the Lord softened the hearts of the creditors until the means were provided to pay the debts.

II. STRENGTHENING SOMEONE

There are scores of examples in the Scriptures where the Lord strengthens his servants. Isaiah would plead, "Strengthen ye the weak hands and confirm the feeble knees (Isaiah 35:3)." When Alma's hand was faltering, he called upon God to strengthen him.

> *ALMA PRAYS FOR PHYSICAL STRENGTH*
> *Alma fought with Amlici with the sword, face to face, and they did contend mightily, one with another.*
>
> *And it came to pass that Alma, being a man of God, being exercised with much faith, cried, saying: O Lord, have mercy and spare my life, that I may be an instrument in thy hands to save and preserve this people.*
>
> *Now when Alma had said these words he contended again with Amlici; and <u>he was strengthened</u>, insomuch that he slew Amlici with the sword (Alma 2:29-31, underlining mine).*

Jesus prayed in the Garden of Gethsemane for the cup to pass from him. Heavenly Father chose instead to send an angel to "**strengthen**" him (Luke 22:43). He was not abandoned as some have supposed. The

Savior made it very clear that the hour would come when all men would abandon him and leave him alone. He said, "And yet I am not alone, because the Father is with me." (John 16:32.)

Sometimes the need is physical strength, such as was Samson's (Judges 16:28) and Nephi's (1 Nephi 4:31, 1 Nephi 7:17-18, 1 Nephi 17:3), and the people fleeing before the armies of King Noah (Mosiah 23:1-3). Other times the need is spiritual strength, as was the case with Jesus and Alma (Alma 31:32-38). The God of all time and eternity stands ready to respond to the prayer of faith. He will strengthen those of a humble and diligent spirit.

III. RAISE SOMEONE UP TO HELP

The examples of raising people up as instruments of Divine Intervention are myriad. Most are not dramatic. They are manifested in the daily lives of millions. Many are unaware of the direct intervention of the Lord as were Sidney Rigdon (D&C 35:4) and the "converted Lamanites"(3 Nephi 9:20) when the Lord was guiding them and "they knew it not." There are dramatic involvements that include the appearance of angels who are raised up by the Lord to be instruments in God's hands. Examples of these angelic appearances include Peter at Joppa (Acts 10:9-48), Paul on the road to Damascus (Acts 91-9), and Alma and the sons of Mosiah (Mosiah 27:14). In the latter case it was not the humility, diligence, or faith of Alma the younger. It was the humility, diligence, and prayers of his father that brought the angel.

AN ANGEL APPEARS TO ALMA THE YOUNGER
Now the sons of Mosiah were numbered among the unbelievers; and also one of the sons of Alma was numbered among them, he being called Alma, after his father; nevertheless, he became a very wicked and an idolatrous man. And he was a man of many words, and did speak much flattery to the people; therefore he led many of the people to do after the manner of his iniquities. And he became a great hinderment to the prosperity of the church of God; stealing away the hearts of the people; causing much dissension among the people; giving a chance for the enemy of God to exercise his power over them. . . .

And as I said unto you, as they were going about rebelling against God, behold, the angel of the Lord appeared unto them; and he descended as it were in a cloud; and he spake as it were with a voice of thunder, which caused the earth to shake upon which they stood;

And so great was their astonishment, that they fell to the earth, and understood not the words which he spake unto them.

Nevertheless he cried again, saying: Alma, arise and stand forth, for why persecutest thou the church of God? For the Lord hath said: This is my church, and I will establish it; and nothing shall overthrow it, save it is the transgression of my people.

And again, the angel said: Behold, <u>the Lord hath heard the prayers of his people, and also the prayers of his servant, Alma, who is thy father;</u> for he has prayed with much faith concerning thee that thou mightest be brought to the knowledge of the truth; therefore, for this purpose have I come to convince thee of the power and authority of God, that the prayers of his servants might be answered according to their faith (Mosiah 27:8-14, underlining mine).

The question may be asked, "Do angels still appear unto men?" or "Would God send an angel to my son, daughter, or loved one?" The answer is yes, if one is willing to qualify by his humility, diligence and prayer of faith. It is also necessary that it be in the "Eternal best interest" of the loved one.

MORONI'S INSPIRED WORDS

Or have angels ceased to appear unto the children of men? Or has he withheld the power of the Holy Ghost from them? Or will he, so long as time shall last, or the earth shall stand, or there shall be one man upon the face thereof to be saved? (Moroni 7:36-37, 44.)

God is always looking for Agents of Change who can serve as Agents of Love. The problem is, those who are called to love are so blinded by the frustrations they feel, love is redirected into improper criticism. Love can manifest itself when a person takes his frustrations to God. Heavenly Father is anxious to reach out to any of His wayward children through a multitude of means.

HOW OFT WOULD I HAVE GATHERED YOU

O, ye nations of the earth, how often would I have gathered you together as a hen gathereth her chickens under her wings, but ye would not! (D&C 43:24.)

VOICES OF THE LORD
D&C 43:25

- Voice of conscience ("by mine own voice")
- Voice of the witness of the Holy Ghost
- Voice of my servants [Prophets, visiting teachers, Agents of Change, and Agents of Love]
- Voice of ministering angels
- Voice of thunderings
- Voice of lightnings
- Voice of tempests
- Voice of earthquakes
- Voice of great hailstones
- Voice of famines
- Voice of pestilences of every kind
- Voice of "the great sound of a trump"
- Voice of judgment
- Voice of glory and honor
- Voice of riches of eternal life

The Lord calls by whatever voice the people are prepared to hear. The issue for Agents of Change is their willingness to be the one raised up by the Lord. Great love is demonstrated by restraint. Agents of Change may be the only voice the loved ones will hear. Is it not worth the effort? Is it not worth ceasing all uninvited, unauthorized, and inappropriate criticism in order to be an Instrument of Love?

The direct approach is man confronting man. When inspired criticism is involved it can be effective. Improper criticism is never effective. When a loved one is unapproachable and possesses a hardened heart, the burden of changing the heart rests with God. Is it not a great relief to lay the burden at the altar of God?

JAMES, THE BROTHER OF THE LORD
. . . and pray one for another, that ye may be healed. The
effectual fervent prayer of a righteous man availeth much.
(James 5:16, underlining mine.)

A righteous man is not a perfect man. A righteous man is one who is at the **right place**, at a **right time**, and with a **right intent** in his heart (Moroni 7:6-14). A righteous man is one who is humble, diligent and exercises the prayer of faith in Christ.

Angels are messengers sent by God on divine missions. They are not always obvious. They may appear as men. In the heat of the day "three men" appeared unto Abraham (Genesis 18:1-22). Jesus said the three Nephite Apostles would tarry as angels. They would minister unnoticed among the Jew and the Gentile (3 Nephi 28:27-32). The Apostle Paul would bear a like testimony about angels.

PAUL TO THE HEBREWS
Be not forgetful to entertain strangers: for thereby
some have entertained angels unawares (Hebrews 13:2).

Angels are not the only ones raised up by the Lord. By far the most frequent one who is raised up as an Agent of Change is a mom, a dad, a grandmother, a home teacher, a bishop, a friend, a brother, a stranger, a neighbor (Alma 1:8, Exodus 3:9-10).

IV. GOD WILL REMOVE ONE FROM THE PROBLEM
EXODUS: HE WILL PREPARE A WAY TO ESCAPE

There are so many examples in the scriptures of the Lord leading away the righteous (Jacob 3:4) and turning the wicked from their pathways that it is only necessary to use the word "exodus." The first Exodus began when Adam and Eve were taken from the Garden of Eden. The great Exodus of righteous and wicked led by Moses through the wilderness may be the one best known. The Book of Mormon is one exodus after another. From Lehi leaving Jerusalem, to Nephi escaping from Laman and Lemuel, to Mosiah fleeing to Zarahemla the story is the same. But will the Lord lead away "my wayward son from his bad friends?" Yes! Just as wayward Alma and his bad friends, the sons of Mosiah, were removed. God will respond to the **diligent, humble, prayer of faith in Christ** of the loving and pleading parent or friend today.

V. GOD WILL REMOVE THE PROBLEM

One of the **least** frequent things the Lord does is to remove the problem. Even when the Lord does remove a problem it is only after longsuffering and many trials on the part of the faithful. Pharaoh hardened his heart ten times after the Lord softened it (D&C 105:27). Ten different plagues were inflicted before he would respond to Moses' pleas, "Let my people go." (Exodus 9-12). Pharaoh and his army drowned in the depths of the Red Sea. The problem was removed after longsuffering and patience. The same is true of Laban and the Plates of Brass. At least three separate attempts were made before Laban was removed as a problem (1 Nephi 3-4).

SUMMARY

Softening the heart, strengthening someone, raising up a mortal or an angel, removing a person from a situation, or removing a person or problem are all ways in which God can and does Divinely Intervene. The very Heavenly Father of all is a living God. Jesus is still the Great Mediator. There is a God. There is a Plan of Deliverance. The principles are eternal.

PAUL TO THE HEBREWS
Jesus Christ the same yesterday, and to day, and for ever (Hebrews 13:8).

Do the principles of Divine Intervention work today? The answer is absolutely, positively, yes. However, the timing is left to the Lord as is the method of intervention. A question frequently asked is this, "If God loves everybody, then why am I needed?" The answer is prayers work. They activate the Powers of Heaven in behalf of a loved one. Also, God needs people who can give love. He needs people who will validate the worth of a soul. The humble, the diligent, and the prayerful are frequently possessed with a greater ability to love.

Humility, diligence, and the Prayer of Faith in Christ are Principles of Righteousness. The Powers of Heaven and the subsequent Divine Interventions are available today. The Lord's way does work, and the change of heart in a loved one is worth the sustained effort in their behalf.

Every child of God can become an Agent of Change. First, the Agent of Change must become an Agent of Love. The Lord's program for Change Agents is clear:

1. Take one's frustration to God in Mighty Prayer.
2. Take one's love to the loved one.
3. Set Boundaries to protect oneself.
4. Be an example of the values one desires.
5. Share to the level of the loved one's willingness.
6. Exercise faith in God's Divine Intervention.
   The Lord will do one of the following:
   - Soften The Heart
   - Strengthen Self or A Loved One
   - Raise Someone Up To Help With The Problem
   - Remove One From The Problem (Exodus)
   - Remove The Problem

Because God is all-knowing and man is not, faith in God's love to act in the eternal best interest of each is important. Humility, diligence, and the prayer of faith in Christ qualify the agent of love to become an instrument in the hands of God to love.

Remember, charity for all is preceded by charity for one. People marry their biggest test in life, give birth to it, or struggle with love for self. Selected charity is picking a "hard to love" loved one and loving him or her. Every soul has two of God's hands to guide them, i.e., The Light of Conscience and the Witness of the Holy Ghost. God loves his children more than their parents love them. Uninvited, unauthorized and improper criticism doesn't change people for the good. It alienates them. The Lord's program can effect real change. It works. Inappropriate criticism must be replaced by respect and common consent. It is the responsibility of each to protect himself or herself form the abuse of others. This includes physical, emotional, verbal or spiritual abuse. Example and sharing are a part of the Lord's way of changing the wayward heart. The combination of these principles of righteousness will make the Agent of Love a true Agent of Change. Notice that becoming an Agent of Love precedes one's ability to become an Agent of Change. With the Light of Christ, witnesses of the Holy Ghost and the responsible love of an Agent of Change, miracles occur. Who knows if one's spirit was not reserved to come to this earth at this time to be an Agent of Change. As Mordecai said to Esther, "And who knoweth whether thou art come to the kingdom for such a time as this?" (Esther 4:14).

CHAPTER SEVEN

MIGHTY PRAYER

Then shall ye call upon me, and ye shall go and pray unto me, and I will hearken unto you. And ye shall seek me, and find me, when ye shall search for me <u>with all your heart</u>. And I will be found of you, saith the Lord (Jeremiah 29:12-14, underlining mine).

Mighty Prayer is obviously different from prayer. A brief discussion of the differences and similarities seems in order. Both Mighty Prayer and prayer assume a relationship between mankind and God. That relationship is Father to child and child to Parent. When the children of God talk to Heavenly Father it is called PRAYER. When God communicates with his children, it is called REVELATION. As with any relationship, it requires communication and the willingness of both parties to listen. The Lord has commanded that His children call upon Him while He is near.

REVELATION TO JOSEPH SMITH
And again, verily I say unto you, my friends, I leave these sayings with you to ponder in your hearts, with this commandment which I give unto you, that ye shall call upon me while I am near —

Draw near unto me and I will draw near unto you; seek me diligently and ye shall find me; ask, and ye shall receive; knock, and it shall be opened unto you.

Whatsoever ye ask the Father in my name it shall be given unto you, that is expedient for you (D&C 88:62-64).

PRESIDENT SPENCER W. KIMBALL
When we pray, do we just speak, or do we also listen? Our Savior. . . stands and knocks. If we do not listen, he will not sup with us. . . We must learn how to listen, grasp, interpret, understand. The Lord stands knocking. He never retreats. But he will never force himself upon us. If our distance from him increases, it is we who have moved and not the Lord (<u>The Teachings of Spencer W. Kimball</u>, p. 125).

Prayer is not just words but communication. If one rises from his knees having merely said words, he should fall back on his knees and remain there until he has established communication with the Lord who is very anxious to bless, but having given man his free agency, will not force himself upon that man (The Teachings of Spencer W. Kimball, p. 124).

HEAVENLY FATHER'S REQUIREMENTS FOR PRAYER ARE SIMPLE.

MORONI'S ADMONITION ON PRAYER
I would exhort you that ye would ask God, the Eternal Father, in the name of Christ, if these things are not true; and if ye shall ask [prayer] with a <u>sincere heart</u>, with <u>real intent</u>, having faith in Christ, he will manifest [revelation] the truth of it unto you by the power of the Holy Ghost (Moroni 10:4, brackets mine, underlining mine).

It is HUMILITY, DILIGENCE, and the PRAYER OF FAITH IN CHRIST that qualifies the **prayer** as coming from " a sincere heart, with real intent." In the parable of the "Unjust Judge (Luke 18:9-14)" the Lord teaches ". . . that men ought always to pray, and not to faint." He uses the importuning widow as an example of <u>diligence</u>. Jesus immediately follows up with the parable of the "Pharisee and Publican (Luke 18:9-14)." The principle herein taught is <u>humility</u>: ". . . he that humbleth himself shall be exalted." Jesus is The Christ. There is a Heavenly Father. The Plan of Salvation is real. Having faith in Christ is believing Jesus will do what He said He would do.

MORONI'S ADMONITION ON PRAYER CONTINUED
For behold, God hath said a man being evil cannot do that which is good; for if he offereth a gift, or prayeth unto God, except he shall do it with <u>real intent</u> it profiteth him nothing.
For behold, it is not counted unto him for righteousness. . . .
And likewise also is it counted evil unto a man, if he shall pray and not with <u>real intent of heart</u>; yea, and it profiteth him nothing, for God receiveth none such (Moroni 7:6-9, underlining mine).

It is counterfeit prayer, false and dishonest prayer, which is rejected by God. Sincere, honest prayer from a sinner is preferable to the self righteous prayers of the Pharisees. (Matthew 23.)

WHY DON'T PEOPLE PRAY?

PRESIDENT SPENCER W. KIMBALL
President Kimball asked this very question of a young man who stopped praying but wasn't sure he could answer the

*question as to why he had stopped praying. The Prophet chided
the young man.*

"Why don't you pray?"

"I am not sure any more."

*"Why aren't you sure anymore? Because you have cut all the
communication lines? You have lost his address? You do not
have his telephone number even, and you do not have any
address? The communication lines have been severed? How do
you expect to know whether he is living or dead? If you went for
two years without ever hearing from your parents and they were
in the opposite end of the world, how would you know if they
were alive or dead? How do you know if God is dead or alive if
you have lost communication? Now, you get on your knees, my
boy. If you want to be happy, get on your knees and crawl on
your knees to the city of happiness. Only there is peace." (The
Teachings of Spencer W. Kimball, p. 127).*

There seem to be two main reasons why people don't pray.
Weakness and unworthiness are their concerns. However, weakness and
unworthiness are not disqualifiers for God. In other words, God is
available to the vilest of sinners, regardless of their weaknesses and
unworthiness. It is fear and doubt that keep the children of God from
the arms of their loving Father. The wonderful Brother of Jared waited
four years before he called upon the Lord. When the Lord appeared to
him, the Brother of Jared was chastened by the Lord.

THE LORD TO THE BROTHER OF JARED
*And for the space of three hours did the Lord talk with the
brother of Jared, and chastened him because he remembered not
to call upon the name of the Lord (Ether 2:14).*

The Brother of Jared repented in spite of his weaknesses and
unworthiness and continued to call upon the Lord. Notice the Brother
of Jared's prayer when he calls upon God to touch the sixteen small
stones to give light to their vessels.

THE BROTHER OF JARED'S PRAYER
*O Lord, thou hast said that we must be encompassed about by
the floods. Now behold, O Lord, and do not be angry with thy
servant because of his weakness before thee; for we know that
thou art holy and dwellest in the heavens, and that we are
unworthy before thee; because of the fall our natures have
become evil continually; nevertheless, O Lord, thou hast given
us a commandment that we must call upon thee. . . (Ether 3:2,
underlining mine).*

One of the most important words in this verse is NEVERTHELESS. In spite of weakness and unworthiness The Brother of Jared prays because weakness and being unworthy do not disqualify the children of God. How is it possible that God, who cannot look upon sin with the least degree of tolerance can tolerate the sinner? The answer is that God has incredible tolerance for His children. The sin and the sinner are separated by the Love of God. While God rejects all sin, repentance is extended to the sinner.

> REVELATION TO THE PROPHET JOSEPH
> *For I the Lord cannot look upon sin with the least degree of allowance;*
> *Nevertheless, he that repents and does the commandments of the Lord shall be forgiven; . . . (D&C 1:31-32, underlining mine).*

THE "I LOVE YOU" PROGRAM
AND THE "I TRUST YOU" PROGRAM OF GOD

Heavenly Father has two approaches to His children. The first is an "I Love You" program and the second is an "I Trust You" program. There are things Heavenly Father does for His children because He is good, not because they are good. For example, even Cain, as a son of Perdition, is going to resurrect. The resurrection is a universal and unconditional blessing (I Corinthians 15:22). God's availability to each of His children in prayer is another. Just prior to Cain killing Able, the Lord appeared to Cain and pleaded with him to do well. (Moses 5:22-23). If God is available in prayer to one who is committed to be a Son of Perdition, He is certainly available to the rest of His children. The Light of Christ and a Witness of the Holy Ghost to the truth of all things are likewise universal blessings available to all of the descendants of Adam and Eve. These are blessings which come from God because they are part of God's "I Love You" program.

The "I Trust You" program of the Lord deals with the laws of obedience and blessings. It is a program that is definitely conditioned upon adherence to correct principles. Obtaining the Lord's intervention through prayer is enhanced as His children demonstrate trustworthiness. As a person, family, or nation these laws apply:

- *OBEDIENCE EQUALS BLESSINGS*
- *DISOBEDIENCE EQUALS CURSES*
- *RIPE IN INIQUITY EQUALS DESTRUCTION*

The entire twenty-eighth chapter of Deuteronomy is a witness to the Laws of God. These Laws apply to individuals, families, and nations. When the covenant people of God are obedient to the Lord's commandments, they are blessed and prosper. When the people of the covenant are in a state of disobedience it brings upon them the curses of God (D&C 101:7). Amulek taught that the curses of God were intended to focus the attention of the people. These curses manifest themselves in terms of "famine, pestilence, and the sword." (Alma 10:20-23.) The people can arrive at a point where they are "past feeling."(Moroni 9:18-20) When this occurs, the Scriptures refer to this spiritual state as being "ripe in iniquity." Such was the case with the people in the days of Noah. The Jaredites and the Nephites both reached a point where they could no longer progress on this side of the veil. The Book of Mormon is a continuous account of these principles in action.

REVELATION TO THE PROPHET JOSEPH SMITH
There is a law, irrevocably decreed in heaven before the foundations of this world, upon which all blessings are predicated—
And when we obtain any blessing from God, it is by obedience to that law upon which it is predicated (D&C 130:20-21).

WHY PRAY?
If any of you lack wisdom, let him ask of God, that giveth to all men liberally, and upbraideth not; and it shall be given him (James 1:5).

"Any" is all encompassing. Additionally it is a commandment to "Pray always. . . (D&C 19:38)." "But ye are commanded in all things to ask of God. . . (D&C 46:7)." However, as president Kimball intimated, God will not force Himself upon His children (The Teachings of Spencer W. Kimball, p. 125). God respects the Agency of man. Wherefore it behooves the children of God to invite Him into their lives and the lives of their loved ones. The importance of this principle cannot be passed over lightly. The prayer of invitation opens the windows of Heaven and authorizes Divine Intervention..

JAMES, THE BROTHER OF THE LORD
Confess your faults one to another, and pray one for another, that ye may be healed. The effectual fervent prayer of a righteous man [or woman] availeth much (James 5:16, brackets mine).

The poem and later Hymn, "Prayer Is The Soul's Sincere Desire" by James Montgomery expresses several purposes for prayer.

PRAYER IS THE SOUL'S SINCERE DESIRE

Prayer is the soul's sincere desire,
Uttered or unexpressed,
The motion of a hidden fire
That trembles in the breast.

Prayer is the burden of a sigh,
The falling of a tear,
The upward glancing of an eye
When none but God is near.

Prayer is the simplest form of speech
That infant lips can try;
Prayer, the sublimest strains that reach
The Majesty on high.

Prayer is the Christian's vital breath,
The Christian's native air,
His watchword at the gates of death;
He enters heav'n with prayer.

Prayer is the contrite sinner's voice,
Returning from his ways,
While angels in their song rejoice
And cry, "Behold, he prays!"

The Saints in prayer appear as one
In word and deed and mind,
While with the Father and the Son
Their fellowship they find.

Nor prayer is made on earth alone:
The Holy Spirit pleads,
And Jesus at the Father's throne
For sinners intercedes.

O thou by whom we come to God,
The Life, the Truth, the Way!
The path of prayer thyself hast trod;
Lord, teach us how to pray.

(Hymns, The Church of Jesus Christ of Latter-day Saints, #145.)

WHAT IS MIGHTY PRAYER?

The key word is mighty. There are twenty-four Hebrew words that have been translated into the English as "mighty." Most of them carry the notion of strong or strength. Of the eleven Greek words translated as mighty, most identify the idea of strong, powerful, or fervent. In relationship to the concept of loving the Lord with all your heart, soul, and might (Duet 6:5) the Hebrew word is "vehemently" or "intensive." The Greek word in the New Testament means "forcefulness, powerful and filled with strength." In either case Mighty Prayer is intense and strong. It is not casual, relaxed, or routine. It is focused and it involves the emotions. It is a prayer which is not only said, but felt. It is not rote nor detached from one's feelings. Mighty Prayer is honest, heartfelt, and emotionally sincere.

THE MIGHTY PRAYERS OF THOSE IN NEED

LEHI
Wherefore it came to pass that my father, Lehi, as he went forth prayed unto the Lord, yea, even <u>with all his heart</u>, in behalf of his people. . . (1 Nephi 1:5).

NEPHI
And it came to pass that I, Nephi, being exceedingly young, nevertheless being large in stature, and also having great desires

118

to know of the mysteries of God, wherefore, <u>I did cry unto the</u> <u>Lord</u>; and behold he did visit me, and did soften my heart that I did believe all the words which had been spoken by my father; wherefore, I did not rebel against him like unto my brothers. . . 1 Nephi 2:16).

And by day have I waxed bold in <u>mighty prayer</u> before him; yea, my voice have I sent up on high; and angels came down and ministered unto me. . . (2 Nephi 4:24).

ALMA

Nevertheless the children of God were commanded that they should gather themselves together oft, and join in fasting and <u>mighty prayer</u> in behalf of the welfare of the souls of those who knew not God. . . (Alma 6:6).

<u>Nevertheless</u> Alma labored much in the spirit, <u>wrestling with</u> <u>God in mighty prayer</u>, that he would pour out his Spirit upon the people who were in the city; that he would also grant that he might baptize them unto repentance. . . (Alma 8:10).

HANNAH

So Hannah rose up, . . .she was in <u>bitterness of soul</u>, and prayed unto the Lord, and wept sore (I Samuel 1:11).

MARY

And Mary said, <u>My soul doth magnify the Lord, and my spirit</u> <u>hath rejoiced in God my Saviour</u> (Luke 1:46-55).

DISCIPLES OF JESUS

And it came to pass that as the disciples of Jesus were journeying and were preaching the things which they had both heard and seen, and were baptizing in the name of Jesus, it came to pass that the disciples were gathered together and were united in <u>mighty prayer and fasting</u>. . . (3 Nephi 27:1).

JESUS

And he called them by name, saying: Ye shall call on the Father in my name, in <u>mighty prayer</u>; and after ye have done this ye shall have power that to him upon whom ye shall lay your hands, ye shall give the Holy Ghost; and in my name shall ye give it, for thus do mine apostles. . . (Moroni 2:2).

Behold, I say unto him, he exalts himself and does not humble himself sufficiently before me; but if he will bow down before me, and humble himself in <u>mighty prayer and faith</u>, in the sincerity of his heart, then will I grant unto him a view of the things which he desires to see. . . (D&C 5:24).

Who will gather his people even as a hen gathereth he chickens under her wings, even as many as will hearken to my voice and <u>humble</u> themselves before me, and call upon me in <u>mighty prayer</u> (D&C 29:2, all previous scriptures underlining mine).

EXAMPLES OF MIGHTY PRAYER

Enos is a great example of Mighty Prayer that is honest, heartfelt, and emotionally sincere.

THE WRESTLE OF ENOS
And I will tell you of <u>the wrestle</u> which I had before God, before I received a remission of my sins.
Behold, I went to hunt beasts in the forests; and the words which I had often heard my father speak concerning eternal life, and the joy of the saints, <u>sunk deep into my heart</u>.
And <u>my soul hungered</u>; and I kneeled down before my Maker, and <u>I cried unto him in mighty prayer</u> and supplication for mine own soul; and all the day long did I cry unto him; yea, and when the night came I did still raise my voice high that it reached the heavens. (Enos 1:2-4.)

THE PROPHET HAROLD B. LEE
I once read that scripture to a woman who laughed and said, "Imagine anybody praying all night and all day." I replied, "My dear sister, I hope you never have to come to a time where you have a problem so great that you have to so humble yourself. I have; <u>I have prayed all day and all night and all the next day and all the next night</u>. . . (Harold B. Lee, <u>Stand Ye in Holy Places</u>, p. 246.)

MIGHTY PRAYER IS ALWAYS
MEASURED BY THE QUALITY OF ITS' SINCERITY.

THE PROPHET SPENCER W. KIMBALL
Could the Redeemer resist such determined imploring? How many have thus persisted? How many, with or without serious transgressions, have ever prayed all day and into the night? Have many ever wept and prayed for ten hours? For five hours? For one? For thirty minutes? For ten? Our praying is usually measured in seconds . . . How much do you pray, my friends? How often? How earnestly? . . . Have you yet found your deep forest of solitude? How much has your soul hungered? How deeply have your needs impressed your heart? When did you

kneel before your Maker in total quiet? For what did you pray—your own soul? How long did you thus plead for recognition—all day long? And when the shadows fell, did you still raise your voice in <u>mighty prayer</u>, or did you satisfy yourself with some hackneyed word and phrase? (<u>Faith Precedes the Miracle</u>, p. 211, underlining in previous quotes mine.)

MIGHTY PRAYER IS NOT ALWAYS A LONG PRAYER IT IS EMOTIONALLY SINCERE AND REACHES TO THE DEPTH OF THE SOUL

HEZEKIAH'S THIRTY WORD PRAYER

In those days was Hezekiah sick unto death. And Isaiah the prophet the son of Amoz came unto him, and said unto him, Thus saith the Lord, Set thine house in order: for thou shalt die, and not live.

Then Hezekiah turned his face toward the wall, and prayed unto the Lord, And said, Remember now, O Lord, I <u>beseech thee</u>, how I have walked before thee in truth and with a perfect heart, and have done that which is good in thy sight. And Hezekiah <u>wept sore</u>.

Then came the word of the Lord to Isaiah, saying,

Go, and say to Hezekiah, Thus saith the Lord, the God of David thy father, <u>I have heard thy prayer, I have seen thy tears</u>: behold, I will add unto thy days fifteen years. (Isaiah 38:1-5.)

JOSEPH SMITH'S MIGHTY PRAYER IN LIBERTY JAIL

<u>O God, where art thou</u>? And where is the pavilion that covereth thy hiding place?

How long shall thy hand be stayed, and thine eye, yea thy pure eye, behold from the eternal heavens the wrongs of thy people and of thy servants, and thine ear be penetrated with their cries?

Yea, O Lord, how long shall they suffer these wrongs and unlawful oppressions, before thine heart shall be softened toward them, and thy bowels be moved with compassion toward them?

<u>Remember thy suffering saints</u>, O our God; and thy servants will rejoice in thy name forever (D&C 121:1-6).

ISAIAH'S INTERCESSORY PRAYER

. . . <u>where is thy zeal and thy strength, the sounding of the</u> <u>bowels and of thy mercies toward me</u>? Are they restrained?

Doubtless thou art our father, though Abraham be ignorant of us, and Israel acknowledge us not: thou, O Lord, art our father, our redeemer; thy name is from everlasting.

O Lord, why hast thou made us to err from thy ways, and hardened our heart from thy fear? Return for thy servants' sake, the tribes of thine inheritance. . . .

We are thine: thou never barest rule over them; they were not called by thy name. . . (Isaiah 63:15-19; Isaiah 64:1-12.)

JESUS' INTERCESSORY PRAYER

<u>I pray for them</u>: I pray not for the world, but for them which thou hast given me; for they are thine. . . .

And now I am no more in the world, but these are in the world, and I come to thee. Holy Father, keep through thine own name those whom thou hast given me, <u>that they may be one, as</u> <u>we are</u>. . . .(John 17, underlining in previous quotes mine).

There are numerous examples in the scriptures of Mighty Prayer. (2 Nephi 4:17-35, 3 Nephi 17:13-22, 3 Nephi 19:7-36).

APPLICATION OF MIGHTY PRAYER

The counsel is to take one's frustration to God in Mighty Prayer. Take one's love to his loved ones. Until one is committed to "Mighty Prayer" this seems idealistically unreal. The truth is, it is the most effective and efficient way to operate. Mighty Prayer calls upon the Lord to Divinely Intervene and leaves the disciple of Christ with the ability to criticize only when necessary and with the Spirit and to love appropriately.

THE SIX ELEMENTS OF MIGHTY PRAYER

I. **Call Upon the Name of Heavenly Father:**
   This is very personal. Each child of God addresses his or her Heavenly Father in one's own endearing terms. This is a relationship between a kind, loving Father and an imperfect child. Such terms as "Holy Father," "Dear Lord," "Our Kind and Eternal Father in Heaven" are appropriate titles with which to call upon the Name of God.

II. **Be Honest In Declaring Feelings At The Time of Prayer:**
People who do not feel their prayers are not being honest. A
declaration of one's honest feelings at the time of prayer brings
reality.

ANCIENT EXPRESSION		MODERN EXPRESSION
"I am weary"	vs	"I am tired"
"My soul hungered"	vs	"My heart aches"
"Groaning in himself"	vs	"I am feeling overburdened
"He cried unto the Lord"	vs	"He raised his voice; He wept"
"I anguish, Father"	vs	"I am impatient, Lord"
"I am brought to naught"	vs	"I am frustrated"
"I did mourn sore"	vs	"I am ready to tear my hair out." "I'm angry; I'm mad; I'm heart broken and disappointed."
"My spirit was troubled"	vs	"I am upset." "I am afraid." "I am worried."
"I am sorrowful"	vs	"I am hurt, Lord." "I am unhappy." "I feel hopeless."
"Succor me, O Lord	vs	"I need help." "I can't do this alone."
"Let this cup pass"	vs	"Help me get through this."

III. **Pray For People By Name And By Specific Circumstance:** Platitudes and general statements create distance
between God and the prayer-giver. "Bless my family and help us
be good" is too vague. Also it is difficult to recognize the Lord's
answers. When people pray by name and by circumstance it is
easier to recognize the answers to one's prayer.

*"Father, I am frustrated with my son, Bob. He is in
trouble with the law. He has dropped out of school and I
know he is experimenting with drugs. Wilt thou Divinely*

Intervene? Wilt thou help my son? Wilt thou raise someone up to reach him. He won't listen to me anymore."

"Heavenly Father, I am embarrassed and ashamed because of my pride. I lied today and I knew it was wrong. I was afraid if I told Mary the truth, our relationship would be over. I am still afraid. Help me, Lord, to do the right thing. Soften Mary's heart. I am sorry and I promise thee I am determined never to buy anything again over $100.00 dollars without consulting with Mary and obtaining her common consent. Strengthen me, Lord."

IV. Express Sincere Love and Gratitude to Heavenly Father. Be Specific:

SOLOMON'S DEDICATORY TEMPLE PRAYER
And he said, Blessed be the Lord God of Israel, which spake with his mouth unto David my father, and hath with his hand fulfilled it, saying,
. . . Lord God of Israel, there is no God like thee, in heaven above, or on earth beneath, who keepest covenant and mercy with thy servants that walk before thee with all their heart. (I Kings 8:15, 23.)

Jesus would use words like "I have glorified thee (John 17:4)." "Father, I thank thee, thou hast given them the Holy Ghost (3 Nephi 19:20)." "Father, I thank thee that thou hast purified those whom I have chosen (3 Nephi 19:28)."

DEDICATORY PRAYER OF KIRTLAND TEMPLE
Thanks be to thy name, O Lord God of Israel, who keepest covenant and showest mercy unto thy servants who walk uprightly before thee, with all their hearts— (D&C 109:1).

"LOVE AND GRATITUDE" TODAY
Holy Father, in spite of my weaknesses and my many sins, and my unworthiness, I am grateful for the Plan of Salvation, for the Atoning Sacrifice of Thy Son, Jesus Christ. I am thankful for the health I enjoy. Even though I am overcome with my own problems, I express my love for Thee. I love Thee, Father. I pray thou wilt strengthen me.

V. Pray In The Name and Worthiness of Jesus Christ:

Jesus prayed to the Father in His own name (John 17; 3 Nephi 19:19-32). All of the rest of mankind are to call upon the Father in the name of Jesus Christ. There are scores of scriptures which instruct the children of God to petition the Father in the name of the Mediator, Jesus Christ.

JESUS INSTRUCTS THE NEW WORLD DISCIPLES
. . . ye shall call upon the Father in my name, . . .
if it be in my name the Father will hear you (3 Nephi 27:7, 9).

MORMON COMMENTS ON HELAMAN
. . .the Lord is merciful unto all who will in the sincerity
of their hearts, call upon his holy name (Helaman 3:27).

When John on the Isle of Patmos saw the glorious vision of the Plan of Happiness, he wept because no man was found worthy to carry out the Atonement and to be Man's Great Example. A strong angel told him to weep no more because Jesus Christ, the Lamb of God was worthy (Revelation 5:1-12). Because of the worthiness of Jesus he became the Great Mediator between Heavenly Father and all His less worthy children (2 Nephi 2:27:28, D&C 76:69, D&C 107:19, Hebrews 8:6, Hebrews 9:15, Hebrews 12:24).

PAUL TO TIMOTHY
For there is one God, and one mediator between God and
men, the man Christ Jesus (I Timothy 2:5).

All people are subject to the Fall of Adam. In the mortal state no man can be worthy as Christ is worthy. To be "temple recommend worthy" means something totally different than the worthiness of Christ. Temple worthy saints are keeping a few fundamental commandments which qualify them to go to the Temple. It is the worthiness of Christ's Atonement which qualifies the prayers of the children of God to enter into the ears of Heavenly Father. This is the principle of Divine Compensation. The worthiness of Jesus compensates for the unworthiness of all. Therefore, one does not pray in his "own" name nor by virtue of his own worthiness.

JOHN WAS A "KNOW YOUR RELIGION" SPEAKER
John and his wife drove up to the Stake Center. This was just prior
to his speaking at a Know Your Religion program. While in the parking
lot, a discussion about money led each to take a hard position. The Spirit
left. In less than fifteen minutes he would have to speak to a large group
of people. Most of these people came to be edified, uplifted, and

instructed by one who was inspired by the Holy Spirit. But the Holy Ghost had left. Recognizing their desperate condition, mutual apologies were exchanged. Here is the essence of the prayer that followed.

"Holy Father, we have been foolish. We have allowed contention over money to drive away thy Holy Spirit. Kind Father, of ourselves we are not worthy of thy Spirit. But Father, there are hundreds of thy children that await one who will speak under the inspiration of the Holy Ghost. This blessing we ask of Thee, that Thou wilt grant the Holy Ghost to rest upon John as he speaks that thy saints may be blessed. We thank Thee, Father, for the principle of repentance. We ask now in the name and worthiness of thy Son, Jesus Christ, to grant this our prayer. Amen."
The Spirit was restored.

VI. Say, "Amen" With Conviction And Determination:
The word amen means "so be it!" or "truly." Various Church leaders have given counsel on the importance of an energetic, enthusiastic, and sincere "Amen!"

ENCYCLOPEDIA OF MORMONISM
In antiquity the expression [amen] carried the weight of an oath. By saying "amen" the people solemnly pledged faithfulness and assented to curses upon themselves if found guilty (Deut 27:14-26). And by saying "Amen" the people also sealed their praises of God (I Chr. 16:36; Psalms 106:48; Romans 11:36; I Pet 4:1, Nehemiah 8:6).

By saying "Amen," Latter-day Saints officially sustain what is said in formal and private prayer, as also in the words of sermons, official admonition, and testimony (See D&C 88:135). (Daniel B. McKinlay, Encyclopedia of Mormonism, Vol 1, p. 38.)

APOSTLE LYMAN
*When these prayers of which I have spoken are offered in the family circle, at church, to open a meeting or to close it, and more especially when blessings are asked upon the holy sacrament, upon the bread or upon the water, there should be silence, a real stillness, all eyes ought to be closed, all heads ought to be bowed, all hearts filled with the prayerful spirit. These appeals are not to be made by one individual, they should be the hope, the faith, the united appeal of all who are present. And if in every heart there burns an earnest hope for Providence to hear, and for the united appeal to be answered, then **every pair of lips should express the fervent feeling of each and every heart by saying, Amen when the prayer is finished** . (Richard R. Lyman, CR, April 1933, p. 51, bold mine.)*
PRESIDENT SPENCER W. KIMBALL
The echoing of "amen" by the listeners is evidence of their accord (The Teachings of Spencer W. Kimball, p. 124.)

I was glad to hear you say "Amen." Sometimes we forget to do that and it is a very pleasing word to those who speak or pray or preach, and we hope that that (sic.) will always be very important in your life and in your sacred services. That sounds better every time. Every time that a sermon is concluded or a prayer is offered, every man, woman, and child should say "Amen," loud enough so that the person next to him or her can hear it. (The Teachings of Spencer W. Kimball, p. 520.)

In a similar talk given at the Priesthood Session of General Conference, President Kimball chided the brethren for their weak and somewhat infirm "Amen." When he concluded his sermon he said stoutly, **"AMEN,"** and turned around to sit down. The Tabernacle resounded with a loud chorus of **"AMEN!"** President Kimball turned around and with a raspy whisper said, "That is more like it!" (Author in attendance.)

Most people make prayer difficult. It is not unusual to hear a myriad of reasons as to why people don't pray. Many simply feel it doesn't matter. Others lack faith in Christ. It's as if the Gospel works for Apostles and Prophets, but not for the average person. This is the issue. There are no average people for God. Heavenly Father is the God of the living **and** the dead. Truly He is no respecter of persons. He hears and answers the prayers of all of His Children whether on earth or in the world of spirits.

"SOMEONE PRAYED ME HERE"

The thoughts of bearing one's testimony at a church of a different denomination without being invited is scarey. Yet, that is exactly what happened. At the time I was serving as the Stake Mission President. In a very vivid dream, I saw myself walking into a certain Church. After a few moments I stood upon my feet and bore witness of Jesus Christ, the Prophet Joseph Smith and the truthfulness of the Book of Mormon. That is where the dream ended.

When I arose in the morning the details of the dream were engraved upon my mind. It was a white building made of wood with a large Oak tree in front. I could see the graveled parking lot and the large sign announcing the meeting times. Try as I might I could not rid myself of this dream. I prayed unto the Lord in mighty prayer to seek his guidance. I asked the Lord to take the dream away and give me peace of mind. If, however, this was of God, I prayed He would open the way before me. I felt a strong confirmation that I should go to this particular church. It was in a town off of the main highway. I consulted with my Stake President and he encouraged me to go forth. I doubted my sanity even though I felt the Spirit.

It was not until I turned the corner and saw the church that I knew for sure this was a mission from God. The sign, the tree, the building and the graveled parking lot were exactly as I had seen them in my dream. I wondered how the Lord would open the door for me to bear my testimony. I thought of Nephi going for the Plates of Brass, not knowing beforehand the things which he should do. I entered the church on a hot August Sunday and sat down on one of the pews.

After a few songs and several prayers there was a period of silence. I felt the Holy Ghost move upon me as I had felt before in a Mormon Fast and Testimony Meeting. It was "time." I stood up, went to the pulpit not knowing what I should say. The moment I opened my mouth to speak, the Lord gave me the words. I witnessed of Jesus, I bore testimony of Joseph Smith and of the Book of Mormon. Still I did not know why I was there. Then it came to me. It was clear. Someone had "prayed" me to the church. I bore testimony that I had bee "prayed" to this meeting and I was there in answer to one of their prayers. At the time, I did not know that the church I was attending that hot August day was built by my Grandfather. He did when I was six and I barely remembered him. He had been a faithful member of that church. Although he was dead and in the Spirit World, his mighty prayer to God had inspired me as his grandson to bear my testimony. It was he who had "prayed" me there.

Several good things happened as a result of that experience. Many of those people, including the minister, investigated the Church. The story is not over. There will come a time when I will meet my grandfather and acknowledge the power of his Mighty Prayer.

At some point, like the "Prodigal Son," each must "come to himself" (Luke 15:17). The intent of Mighty Prayer is to accept the Lord as the changer of the human heart. When someone is frustrated with a loved one, it is hard to focus on loving them. The Mighty Prayer takes the frustration to God. It empowers a person to bring his love to his loved ones. Before a person reacts to their frustration and gives uninvited, unauthorized, and inappropriate criticism, he should go to the Lord in Mighty Prayer. The Father will direct which of the Divine Interventions He will use and when. He may decide to soften the heart of the prayer giver (1 Nephi 2:16). He will strengthen, raise someone up, remove the problem, or remove the person from the problem. Humility, diligence, and the Prayer of Faith qualifies the petitioner. The Atonement of Jesus Christ, his love and His Worthiness, divinely compensates for the lack of worthiness on man's behalf. The Mighty Prayer is notarized by The Holy Ghost. It is sent directly to the Father for doing that which is in the eternal best interest of each of His children. It allows the prayer-giver to act out of love and in harmony with the Holy Ghost.

CHAPTER EIGHT

ACTING OUT OF LOVE

No power or influence can or ought to be maintained by virtue of the priesthood, only by <u>persuasion</u>, by <u>long-suffering</u>, by <u>gentleness</u> and <u>meekness</u>, and by <u>love unfeigned</u> (D&C 121:41, underlining mine).

PAUL TO THE GALATIANS
But the fruit of the Spirit is <u>love</u>, joy, peace, <u>longsuffering</u>, <u>gentleness</u>, goodness, faith,
<u>Meekness</u>, temperance: against such there is no law.
And they that are Christ's have crucified the flesh with the affections and lusts.
If we live in the Spirit, let us also walk in the Spirit.
Let us <u>not</u> be desirous of vain glory, <u>provoking one another</u>, envying one another (Galatians 6:1-2, underlining mine).

Acting out of love requires that the intent of the heart be consistent with the manner in which one is treated. Righteous intent and unrighteous means will never convince anyone he is loved. If the only attention one receives is negatively imbalanced, the words "I love you," fall on deaf ears. There must be an "I Trust You" program as well as an "I Love You" program.

CHARITI AND HER FATHER
Chariti was a fourteen year old girl with a passion for animals. Horses and dogs seemed to be her obsession. Since they lived in a suburban area on a quarter acre lot, the horse was out. Weeks were spent by Chariti going to the library and reading about every breed of dog. Finally Chariti decided she wanted a Schipperke. She had pictures on her walls of this little, black dog without a tail. It looked very much like a black fox and about that size. Every Saturday Chariti and her father would drive around looking at pet stores and checking out the newspaper ads.

Then Chariti broke one of the family rules. It was not a difficult rule to remember. The rule was if the children's plans changed while they were with their friends, they must contact either parent in person or over the phone. If the parents could not be reached, the answer was "No!" The penalty was two weeks of being grounded from all activities except school and church. Chariti knew the rules. One Friday night she and a girlfriend were going to the movies. At the last minute her girlfriend canceled and Chariti called another girlfriend and spent the night at her house without informing her parents. When the mother and father came home at midnight they did a bed check. They found the other seven children sound asleep in their beds. Chariti was gone.

The mother called up the first girlfriend's parents and was told the girls never got together. The plans had been canceled. The mother began to imagine the worst. Maybe she was dead. Maybe she got hit by a car and was in the hospital. All of Chariti's friends were called except the one at whom she was mad. This happened to be where she was. The police were called, the hospitals were called and the mother got in the car to see if she could find her. It was 4:00 a.m. when the mother and father commended her spirit to God and went to bed.

Chariti had spent the night less than one half block from her home with Jeannie. About 9:00 a.m. on Saturday Chariti came bounding through the front door all smiles and cheerful. After the gravity of her insensitivity was explained to her, she was grounded for two weeks. Chariti cried. Through her tears she said to her father, "Does this mean we are not going to look for a dog today?"

The father replied, "We are still going to look for a dog today because I love you. You are still grounded for breaking the rules but this is a different thing." This was the father's "I Love You" program. It was independent from the "I Trust You" program. It was part of the father's unconditional love. Each week the father would hold a sharing time with each child. It was a time to talk or play games. In Chariti's case the time had been allocated to looking for a dog. It was not a time to be withdrawn as a punishment or taken away at any whim or infraction. This was an unconditional act of love.

In the foregoing story the father was acting out of love. The message is one should not use "love" as a "punishment." When people withhold love as a punishment they become emotionally unsafe. The one being criticized withdraws. The critic becomes less and less effective. The distance increases with each new critical statement and subsequent withdrawal of the one being criticized.

THE CRITIC——THE CRITICIZED
(More criticism equals greater distance)

THE CRITIC——————THE CRITICIZED
(More criticism equals greater distance)

THE CRITIC————————————THE CRITICIZED
(More criticism equals greater distance)

Now the critic screams or yells in order to be heard because the emotional distance is so great. The more out of control the critic becomes the more emotionally unsafe they are to the one being criticized. What the critic doesn't realize is that the one being criticized is not focusing on the message but the messenger. The only message being received is that he or she is not acceptable, worthwhile, or valuable. The critic's frustration is only intensified. However, if someone doesn't understand Spanish, whether it is whispered or shouted doesn't matter. Until the one being criticized is confirmed, validated, and secure in the love of the critic, the message will never be the focus, only the messenger.

The essence of the Gospel of Jesus Christ is to love. It is to help others become their highest and best selves. This is not psychobabble or some socially acceptable thing to do. It is not about being politically correct. It is a Gospel principle. "Reproving betimes with sharpness, when moved upon by the Holy Ghost; and then showing forth afterwards an **increase of love** toward him whom thou hast reproved, lest he esteem thee to be his enemy." (D&C 121:43, bold mine.)

It is important to love before the reproof is given. A solid "I Love You" program complete with weekly shared time experiences may be necessary. Treating a loved one with respect enhances the possibility of not being perceived as an enemy. The kindness of a "thank you" and "please" engenders respect. If one is treated consistently with respect, the credibility of the critic increases. The critic who is unwilling to develop an "I Love You" program and an "I Respect You," disposition will almost certainly to be viewed as an enemy.

In an interview with a young man who had been verbally and spiritually abused, President Gordon B. Hinckley was stunned. This young man was convinced his father hated him and was his enemy.

PRESIDENT GORDON B. HINCKLEY

I happened to know his father, and I know that his father did not hate him. He loved him and mourned and grieved for him, but that father had an uncontrolled temper. Whenever he disciplined his children, he lost control and destroyed both them and himself.

As I looked across the desk at that trembling, broken young man, estranged from a father he considered his enemy, I thought of some great words of revealed truth given through the Prophet Joseph Smith. They set forth in essence the governing spirit of the priesthood, and I believe they apply to the government of our homes. Let me read them to you. "No power or influence can or ought to be maintained. . . only by persuasion, by long suffering, by gentleness, and meekness and by love unfeigned by kindness and pure knowledge which shall greatly enlarge the soul without hypocrisy and without guile ."

I believe those marvelous and simple words set forth the spirit in which we should stand as fathers. Do they mean that we should not exercise discipline, that we should not reprove? Listen to these further words:

"Reproving betimes with sharpness (When? While angry or in a fit of temper? No—) when moved upon by the Holy Ghost; and then showing forth afterwards an increase of love toward him whom thou hast reproved, lest he esteem thee to be his enemy;

"That he may know that thy faithfulness is stronger than the cords of death (D&C 121:41-44)."

This, my brethren of the priesthood who stand at the head of families, is the key to government in the home directed by the Holy Spirit. I commend those words to every man within the sound of my voice and do not hesitate to promise that if you will govern your families in the spirit of those words, which have come from the Lord, you will have cause to rejoice, as will those for whom you are responsible. (Gordon B. Hinckley, Conference Report, October 1967, pp. 91-92.)

The term enemy is such a strong word. Enemy! Is it possible that which the Prophet Micah said is true across all time?

MICAH THE PROPHET

Trust ye not in a friend, put ye not confidence in a guide: keep the doors of thy mouth from her that lieth in thy bosom.

*For the son dishonoureth the father, the daughter riseth up against her mother, the daughter in law against her mother in law; **a man's enemies are the men of his own house** (Micah 7:5-6, bold mine).*

Jesus quoted this scripture in Luke 12:53 and taught a higher law. This higher law will create a division. The division is between those who treat people with love and respect and those who do not.

This is not just about how to give and receive criticism in the Lord's own way. It is about loving and being loved. It's about eliminating a self-defeating behavior and empowering love. It's about letting the feeling of love get through an aura of negativism. It's about being an emotionally safe person. It's about being a more effective communicator. It's about helping loved ones become their highest and best selves. It's about better relationships at work and at home. It's about self-mastery. It's about becoming a disciple of Jesus Christ.

The admonition of Jesus was to love one another. Sometimes people don't understand what love is. It is affection, acceptance, and appreciation. Acting out of love ought to include hugs of affection. Words of sincere praise and approval are necessary. Little acts of kindness visually reinforce the loved one. How hard one works at employment or as a homemaker does not compensate for neglect of affection, acceptance and appreciation. Courtesy, a smile, and concrete expressions communicated daily are the things of which love is made. Each relationship stands on its own merits. It will rise or fall on the mutual love, respect, and caring concern that each invests into the relationship.

FOR A RELATIONSHIP TO GROW
REQUIRES COMMON CONSENT

Acting out of love does not require common consent. One party acting unilaterally can gift love to another. However, for a relationship to grow requires common consent. When two free agents choose to interact, a relationship is born. Once a relationship has been established, there is no such thing as not communicating. Silence and not being available for a relationship sends a loud message of indifference, apathy, or abandonment. Common consent is the basis of all healthy relationships. Mutual agreement is a key principle.

ISAIAH, THE PROPHET
Come now let us reason together (Isaiah 1:18).
AMOS, THE PROPHET
Can two walk together, except they be agreed?
(Amos 3:3.)

Frequently one party or both do a lot of compromising in order to share the world of a friend, a spouse, or a child. The best relationships are built by sharing. They share time together. Often they share their hopes and dreams. The nature of a relationship will be a function of age difference, varied interest, and mutual respect. Sometimes the best way for a relationship to grow is by taking turns in choosing the shared activity. However, priorities prevail and some relationships have to settle for the best efforts of each.

ELLEN AND SUSIE, FRIENDS WITH SO LITTLE TIME
Ellen and Susie had been roommates in college. They both worked and had very busy, but separate, lives. Each would like to have spent more time together but their schedules never seemed to match. The years went by and each lamented the loss of contact. They finally decided on a luncheon date once a month and a phone call every other week. This was all the time they had for each other. Because it was mutually agreed upon by common consent, it was a good relationship.

"I Love You" programs come in all sizes and shapes. The one thing any successful relationship has is shared time by common consent. Another factor to consider is age appropriate activities. Frequently adults try to bring children into an adult world instead of the adult entering the world of the child. Grand Daddy learned this lesson the hard way.

GRAND DADDY AND THE GRANDSON

Grand Daddy wanted to take his grandson to a football game. The Grandmother asked the Grandfather if he was sure he wanted to take a four year old to a football game. "He will get bored, he won't understand, and he will be going to the bathroom all the time," she said.

The Grandmother could not have been more right. It was a terrible experience for both of them. Grand Daddy had purchased root beer and popcorn for the little guy. He spilled all the popcorn on the people below them. However, he did drink the pop. Grand Daddy had to leave the game at exciting times to take his grandson to the bathroom.

Upon their return the Grandmother didn't need to ask how it went. She could see it upon their countenances. Grand Daddy was frustrated because he tried to bring a four year old into an adult world activity. The grandmother suggested the grandson would have been happy just to go to the park and play on the swings. The next time they went into the world of a four-year-old. It was wonderful. Grandmother winked at her husband and said,"If you want to build a relationship with a four-year-old, you have to think like a four-year-old." Grand Daddy said the way his memory was slipping he would catch up with their grandson in no time at all. They laughed.

There is an old saying that goes, "If you don't have time to do it right when will you have time to do it over again." There is time now to love. There is time to develop, if necessary, a one-sided, unilateral "I Love You" program with each person in one's life. Maybe its a card, a phone call, an enthusiastic hug, a smile. Acting out of love doesn't always have to cost money. It does require thought, effort and some time.

SOME RELATIONSHIPS REQUIRE STRATEGIC RETREAT

A relationship cannot grow beyond the willingness of each to participate. This means one party or the other will have to sacrifice and compromise in order for the relationship to progress. God was willing to have the children of Israel behold His face. He was ready for a better relationship. However, the children of Israel were not. Moses came down from the mountain with the higher law written on tables of stone. The children of Israel were not willing nor prepared for this higher relationship.

MOSES
Now this Moses plainly taught to the children of Israel in the wilderness, and sought diligently to sanctify his people that they might behold the face of God;
But they hardened their hearts and could not endure his presence (D&C 84:23-24).

Rather than abandon the children of Israel altogether, the Lord agreed to a lesser relationship called the Law of Moses. This is called STRATEGIC RETREAT. It is not abandonment. It is common consent. It is working at the level of mutual agreement. It is sharing at the level of one's willingness to share. A relationship cannot be forced.

Modern day Israel was commanded to gather to Zion in Independence, Missouri (D&C 57:1-3). However, they were not spiritually prepared to do so and were driven out. Once again they lacked the commitment necessary to live the higher relationship. Joseph Smith was told why they were driven out.

A ZION PLACE
DOES NOT A ZION PEOPLE MAKE
Behold, I say unto you, there were jarrings [harsh discordant speech], and contentions, and envyings, and strife, and lustful and covetous desires among them; therefore by these things they polluted their inheritances. (D&C 101:6, underlining and brackets mine.)

Going to a geographical location called Zion does not a Zion people make. It requires the people to live a Zion law wherever they are. One might just as well assume that all should go to the temples without recommends. Being at a holy spot does not make one holy. Modern Israel, i.e., mothers, fathers, brothers, sisters, sons and daughters, friends and companions, must learn to exist with respect and common consent. This is acting out of love.

Notice the characteristics which caused the chosen to pollute their inheritance. There were "jarrings [harsh discordant speech], and contentions and envyings and strifes. . . by these things they polluted their inheritances." Common consent respects the preparation of each party in the relationship to function at their level of willingness. To criticize another requires common consent. Compulsion, appeal to one's position of authority and improper criticism will not achieve common consent. It is only when one is acting out of love that real progress can be made.

APPLICATION

- Develop an "I Love You" Program, independent of an "I Trust You" Program.
- "Gift" respect to all people because you are a good person.
- Work by Common Consent.
- Learn to "Strategically Retreat."
- Work at the level of the preparation of each person.
- Work at the level of the willingness of each person.

CHAPTER NINE

THE ART OF GIVING
APPROPRIATE CRITICISM

Dr. John L. Lund's
QUICK CHECK GUIDE TO APPROPRIATE CRITICISM
THE ART OF GIVING APPROPRIATE CRITICISM

☐ STEP ONE:
- BEFORE YOU SPEAK ASK YOURSELF TWO QUESTIONS:
  1. Is the criticism a part of my stewardship or business?
  2. Is the criticism not only true, but is it necessary?
- If the answer to EITHER of the foregoing questions is "No," then BACK OFF!
- If the answer to BOTH of the questions is "Yes," then proceed with the following:
☐ STEP TWO:
- Ask for, and receive, permission to criticize.
- Be alone with the one being criticized at a mutually agreeable time and place.
- Be in emotional control and logically explain your concerns. No yelling, crying, swearing, threats, physical, or emotional intimidation.
- Stay focused on the issue or behavior in question. DO NOT ATTACK SELF-WORTH! Separate the issue from EGO. Protect their self-esteem.
☐ STEP THREE:
- AFFIRM THEIR WORTH TO YOU !

STEP ONE:
Before One Speaks: Before one opens the mouth with "you should, you need, you ought," consider the consequences of one's words. The uncontrolled critic destroys his own credibility and effectiveness. Some refer to this as the "Ready-Fire-Aim" approach. They are always **READY** to criticize with no regard for respecting the feelings of the one being criticized. They **FIRE** their mouth off without thinking of the

time, place, circumstance, nor the ability of the one being criticized to receive it. The consequences are usually disastrous and create unnecessary fallout. In the process of justifying their criticism they now try to **AIM** their comments to some productive purpose. Ego-centric and insecure people refuse to admit their approach was insensitive, nonproductive, and poorly handled. They persist in putting the blame on others. They live in denial of their toxic behavior.

Respect is not earned. It is gifted as a reflection of one's goodness. Appropriate criticism will always respect the time, the space, and the ability of the recipient of criticism to manage it. Before one speaks, it would be wise to mentally walk through the experience and anticipate the reaction and the desired outcome.

Before one proceeds there are two questions that need to be answered in the affirmative.

QUESTION # 1: IS THE NEGATIVE BEHAVIOR OR ISSUE A PART OF ONE'S BUSINESS AND DOES IT FALL UNDER ONE'S STEWARDSHIP TO DO ANYTHING ABOUT IT?

If the answer to either of the above questions is "No," allow others their own lousy relationships and their right to fail. If one's concerns are serious enough to warrant outside intervention, then report the information to one who has the appropriate authority and BACK OFF!

In a family of eight children the youngest child frequently grows up thinking he has nine parents. They include Mom and Dad, and seven brothers and sisters. In spite of having two real parents, his brothers and sisters feel authorized to tell the youngest what he should, needs, and ought to do. The siblings give themselves permission to criticize because they are older. Some assume the right because they are bigger, faster, smarter, or stronger than the younger brother. There are those who feel they have a right to criticize absolutely anything that any family member may do which might negatively reflect upon them, and therefore they are constantly correcting others and interjecting what "should," "need," and "ought" to be done in the stewardships of others. When someone assumes a stewardship they do not have or if they have the stewardship but act inappropriately, it is call "unrighteous dominion."

The concept of individual stewardship is an important one. Each person is entitled to his own space and the right to manage his life within that space. This includes the right to succeed and the right to fail. There is much to be learned by both success and failure. There are only three major ways of learning, i.e., observation, instruction and bumping into boundaries. It is important to allow reasonable consequences to perform their function.

In regards to human relationships, it is important to allow people their own lousy (or good) interaction. Any form of abuse is not accepted. However, if a father and son have a poor relationship because neither of them is willing to make the effort to improve they need to accept responsibility for what they have. It is an illusion for a third party, like the mother, to try to compensate for their lack by being a "go-between" This type of mediator is eventually blamed by one or both for contributing to the poor relationship. She winds up being a judge or umpire. The real damage done by the third party interventionist is to take away the responsibility which the father and the son have to make the relationship work. Also, it creates an illusion that the relationship is somehow better than it truly is.

On occasions, a counselor will ask this question to the well-meaning and well-intentioned meddler, "Where would this relationship be if you were killed in a traffic accident tomorrow?" The answer is the relationship would be where it was before the meddler got involved. Assume the father stopped communicating with his son when the boy was a teenager. All messages were carried between them by the mother who served as a mediator, negotiator, and arbitrator. They were more than willing to let her carry the messages. Although she was frustrated, it gave her a sense of being needed.

In this case, the mother did die when the boy was eighteen. The father and his son had to go back to the point where the relationship was abandoned. From that point they had to communicate to make it better. They were willing to do so. If one or both of them had been unwilling to communicate it would have revealed the true nature of their dysfunctional relationship. They needed to face reality. The basic truth has always been a third party cannot have a relationship for two other people who need to have their own relationship.

MOM AS A "TRAFFIC COP"

The mother was acting out of her stewardship. She was simply trying to compensate for the "lousy" relationship of the father and the son. The mother should have felt free to communicate with her husband and to communicate with her son as two separate relationships. In a situation like this the best alternative for the mother would have been to become a "traffic cop." This means she should have directed the negative, verbal traffic to its proper destination. When approached by her husband with a complaint about the son, a more appropriate response would have been, "You are so right, dear. May I suggest that you go to him and tell him what you have just told me." The mother would offer understanding, but she would not accept responsibility to communicate for her husband. In like manner, when the son brought his concerns to the mother she should have directed him to his father. This could have been done by her sympathizing with the son. "It must be very hard for you, son, not to feel like you can communicate with your father. However, I think you have a point. It's important that he hear from you. Perhaps you may want to write him a note." This way the mother would have been free to love her husband and to love her son independent from feeling the responsibility to make the relationship better.

EXCEPTIONS TO THE RULE

Sometimes the question is asked, "What about verbal or emotional abuse? Would I not be justified in intervening in a dysfunctional relationship if my husband were verbally or emotionally abusing my son or daughter?" In the case of a child, the mother does have a stewardship to protect her offspring. This does not give her license to act unrighteously nor inappropriately. It does not authorize her to assume responsibility to communicate for the husband or the son. Each situation is unique. All of the circumstances need to be considered carefully and prayerfully. There will be times when insertion under serious verbal and emotional battering is an appropriate response.

If someone is so emotionally unhealthy as to be constantly assaulting their spouse or children with verbal and emotional abuse, the questions should be asked, "What is being done to protect the child? What is being done to obtain help for the abusing spouse?" Most want to run off and get a divorce. The nonabusing mate needs to approach the Lord in Mighty Prayer and petition for Divine Intervention. The Gospel has clear guidelines for approaching an offending party. It is the responsibility of the one offended to attempt reconciliation. This is to be accomplished in the spirit of helpfulness (D&C 42:88-89.) Assume this attempt were rejected. According to D&C 98:34-45, an "offer of peace" is to be made at three separate times. Between each attempt, Mighty Prayer is offered unto God for Divine Intervention. Wisdom indicates that consulting with a bishop and priesthood leaders is in order. After the fourth offense, these testimonies are to be brought before the Lord. They will not be blotted out until the abuser repents. The Lord will choose which of the principles of Divine Intervention He will use. This does not mean that in the case of physical abuse someone is to tolerate being "beat up" three times before they protect themselves. What is being examined here is verbal and emotional abuse.

The nonabusing spouse has to be willing to put his or her relationship with the abusing spouse on the line and say, "You cannot verbally or emotionally abuse these children anymore. If you do not go and get professional counseling help, I am leaving you for a week, a month, etc.," and then do it. A decision of this magnitude should only be made after Mighty Prayer and consultation with priesthood leaders. This is a proper response to someone who is out of control with verbal or emotional abuse.

People will say they can't leave because they have no where to go, they can't afford it, they fear for their safety, etc., etc, etc. Seldom are these valid reasons. There are women's shelters in every major city and anyone with determination will find religious and charitable groups willing to help. The Lord does not lead people away from a problem until His ways have been followed.

The purpose of this entire explanation is to give permission to leave when necessary. In general, this will not be the rule. It is more appropriate to approach the Lord in Mighty Prayer and call upon the powers of Divine Intervention and to consult with priesthood leaders. Professional counseling may be in order. The more people are in tune with the spirit, the greater will be their confidence in the outcome.

DEALING WITH THE VERBALLY ABUSIVE

Harry is a verbally and emotionally abusing father and husband. He always criticizing his wife and children. He is constantly calling them names like "stupid" and swearing at them. Wendy, his wife, has managed to deal with Harry, but fears the children will suffer irreparable damage. Every time Harry begins to criticize the children, Wendy jumps in to defend them. Then Wendy and Harry wind up in a fight. Harry is not justified in being verbally abusive. Wendy's issue is his verbal and emotional abuse. Harry has an issue with Wendy interfering with his relationships. He also feels she is parenting him by telling him what he should, needs, and ought to do. He sees Wendy as being disloyal to him in front of the children. Furthermore, he accuses her of choosing the children over him. Harry is right that Wendy has been mothering him. There is another way that Wendy could handle this situation that would have taken away all of Harry's complaints about her.

Unwittingly, Wendy, by mishandling her response, gives Harry issues to argue, and thereby escape focusing on his abusive behavior. Because she parents him in front of the children she is viewed by Harry as being the problem. This is typical of most arguments. Each party is arguing a point of view they can defend. Wendy wants to talk about Harry's abusive actions, while Harry wants to talk about Wendy's inappropriate reactions. What if Wendy had asks Harry for permission to criticize him. Maybe a letter or note could be written by Wendy asking for permission to meet with Harry to discuss a painful issue which threatens their relationship. It is not a good time to ask someone in the middle of an emotionally charged encounter if now would be a good time to discuss their inappropriate conduct.

When Harry and Wendy do meet alone, at a mutually agreed upon time and place, Wendy is nervous and maybe a little afraid, but she says to Harry, "I've asked to meet with you privately because I did not want to criticize you in front of the children. It's my way of respecting you. Also, I did not want you to think that I was choosing the children over you. Our relationship is worth working on and I love you. I know that the children are frustrating you and I want to help. I have a problem with the way you talk to the children. I'm concerned about their self-esteem. Also, I know I'm not perfect myself, and I am willing to work on being better. I'm really looking for solutions, Harry. You love the children and you work hard to provide for us. I will try to help them be appreciative of what you do for all of us. I worry when I see either fear or despair in the children's eyes when you swear at them or call them names."

"This is the issue I have, Harry, and I honestly believe it's hurting your ability to have a good relationship with the kids. But you are entitled to have a poor relationship if that is what you want, but not an abusive one. I fear for their self esteem when you call them names or swear at them. I love you and I love them, and I want to help if I can. What can I do to help? I have made several phone calls and I know where and when different anger management groups meet. I'll go with you if you would like. Think about it and we can talk later."

Some will say, "Harry will never let me complete the first sentence without interrupting me. In such cases, write out the whole concern and the consequences in a letter. Obviously Harry is going to be defensive. However, Wendy has not compounded the problem with insertion, disloyalty, and face-loss for Harry. If Harry is a good man, he will think about it and try to improve. Wendy needs to go to the Lord in Mighty Prayer. She needs to bring the same calm spirit to at least three such encounters. If he is a "bad" man then Wendy needs to confront him with an ultimatum to get "professional help" for anger management or leave for a specified period of time. Most do neither, instead they gripe and moan about what is, but make no attempts to positively effect change. What Wendy attempted to do falls under the category of seeking for common consent. By following the Lord's approach the focus is taken off of Wendy and placed directly in Harry's lap.

Earlier, it was pointed out that one can only share to the level of willingness of the other person. In the illustration, Wendy did what she could. She went to the Lord in Mighty Prayer and consulted with the Bishop. Next, she asked for and received permission from Harry before she criticized him. She made sure she and Harry were alone at a mutually agreeable time and place. She was in emotional control of herself and logically explained her concerns over Harry's abusive language and her fear of its impact on the children's self-esteem. Also, Wendy gave Harry a viable alternative. She prepared a way for him to be successful. Wendy is only one half of this relationship. She can only control her actions and her reactions. She can model proper behavior for Harry in interacting with the children. She can love Harry for the good he does in generally protecting and providing for the family. She may not feel she can trust Harry and his abusive relationship with the children, but Wendy can have an" I love Harry Program" and do an unconditional deed of love every day for him independent of Harry's language with the children. She will do this deed of unconditional love, not because Harry deserves it, but because Wendy is a good person. She wants to be a loving individual. By strengthening the overall relationship with Harry, Wendy creates a supportive environment conducive to change. Her phone calls showed effort to find a solution. All of her efforts could be defeated by Harry's lack of willingness.

Some might ask, "Isn't it a form if intimidation to threaten Harry with leaving if he does not change his abusive language?" Yes, and it depends on how serious Wendy is about the issue. This should not be a ploy. Wendy cannot threaten to leave over everything, or she is simply trying to emotionally blackmail Harry. Her saying that she will leave if Harry continues to verbally and emotionally abuse the children is a simple statement of fact, not an idle threat. Wendy may want to leave for a month or a week to underscore her words if Harry's behavior is not modified. This is setting boundaries to protect oneself and the children.

For Wendy, this is a preferable and more appropriate overall response than to insert herself into every conversation that Harry has with the kids and wind up always arguing with Harry. Even if Wendy divorces Harry, he is still going to have some kind of relationship with the kids. This may include every other weekend, six weeks in the summer, and alternative holidays. In the end, Harry has to be responsible for his own lousy relationships. Wisdom would dictate that Wendy criticize sparingly so that when she does speak to Harry, her input will be considered, evaluated and weighed. Otherwise, Wendy will be perceived as a "nagging," "never-satisfied" person and the content of her messages will never be given sincere consideration. She dealt with Harry as a wife. She also dealt with Harry as the mother of their children. What she did not do was to constantly interfere directly with Harry's relationships. By acting the way she did, Wendy stayed in stewardship.

QUESTION # 2: IS THE CRITICISM NECESSARY?

It may be true but is it edifying and in another's best interest to hear it? Just because something is true does not mean that everyone needs to know it. An aging mother does not need to hear about all of the sins of her children while they were teenagers. In the same way, it is foolishness for parents to confess all of their transgressions to their children in the name of truth. Many of these facts only become "brain clutter."

> *REVELATION TO JOSEPH SMITH*
> *And that which doth not edify is not of God, and is darkness (D&C 50:23).*
>
> *ALMA*
> *It is given unto many to know the mysteries of God; nevertheless they are laid under a strict command that they shall not impart only according to the portion of his word which he doth grant unto the children of men, according to the heed and diligence which they give unto him (Alma 12:9).*

Wisdom would dictate that the sharing of truth be appropriate to the ability of the receiver to appreciate it. There are many truths which should never be spoken. Just because they are true, does not justify their publication. This is not a justification for lying. The real issue here is the matter of a higher law than, "Is it true?" The higher law asks, "Is it edifying?"

> *TRUE OR EDIFYING?*
> *A neighbor girl went away to have a child out of wedlock. She then decided to have the child adopted to a caring couple. She later returned, and desiring, with all of her heart, to start her life over.*
> *The girl is now doing well and the truth is only known by a small circle of family and medical personnel. Quite by accident her neighbor stumbles across the fact by being in the other town and encountering the couple who adopted the child. Putting the information they casually gave with some knowledge about the neighbor girl, the neighbor concludes the truth. A little investigation confirms it.*
> *Now the neighbor is involved in a conversation with a someone who asks what she thinks about the girl. If she were to tell all she knows it would not be a lie. It is, after all, "only the truth." She would only be relating what she knows. It is gossip, however, and to spread the tale of what one knows could impact on the young girl's future.*

If one's standard of judgment is, "Is it true?" Then one could prattle away and tell all. If, however, one's standard is a higher one, a standard that asks, "Is it edifying?" Then one's lips will be closed and she will not speak it. It is not necessary. It is not needed or called for; it is a truth which never needs to be spoken.

In conjunction with the question, "Is it edifying?" is the issue of whether or not it is in another's best interest to hear it. If the knowledge and criticism one has to share is truly in another's best interest to hear, then have the courage to share. If, however, no good thing can come of it, then exercise restraint and control the impulse to share it with anyone. A very important part of self-mastery is the ability to keep harmful knowledge from being said. People are more respected for constraint than indulgence. One will possess greater self-respect and self-mastery when he only speaks the truth which edifies.

AN OLD LIE

Barbara and Doris have been best of friends since junior high school. Now, both are married and preparing to attend the same ten-year class reunion at the old high school. Barbara has found out that Doris didn't make the cheer leading squad in high school because of a false rumor. It's newsy, it's informational, and it is just plain interesting. It certainly is true that Doris suffered as a consequence of a false rumor. Is it edifying for Barbara to tell Doris? What earthly good could it do for Doris to know that now? Would it change the past? Will Doris feel better about herself just knowing she might have made the team had someone not spoken ill of her to the teacher? Will it impact on Doris' self-concept for the good? Will it impact on Doris and her former teacher who acted on false information? Currently, Doris doesn't feel badly about the teacher, nor about the gossiping classmate whose lie kept her from the cheer leading squad. The teacher is the class advisor. Both Barbara and Doris will see her at the reunion. Also, the girl who spread the false rumor is the class vice-president and she will be there also.

What do you think would happen if Barbara told Doris? Would the ten-year reunion be edifying for Doris? Would it be in Doris' best interest to hear this information about the past, and would it wise for Barbara to disclose all she knows? The answer is if it would not edify DON'T SAY IT. LET IT GO !! If it were a situation where the answer would be "Yes," it is in one's stewardship and it is necessary then one would proceed with Step Two.

read top of page

STEP TWO:
#3 ASK FOR AND RECEIVE PERMISSION TO CRITICIZE

Asking for permission to criticize does not mean permission will always be given. It is as important to receive permission as it is to ask for it. If one criticizes without asking for <u>and</u> receiving permission he is not treating the other person as a co-equal, nor as an adult, nor with respect. If one criticizes without permission, he is assuming a parent role over the other person. No one has a right even if they have authority to treat another with disrespect. If one does not receive the permission to criticize verbally he may ask for permission to communicate his criticisms in writing. The one being criticized could then read them and respond within a certain amount of time, perhaps twelve hours. This option gives the frustrated critic a place to take his criticism. Writing down criticism removes much of the intimidation factor and allows the one being criticized to focus on the content of the criticism. Otherwise, the packaging of the criticism and the delivery system supersede the message. Remember, people interpret meaning by looking at a person's facial expression and interpreting their body language. Tone of voice also distracts from the content of the message. Writing down the criticism provides focus for the critic and greater emotional safety for the one being criticized. It is an art and skill to communicate verbally and keep the focus on the message and not on the messenger.

#4 BE ALONE WITH THE ONE BEING CRITICIZED AT A MUTUALLY AGREEABLE TIME AND PLACE.

Once permission to criticize has been verbally received, decide when and where the parties can be alone. The meeting should be at a mutually agreed upon time and place. For the disrespectful and the impatient these are a waste of time. Most want to dump their criticisms in the here and now and move on to other matters. Criticizing anyone in front of others is a bad idea. A person criticized in front of others suffers face-loss and humiliation. They feel belittled and are more concerned about other people who may be present than they are about the content of the criticism. This is especially true of children being criticized in front of their friends. If the critic is truly concerned about efficiency, he will be alone with the one being criticized at a mutually agreed time and place. "Johnny, I would like to talk to you right after dinner, before your friends come to play," or "Mary, I can see this is a bad time, could we talk before you go to bed, about 9:00 p.m. ?"

A parent, employer, or one who is in a position of authority may ask, "What if he or she refuses to give permission to criticize?" An appropriate response would be, "That is not an option. I was asking out of respect for you. Your options are to choose within the next twenty-four hours a time and a place that will be convenient for both of us."

It shows respect and restraint when one is willing to be alone at a mutually safe place. The opposite is also true. It shows disrespect and lack of restraint when the critic insists on the here and now. For those who want to enjoy a close-bonded relationship, being emotionally safe is enormously important. In addition to respect and restraint, the critic who is willing "not to criticize" in front of others is displaying loyalty to the relationship. It is such a hypocrisy to expect loyalty from others when loyalty is not given. A common complaint expressed by men and women is to be criticized in front of their co-workers, friends, or children. The focus is not on the message but on the messenger's insensitivity. It is as if the critic had broken an unwritten rule by criticizing in front of others. He or she becomes emotionally unsafe and disloyal. Most people expressed feelings of resentment for the critic whose public displays of criticism were seen as violations of loyalty. Criticism in front of others is an emotionally unfaithful act. It is astounding to those being criticized that the critic could do so with such impunity.

There are consequences for humiliating someone in front of others. Emotional closeness will suffer. Respect will be replaced by resentment. Most critics are either unaware of these consequences or it simply doesn't matter to them. It is as though the critic felt justified for giving the ridicule or criticism in public. Therefore the critic feels he has done nothing to deserve alienation. He expects that being "right" gives him permission. The critic assumes there will be no consequences for his self-justified behavior. His criticism was just compensation for the behavior of the one who is being criticized.

If "making the point" is his objective, if giving criticism in front of others represents a point of emphasis, then the rules for verbal warfare include public humiliation as a part of the escalation. Humiliation is an attempt to force a change in behavior. Those who agree to these rules of engagement should not expect to be loved for this counter-productive behavior, nor should they expect to be seen as emotionally safe. Disloyalty will breed disloyalty in return.

Behavior which says, "I am free to criticize anytime, anyplace, and in front of anyone I choose," is naive and could be amusing, except for its tragic consequences. Ironically, even when the critic is right, he is wrong in not being alone to share the criticism. To criticize in front of others and hope that social pressure will be on the side of the critic is foolish. The sympathy goes to the one being criticized.

Imagine in a classroom setting, a misbehaving boy who is truly guilty of rude and insensitive conduct. The teacher calls him by name and chastens him in front of the other students. In spite of the fact that the student is wrong and the teacher is right, the students will sympathize with the one being embarrassed in front of others. In this case the teacher is right in principle, but wrong in delivery.

#5   BE IN EMOTIONAL CONTROL AND LOGICALLY EXPLAIN YOUR CONCERNS. NO YELLING, CRYING, SWEARING, THREATS, PHYSICAL, OR EMOTIONAL INTIMIDATION.

Facial expression and body language represent more than half of how communication is interpreted. It is vitally important to be in control of these bodily signals. When neck muscles are taut and the blood vessels at the temple are bulging, the focus is going to be on the messenger and not the message.

> ### SUE AND HER FATHER
> *Sue is a runaway. Her father had caught her breaking curfew, not doing her chores, and lying to him. He began yelling at her, grabbed her arm, and pulled her downstairs. Sue tripped and broke her arm in the fall. Child Protective Services was called and the father was mandated to take an anger management class by the court. He was required to report for regular counseling. As the counselor talked with Sue and her father, it was obvious the hostility that each had. Sue confessed she was wrong. She fully expected to lose the privilege to use the phone and to be grounded for the weekend, which were the punishments prescribed by the father. With child-like wisdom she said, "But I didn't deserve to be treated that way. Certainly I would not have broken my arm if you had not pulled me down the stairs."*
>
> *The father was in bewilderment that somehow he had become the focus. He felt that Sue's misconduct justified his behavior. It was explained to them what it means to be emotionally healthy. It is important that each accepts responsibility for his or her behavior. They role played the situation over again as to what should have happened. Sue accepted reluctantly the responsibility for each poor judgment decision she had made.*
>
> *Then it was the father's turn. He had a very difficult time accepting responsibility for getting angry and acting out his aggressive behavior. It took several tries before he could admit that her behavior did not justify his reaction. The "abuser mentality" was explained to him.*

THE ABUSER MENTALITY

A man hit his wife because she had not done something he had asked her to do. The abusive man felt justified. He tried to explain he would not have done it had she only accomplished his expectations. This of course, negates individual accountability. Each person is responsible for his or her own behavior regardless of the actions of others. Each has a right and opportunity to act and to react. One cannot always choose the circumstances, but they can always choose their response. When one party tries to say that someone else made him do it, he is not accepting responsibility for his own behavior. He violates the first principle of emotionally healthy people, i.e., to accept responsibility for one's own happiness, unhappiness and behavior and to respect the boundaries of others. Abuse is never justified.

It was important to talk about how the father could have handled the situation differently. He agreed that in all future encounters he would be in emotional control before he spoke to her. This might mean a time out, a walk, or any number of anger-control mechanisms, i.e., deep-breathing exercises, counting backwards, going for a trip in the mind or actually walking around the block.

For some, it is more effective to write down what the consequences for misconduct will be. This removes all language and tone of voice and allows the one receiving the restrictions to focus on the content of the message. Writing it down also releases energy and serves to take it out of the body and mind and place it on the paper. It also requires some organization of thought.

When someone logically explains his concerns, it removes the element of emotionalism with its attendant distractions. Credibility is on the line when someone says they are being logical, although their behavior says otherwise. Criticism is difficult to receive under the best of circumstances. Adding emotionalism to the criticism only confuses the matter. The focus is the issue or behavior in question. It is best not to become angry, to swear, or to cry. Some feel this display of emotionalism adds emphasis to their point of view. The critic only succeeds in making himself the focus. Those who use physical or emotional intimidation as a part of their presentation, once again dilute the message and divert the focus to the messenger.

It is a dysfunctional and a self-defeating behavior to criticize anyone in the heat of emotionalism. If it is too sensitive an issue and tears cannot be restrained, it would be better to write it down. A third party professional, or priesthood leader can deliver the content in such a way the emphasis remains on the issue or behavior in question. Men feel manipulated when women cry. They resent it. They feel diverted from the true issue. Many women have this same response when men yell at them. Both yelling and crying shift the focus to the person and away from the issue. This is so frustrating that many men and women just give up. Breaking the nonproductive behavioral pattern of joining criticism and negative emotionalism is a difficult habit to modify. Nevertheless, logically explaining one's concerns can be practiced. It develops into a skill and contributes to the process of better communication.

#6 IS THE CRITICISM AN ATTACK ON SELF WORTH? PLEASE FOCUS ON THE ISSUE OR BEHAVIOR. BE SPECIFIC IN SEPARATING SELF-WORTH FROM THE ISSUE OR BEHAVIOR.

Part of the art of giving criticism relates to this important ability to separate EGO from ISSUE.

EGO

Ego means the whole person, the self, the "I." It represents one's personal identity. Ego is expressed as "my opinion" or "I feel this way." Self-worth or ego-worth is the value one places on his or her personal identity. It manifests itself by asking three questions:

- What is my worth?
- Is my input, effort, and time appreciated?
- Am I loved; am I lovable?

It has often been said that one is born into his greatest test in life, marries it, or gives birth to it. Some have all three. Others struggle with the worth of their own soul. Self esteem is how a person feels about himself or herself. Each relationship helps a person to evaluate his self concept. The sum total of all the messages received from others assists in forming "self perception." Job satisfaction, marital happiness, and self acceptance are all impacted by "self perception."

One's primary family is the greatest contributor to self esteem and self perception. A child who is raised with a constant bombardment of "you are worthless," "you are no good to anybody," "you are dumb, stupid, and lazy" is going to have a problem with ego and with low self esteem. In a family where these messages are constantly sent, the child will seek for acceptance outside of the home. Even in a home where "positive ego strokes" are given a child will look outside the home for validation to friends and acquaintances. The combination of friends, school, marriage or no marriage, work, church involvement, and feedback from society either reinforce the perception of self received from the home or negate it. One of the most important contributions a parent, a family member, or a friend can make is to teach a child his or her worth to God. The next important contribution would be to reinforce that teaching by treating the child, spouse, or friend with respect and love.

The Atonement of Jesus Christ in Gethsemane established the worth of a soul. Imagine facing the Savior on Judgment Day and explaining to Him one's right in attacking the worth of a soul. All are valuable unto God. There can be only one standard that is universally acceptable and that is to respect the worth of each as intrinsically valuable. Once again, the only defensible goal is to help each child of God to become his highest and best self. Anything less is an insult to the Atonement of Christ.

In order to be a disciple of Christ in the Art of Giving Appropriate Criticism, it is never justified to belittle the worth of another. NEVER! It cannot be tolerated. One never has the right to attack the inherent value or self esteem of another, not in jest, not in the heat of anger, not out of frustration, not out of one's own weakness, NEVER! NEVER! NEVER! This means no name calling, no swearing at someone, no epitaphs. It means no spiritual, physical, nor emotional abuse. This is a nonnegotiable. When someone is called "dumb" or "stupid" it is an attack on their worth. To attack self esteem is presuming a right that the critic does not have.

It is a testimony to the futility of criticism when people lash out at another and attack their worth as human beings in an attempt to deal with an issue or behavior. People in an emotional, irrational state of frustration, are seldom possessed with enough presence of mind to separate the real issues from the self esteem of the one being criticized. The struggle to learn charity for self and others is the way God meant it to be. Remember, charity for all begins with charity for one.

Appropriate criticism is that which separates self-worth from the unacceptable behaviors of the one being criticized. The difficulty of this task is enormous because so many have been programmed from their youth to equate their own worth with the criticism from others. He may be so hypersensitive to criticism that it would take a master in the Art of Giving Criticism to separate the issue from his sense of self-worth. It can be done. The "ART" of Giving and Receiving Criticism is the "ART" of separating the self esteem from the behavior or issue to be criticized.

THE "ART" OF SEPARATING
SELF ESTEEM (EGO) FROM THE ISSUE
This is a personal story and relates to my wife, Bonnie, who possesses a natural gift for separating her love from the

obnoxious behaviors of others. As a young married couple, there was considerable latitude given by both parties for each other's shortcomings. However, I possessed a habit that truly made life difficult for Bonnie. We were both college students and took turns with cooking, housekeeping and the washing. However, I was in the habit of taking my dirty stockings, rolling them together to form a ball, and then throwing them from wherever I was to the closet in the bedroom. Frequently this would require a bank-shot off a wall. Just as frequently, the stockings would miss the closet and roll under the bed or down the hall or wherever their final destination would take them. Bonnie's newly-wed patience wore thin as days of this became weeks. Apparently, the final straw was a missed shot that wound up on top of the refrigerator. The stockings rested unnoticed on top of the refrigerator until the next day. Some of my wife's friends were sitting around the kitchen table, when my wife opened the refrigerator door, releasing the stockings and sending them on a downward flight, giving the appearance they had emerged from the refrigerator itself. This might be a difficult thing to explain to friends, i.e., why do you keep your husband's dirty stockings in the refrigerator?

I know not what Bonnie said. I do know that night, when I returned home from an evening class, that there was something unusual about her countenance. I sat on the couch, removed my shoes and stockings and began to roll my stockings up into a ball. Bonnie was standing in the pathway of the projectile. While I still had the germ-riddled stockings in my hand ready to fire, Bonnie asked permission to share a concern of hers. She said something like this, "Honey, there is something silly I would like to talk to you about. It really is a small thing, but it is something that would mean a lot to me."

"What is it," I asked, totally unaware of the stockings in my hand.

"I bought a clothes hamper today and it would really, really mean a lot to me if you would throw your stockings in the hamper." Somehow she had managed to separate my self-worth from a habit of throwing stockings.

There are a number of unproductive ways to approach this same situation. She could have attacked me and criticized me and said, "You have a disgusting habit of throwing your stockings all over the house. It's a sick behavior. Your mother never taught you anything. I'm not your slave, you know, I'm not here to pick up after you. How dumb are you anyway? Don't you know it's only common courtesy to pick up after yourself?" She could have, but she didn't. She spoke to me with respect. She was very much in control of her emotions. She had asked for and received permission to express herself. She logically explained her concern. We were alone at a mutually agreeable time and place. I felt no intimidation. She owned her expectation. The issue was indeed one that was a part of her business as well as mine. It was, after all, a shared stewardship. The criticism was not only true, but it was in my best interest to hear it. Eliminating the behavior in question was edifying to us both. There was no attack on my self-worth, she had focused on the issue with great clarity. I almost felt like a hero for putting my stockings in the clothes hamper.

Learning how to separate "Ego from Issue" on the little things prepares the way to deal with more serious matters.

JASON WAS IN THE HABIT OF LYING

Jason lied even when he didn't need to lie. When he wasn't lying he was exaggerating. His friends were concerned because of this self-defeating behavior. Jason was being laughed at behind his back. Marion, his best friend, approached Jason and said ,"Jason you know, you are my best friend."

"Yes," he replied.

"I feel I need to talk to you about something that is serious," Marion said.

"Shoot," answered Jason.

"Not here where we can be interrupted. Let's go for a ride in my car." requested Marion.

Marion stopped the car and turned to face his friend. "I've been wrestling with this for days, Jason, and I've felt I just had to talk to you."

"What is it? Do I have bad breath?" retorted Jason.

Marion said,"It's more serious. I've chosen to overlook it, because I understand you and I'll always be your friend no matter what."

"What is it?" demanded Jason.

"People are laughing at you behind your back, because you have no credibility. You lie even when you don't need to. And you exaggerate all the time. Jason, you are really a neat guy. People like you just for you. It's not necessary , Jason, to lie. You are only hurting yourself. Well, there I said it. Will you still be my friend?"

Jason looked chagrined, "It's that bad?"

"Yes, Jason it is," responded Marion. "I've been thinking a lot about this, Jason, and I've come up with an idea. When I'm

around you and I can see you're lying or exaggerating, I'll give
you a key phrase and it will alert you."
Jason said, "I don't know if I can do it, but I'll try."

Is there an art and a skill to the giving of criticism? Yes, very definitely. It is time to practice. Remember, like bowling or golfing, or anything one does for the first time, it will feel awkward. And just like playing the piano or violin the first time, it sounds awkward. In spite of feeling clumsy and a little embarrassed, and ill at ease, do it! It is time to put it all together. It is time for a profound adventure into self-mastery. When beginning to practice the "ART" of giving criticism, it is a good idea to say, "I'm very concerned about saying something that will hurt your feelings. I would like to be able to talk to you about an issue or behavior without you feeling I'm attacking your self esteem." " I love you," or "I care about you" or "I'm sincerely concerned and I just want to help you be an even better person than you already are. This is why I'm not yelling or crying, I am genuinely concerned." One may want to copy the guidelines for giving criticism onto a card and carry it in a pocket or a purse. Here they are, one more time:

☐ *Think before you speak. Is the criticism within your*
  stewardship and would it be in the best interest of the
  other person to hear it ? If not, don't say it. If it is then
  proceed.
☐ *Ask for and receive permission before criticizing.*
☐ *Be alone with the person at a mutually agreeable time and place.*
☐ *Be in emotional control and logically explain the concern. No*
  yelling, crying, swearing, physical, or emotional intimidation is
  allowed.
☐ *Do not attack the self-worth of any human being. Focus on the*
  issue or behavior. Be as specific as one can in separating self-
  worth from the issue or behavior.
☐ *Affirm their worth to you.*

It is a very good idea to invite a friend or a loved one to practice the process together. It can be a very bonding experience to develop this art and skill with a spouse. Sometimes it is impossible because one's friend or spouse is unwilling or unprepared to do so. Co-workers are a potential resource. A question that is often asked is, "What if I am the only one to do this?" This is a talent to be developed whether anyone else chooses to do so or not. Think of it as a spiritual mission. Remember, one is never alone. Self-mastery is a journey that ultimately must be taken with the help of Jesus.(John 16:32-33.)

RELATIONSHIPS

All relationships stand on their own merit. Any person is only one half of any relationship to which he or she is a part. Younger children need to be protected from abusive older brothers and sisters. If not, an abusive "pecking order" will ensue. Abuse cannot be tolerated. It matters not whether that abuse is physical, sexual, verbal, emotional or spiritual. It is the height of idiocy for parents to be abusive in stopping abuse. Parents are best served by being an example of the desired respect.

MOM AND BILLY

Billy was ten, the older sibling. The youngest child, Micky, came into Billy's room and, without permission, took his remote control car and hid it. Billy confronted Micky, age five, and Micky lied about taking it. Angry and upset, Billy hit Micky then he came to his mother to make Micky give him back the expensive toy. Micky was crying, "Billy hit me, Billy hit me!"

The mother comforted Micky and then said to Billy, "Why did you hit him?"

Billy responded, "Because he stole my remote control car. Make him give it back, Mom! Right now, or I will go into his room and break his toys!"

Mother sends Micky downstairs with these words, "I'll be down in a few minutes and we can talk about it."

Before Mother speaks, she thinks about the desired outcome. Next she says to Billy, "I'm sorry that Micky took your car without permission. That was wrong and I will get it back for you. Billy, I need to talk to you about hitting Micky. Would now be a good time or would you like to wait ten minutes?"

Billy responds, "I just want my car back,"

"So would you prefer we talk about you hitting now or in ten minutes?" repeated Mom.

"In ten minutes," grumbled Billy.

"Fine, I'll set the timer on the stove for ten minutes. When it buzzes I expect you to be ready to talk to me," declared Mom.

The buzzer went off and Billy and Mom sat on the edge of Billy's bed. "Billy, what Micky did was wrong," said Mom, "but what you did in hitting him was also wrong. Two wrongs don't make a right."

"He deserved it, Mom, he is just a little thief. He's always taking my things," blurted out Billy.

"Right now, Billy, we are talking about your behavior. I love you son, and I know you will grow up to be a fine man. For now, I want you to know that it is never right to abuse someone. You

must accept responsibility for what you did in spite of what Micky did. After I talk to Micky, I want you to apologize to him for hitting him. Also I want you to take a time out for fifteen minutes for hitting your little brother. I meant what I said about loving you. I know a good boy like you will want to overcome a bad habit like hitting when you are angry. You go and set the timer on the stove for another fifteen minutes. Then sit at the kitchen table while I talk to Micky. When the buzzer rings, you turn it off and come and find me."

Billy was reluctant, but did it. Mom went to Micky and said, "Micky, may I talk to you now or in two minutes?"

Micky looked puzzled and said, "Now, I guess."

Mom responded, "Thank you, for letting me talk to you. Micky, right now there are only three people in the house—you, me, and Billy. I didn't take Billy's car. That means you had to take it. Don't lie to me because it will only make matters worse for you. I want you to go and get Billy's car right now and bring it to me." She was firm and looked him directly in the eyes. Micky returned with the car.

Mom continued, "It is wrong to take things that don't belong to you. Do you know that, Micky?" Micky nodded his head, yes. "Would you like to get one for your own?" Micky again nodded, yes. "I will talk to you later about some work I need done and maybe you can earn some money and you can buy one. Micky, I love you. You will always be special to me because you are my little caboose. Someday, when you grow up, you will be a missionary and you will teach people about Jesus. So you need to act like a little missionary right now. Missionaries don't take things that don't belong to them. You are a wonderful boy. A good boy like you doesn't want to do a bad thing like take someone else's toy without permission." Micky shook his head from side to side. "Here is the right thing to do. First, I want you to give the car back to Billy. Next, I want you to say you are sorry to Billy for taking his car. Afterwards, I want you to take a fifteen minute time out and think of something nice you could do for your big brother. Billy should not have hit you. That was wrong. Two wrongs don't make a right. He is going to apologize for hitting you. Right now he is taking a time out for fifteen minutes."

The buzzer sounds and Billy appears at the door. "Come in, Billy. Micky has something he wants to return to you."

Micky hands the remote control car to Billy and says, "I'm sorry, Billy."

Mom says, "I'm sorry I took your car without your permission." Micky repeats it.

"Billy, I want you to say 'Micky will you forgive me for hitting you?'" Billy said it.

"Now, Micky, I want you to say, I forgive you, Billy." Micky does so.

"All right, Billy, I want you to say, 'Micky, I forgive you for taking my car without permission.'" Billy repeated it.

"Ok," said Mom, "Now Micky is going to take a fifteen minute time out and think about what has happened here. Afterward I thought I would go for some ice cream. Would my two future missionaries like to go and get some ice cream with a mother who loves them both very much?"

In this story all the elements of "Reproving betimes with sharpness" were present.

☐ *It was in the mother's stewardship and the criticism was necessary.*
☐ *She asked for and received permission to criticize them.*
☐ *She was alone with each one at an agreeable time and place.*
☐ *She was gentle and direct.*
☐ *She stayed in emotional control There was no yelling, crying or abuse. She logically explained her concerns.*
☐ *She focused on the improper behavior and she separated the issue from the worth or self esteem of each. She was fair and evenhanded.*
☐ *She confirmed their worth to her. She showed forth an increase of love.*

STEP THREE: AFFIRM THEIR WORTH.

Affirming worth is another way of saying that after one has reproved or criticized he needs to show "forth afterwards an increase of love toward him whom thou hast reproved, lest he esteem thee to be his enemy (D&C 121:43)."

How does one follow up a message of rejection with a message of love? It is made more difficult by the fact that the one criticized may feel rejected, withdrawn, and alienated by the giver of criticism. Human nature being what it is, inappropriately given criticism will add to the difficulty of showing forth an increase of love. The critic will often find that before he can show forth love, he has to apologize for the inappropriate way the criticism was given. He is not apologizing for the content but the delivery. If the critic allowed himself to be angry or to lose emotional control by yelling or by attacking the worth of the one being criticized, he has a self-imposed higher mountain to climb. First, he must undo the damage done by improper criticism. It may take an hour or so for the one criticized to be receptive. The very pattern of improper criticism destroys the credibility of the critic. Words of love mean little when loving behaviors are absent. To the one criticized, words of love seem hollow and empty, even hypocritical.

What if the critic appropriately criticizes, shows forth sincere love, and is totally rejected on a consistent basis? Assume the one being criticized is not only hostile, but interprets loving behaviors as a mockery. Under these circumstances the appropriate giver of criticism must realize that he or she is dealing with a toxic person. This means one will not be able to say enough, be enough, do enough to ever satisfy the toxic person. However, when one gives criticism in the Lord's own way he or she has the satisfaction of pleasing God. It is consistency and patience that will ultimately triumph. It may take years. The power in the principles of the Gospel of Jesus Christ will overcome the most hardened heart. No one, except sons of perdition, can resist forever the power of unconditional love.

HOW MUCH DOES ONE HAVE TO SUFFER
BEFORE CHANGE BEGINS?

How much unnecessary suffering is enough? How many tearful nights are enough? How much hurt, heartache, and sorrow are enough? The heavens weep. Agency belongs to mankind. When will they ever learn? At what point does one cry out, "It is enough!" "Uncle!" When will the children of God come to treasure the worth of a soul? When will improper criticism stop? When will the natural man yield to the Holy Ghost? When will the words of love be matched with loving behaviors? When will the critic look to reproving in the Lord's own way?

The greatest thing the critic can do to convince the one reproved of his or her worth is not to repeat inappropriate criticism. The critic needs to show respect by restraint. When necessary, the criticisms could be written down on paper. This keeps the verbal airways clear of criticism. By using the verbal channels for normal and positive communication trust can be established. This extra effort may be required by critics who have a problem maintaining a civil tongue. Criticism is a hard habit to break. Nevertheless, there is power in the principles of the Gospel to change the most ingrained habits. All of this bears testimony to the need of criticizing "in the Lord's own way."

A word of wise counsel seems apropos. It is generally not a good idea to announce that one is going to change a behavior. One is setting himself up for failure by raising the expectations of change in the eyes of the loved one. Greater frustration and disappointment will follow the failed attempts to perform to the stated objectives. Promises of change are meaningless. "I'll stop drinking, I promise, if you will only come back." "I'll stop smoking." "I'll stop yelling." "I'll stop improperly criticizing." Since credibility is already a problem it makes no sense to set up oneself by announcing behavioral changes that have not yet occurred. A more excellent way than announcing a behavioral change is to let action speak for itself. Behavioral change will be noticed, especially if there is consistency in the new behavior. After the new behavior has established itself in a pattern of interaction, the credibility of one's words may return. Creating "emotionally safe time" is one behavioral change that can establish credibility.

EMOTIONALLY SAFE TIME

Many people have appreciated the concept of placing time limits on the amount of negative interaction. This gives them emotionally safe time. For example, Charles and Elsie agreed they would only criticize after dinner, between 7:30 p.m. and 7:45 p.m. Each had seven and one-half minutes. The timer on the stove was set. By limiting the time to only seven and one-half minutes each, it forced them to prioritize their concerns. For some people listening for seven and one-half minutes is an eternity. It is like having a "root canal on one's tooth without novocaine." However, seven and one-half minutes a day each leaves one with twenty-three hours and forty-five minutes of time free from criticism. Elsie was much less frustrated knowing she had a time and a place to express her concerns, frustrations, and expectations. It bothered her that Charles frequently would have nothing to say during his seven and one-half minutes. This, however, was his choice. Elsie eventually adjusted and continued to relish her seven and one-half minutes.

Some people have chosen to limit their criticism to one day a week. Marv and Lexus set aside one-half hour on Sundays after dinner to deal with their criticisms. They stayed out of the bedroom. They did not want to associate their bedroom with criticism. Although it was only one-half hour, they referred to it as "The Red Hour." This gave them six days and twenty-three and one-half hours a week of emotionally safe time. They quickly learned to write down their concerns. They eliminated the ones that seemed frivolous by the time they came to the Red Hour. The key was to honor the commitment to stay within the agreed upon time frame. This behavior established credibility for the words of Charles and Elsie and Marv and Lexus.

WHAT IS LOVE?

The greatest revelation that God has ever given to man says "**showing** forth" an increase of love. It does not say "**talking** about" an increase of love. (D&C 121:43.)

What is love? To some, love is a romantic ideal. To others, love is a feeling. Music, poetry, and the movies have removed love from reality. Conceptually, love is a nebulous, illusive, and difficult concept to understand. Behaviorally, love is easier to understand. Love is acceptance, affection, and appreciation. True love is manifested by acting in the Eternal Best Interest of a loved one. It is also loving in a manner that is consistent with the principles of righteousness.

The phrase "that he may know that thy faithfulness is stronger than the cords of death (D&C 121:44)," bespeaks of an eternal perspective. Love is not lust in the selfish present. It is confirmed with a view of eternity. Love that is "stronger than the cords of death," is a commitment to the soul of the loved one. It is a willingness to lay down one's life, if necessary, to help another on his journey to his highest and best self. Love is treating people with respect. Love is kindness, gentleness, meekness and, at times, long suffering. (Galatians 5:22-23.)

JESUS TO HIS DISCIPLES
This is my commandment, That ye love one another, as I have loved you.
Greater love hath no man than this, that a man lay down his life for his friends (John 15:12-13).

People deserve to be loved because they are children of God. Love should not be the reward only for behaving well. One is still loved even if the deeds are not looked upon with the least degree of allowance. What kinds of behaviors are consistent with that love? The answer is behaviors that reflect the acceptance of the person's worth to the critic. Respect, smiles, and sincere praise are concrete evidence of appreciation. For those who are comfortable with them, hugs and kisses are great signs of affection. Love is a reward for being, not a reward for behaving. Encircling loved ones in robes of acceptance, affection, and appreciation will keep them warm during the winter of reproof.

CHAPTER TEN

THE ART OF RECEIVING CRITICISM

Dr. John L. Lund's
QUICK CHECK GUIDE TO RECEIVING CRITICISM

☐ STEP ONE:
  • STOP! Immediately remove your EGO from the issue or behavior being criticized.
  • LOOK at the person.
  • LISTEN. Do not defend, make an excuse or apologize. Don't speak, LISTEN.
☐ STEP TWO: Write it down where you can evaluate it.
☐ STEP THREE: Feed it back without emotion.
☐ STEP FOUR: Excuse yourself from immediate response and set a time and place to respond.
☐ STEP FIVE: Evaluate the criticism and your resources for dealing with it, i.e., time, energy, will.
☐ STEP SIX: Respond at appointed time and place. The response will fall into one of three categories:
  • I will change.
  • I disagree and this is why.....
  • I will not change. I am unwilling or unable to do so.

STEP ONE: STOP! LOOK! and LISTEN!

STOP!
Betty felt as though her husband was hypercritical. She felt his criticism was a blind spot. He was a good man in so many ways, but he was emotionally unsafe for her. She wanted to know what she could do to fix him, because his pride would not allow him to come in to see a counselor. Ed, her husband, was a critiholic and negative about most things and people. I asked Betty if it were also true that she was hypersensitive to being criticized. She confessed she was, and admitted this compounded the difficulties in the marriage. I asked Betty if she would describe for me a typical evening with Ed.

"First, even before he sets foot in the house, he will be upset about bikes in the driveway or the yard, and comes into the house mumbling. I've gotten to the point where I feel sick to my stomach when I know he

is coming home. He seldom has anything pleasant to say at all. Immediately he will begin to check to see if I did all the things he feels are important. It's like a Gestapo going over a checklist. He thinks we are talking, but I feel like it's an inquisition. If I fail to do one thing, I get a lecture. When I try to explain my schedule or my reasons, he gets angry and I cry. It's the same pattern day after day. If we make it through the checklist, we have some kind of dinner. I hate to cook anymore. He criticizes everything, and now he criticizes the fact that I don't cook as often. After dinner, he will go into his computer room until it's time for bed. If he ever comes out to watch a ball game on T.V., he yells and criticizes the entire time. Our intimacy is almost nonexistent. I don't want to be seen by him. I never feel like I perform to his expectations. I find myself making excuses to stay up until he has gone to bed, so I won't have to be with him. He knows something is wrong. He is always telling me I don't appreciate what he has provided for me and the family. He is a good provider and a hard worker. In his own way, I know that he loves me and the children. I'm getting to the point that if something doesn't change, I'm going to leave. I just can't take it anymore. That's why I am here."

"Betty, there are two things you can do immediately to improve your situation. First, protect yourself and second, learn how to live with a 'toxic personality.' Do you accept responsibility for protecting yourself against uninvited criticism or unwarranted criticism?"

"What do you mean?" she asked.

"You are choosing to be hurt. You are giving him a perfect target at which to shoot. What you have told me is that you have a whole series of expectations of how a loving person would treat you if he truly loved you. For example, if someone truly loved you, he would never criticize you, or your weight, or your efforts. You said it yourself, Ed does love you. It is also true that Ed is hypercritical. These are co-existing truths and they are not mutually exclusive. If you were to say Ed doesn't love me because he criticizes me all the time, I would say your conclusion is false. 'Ed loves you' and 'Ed criticizes you' are both true statements. Betty, I want you to focus on Ed loving you, and for now ignore any thought to the contrary. As much as anything, you object to how Ed packages his criticisms and their quantity.

"Let me teach you about criticism, about the art and skill of giving and receiving criticism. Giving criticism deals with the ego or self esteem of others, while receiving criticism relates to your own ego. Developing the art and skill of receiving criticism is more difficult than applying the principles involved in giving criticism. Those truly skilled in giving criticism have the ability to empathetically walk in the self-esteem moccasins of others. Giving criticism properly has been defined as the art of 'telling someone they are going to hell in such a way they look forward to the journey.' They possess the art of focusing on a negative

issue or behavior in a way that preserves the sense of self-worth of the one being criticized. This acquired talent of 'giving' criticism while respecting the value of the individual, happens because of being 'other centered.' The art and skill of 'receiving' criticism requires that we extend to ourselves that same respect for our self-worth. Appropriate self respect means we do not empower other to devalue us.

"I know that you are a deeply committed religious person. I want to appeal to the ultimate worth of your soul. Do you have any idea how precious you are to Heavenly Father? Your worth has been established by the atonement of Jesus Christ. He paid a price beyond death for your soul. We may never know the height and breadth of His Atoning sacrifice until we resurrect. A price has been set on the worth of your soul, Betty. It is above all the combined wealth of a million worlds. No mortal man can even begin to match the price that Jesus paid for the worth of your soul. Do your believe that?"

Betty responded, "Intellectually I do, but frankly, I am not sure I feel it."

"Because we share a common faith, let me tell of a personal experience. I didn't feel it either, until I went to the Lord in fasting and mighty prayer. I asked Heavenly Father in the name of Jesus to fill my soul with His love. A few days past, I awoke one morning and I was absolutely confident that Jesus Christ would have come to this earth if I were the only son of God that needed the Atonement, I knew that the worth of my soul was great, but now I felt it. Our worth is not a topic for debate nor discussion. Those who want to do so are out of stewardship. It is not their right to pass judgement upon our worth. It has been said that no one can hit you over the head with an emotional club that you don't first put into his hand. Being able to protect yourself from the negative effects of criticisms is a part of the art and skill needed.

'There is a desire you must possess. It is the desire to become your highest and best self. Without that desire you will never be able to truly learn the art of receiving criticism. What if the criticism is valid? If you are not committed to become your highest and best self, you will not even evaluate the criticism on its merits. Instead you will be distracted by the way it was said. Your desire to defend your self esteem, your worth, your ego will prevail.

'These two items are absolutely essential if you are to get past the messenger and focus on the message. First no one has a right to comment upon your worth. If anyone other than God does so disregard it. He or she is only trying to manipulate you. The only power that person has is the power you give by believing them. When Ed becomes abusive excuse yourself from his presence. Say to him, 'when you are ready to focus on the issue I'll be back'. Do it. Don't let your fear and doubt rob you of dignity. Second, in order to handle criticism at any level you must possess a deep yearning to become your highest and best self.

"If you are going to be successful in receiving criticism from others, it will require that you live a higher law. The single greatest challenge to receiving criticism is the Ego. The higher law you will be asked to live demands that you place your ego in a safe place, remove it as an issue. Protect yourself. Otherwise, every conversation with anyone about anything becomes an issue for ego validation, i.e., they must agree with you, you must be right, or you have no value. This means you become so emotionally involved in defending your ideas, behavior, and really your ego, you cannot receive valid criticism. You wind up defending your sense of worth, your self-esteem and you are not open to hear what the real issues are. Taking your ego out of the picture is a necessary step.

GOING ON A "MIND WALK"

"Let me tell you what I do. I have a very special box. When anyone criticizes me, I immediately take my ego, my sense of worth, and put it mentally in the box. It takes me a half second. Then I go in my mind to the temple and place the box on the altar for Jesus to take care of it until I return. It works for me. However, each person has to find a way that works for him or her."

I asked Betty if she would like to know how some people handle criticism by taking a *"mind walk."* A *"mind walk"* is a mental journey you take the moment someone begins to offer uninvited criticism. Imagine in your mind an alarm going off, just like those noisy irritating car alarms that go off when someone touches the car. Or think of your ego being in a bank vault, and when the alarm sounds, all the doors automatically close. Huge impenetrable solid steel doors, two feet thick, close off every window, door, or exit. Like the precious Mona Lisa, an art treasure beyond price, your ego is protected. It is safe. Now you can venture outside the bank, because your ego is safe within the vault.

One man said his "mind walk" included a visual image of the critical person asking for the combination to the safe, and he would say, "I'm sorry, it's not available to you." He saw himself putting a package containing his ego into the safe and closing the door and spinning the dial. A very inventive woman said she had a secret Personal Identification Number (pin #) like one finds at all automatic bank teller machines that represented her ego and she didn't let anyone who was toxic know it, or if someone became ego-toxic she changed her secret number.

"This doesn't work for everyone, but living a higher law requires that you develop a system to protect your ego. There are unproductive and relationship-defeating behaviors like becoming confrontational, abusive and more toxic than the giver of criticism. Becoming totally passive and becoming a doormat to be verbally abused, is equally unacceptable. The fight or flight alternatives are not as productive as a *"mind walk." Some simply choose to ignore any unauthorized criticism. In other words, don't sign for the critic's 'registered mail.'*

"I suggested to several people that they reward themselves twenty-five cents each time they were criticized. One woman said it wasn't enough. but a dollar would be! Each time she was criticized a dollar sign flashed in her eyes. Her ego was safe in the cash register. One man bought himself a new fly rod. At twenty-five cents a criticism, one young married wife bought a new pair of shoes in only a month.

"Let's assume that you develop an effective "mind walk" that works for you. Your ego is safe. This means that you have removed self-esteem as an issue, thereby avoiding any emotional melt-down. You are Spock on Star Trek. Professor McCoy comes ranting and screaming at you because you are not responding to his emotionalism. Although he calls you names like a pointed-eared, green-faced, half-human freak, it doesn't bother you. You look at him and say, 'Very interesting, but quite illogical.' Can you imagine how long a court reporter would last if he or she kept getting emotionally involved in each court case? If the court reporter cried and wept and asked the judge for a moment to compose himself or herself, that person would be fired. You are going to fire Ed every time his negative emotions flair up. You do so by ignoring his packaging. Disregard the 'how' and examine the 'what.' This takes practice and is a highly developed mental skill, to separate your ego from the criticisms of others. It can and must be done.

"Your objective with Ed is to focus on the content of his criticism. If the content of his criticism is an attack on your worth, you must protect yourself by leaving or ignoring it. You are Spock, the Court Reporter. Now, bring on the criticism, for "sticks and stones can break your bones," but words shall never harm you. You are going to pan for gold. You are going to separate the mud from the gold nuggets. The packaging of the criticism is the mud and the golden nugget is a truth covered in mud. Accepting that truth may help you reach your objective of becoming your highest and best self. Yes, it is a lousy job of packaging. However, by separating your ego and placing it in a safe place, you are prepared to logically evaluate the criticism and pan for gold. If there is no substance to the comments, they can be disregarded as having come from frustration, or a contentious spirit. If there is merit in the criticism, regardless of packaging, it can be evaluated for future benefit.

LOOK!

"Remember, the art of receiving criticism is much more difficult than giving reproof. It will take a concerted effort to separate your self-esteem, worth, and ego from the criticism. It will take practice and time and more practice and more time. However, the process works.

"With practice, you can separate your ego and put it in a safe place, then you are ready to focus on the message. Remember, you do not have to tolerate abuse. Walk away, go to another room, just say, 'Excuse me please, I'll be back when you are ready to focus on the issue.' If Ed gets physically abusive, call the police. He is out of bounds. If you tolerate it, he will give himself permission to continue.

"Let's assume Ed is frustrated and criticizing you. You are going to de-fang the tiger. Here is what you do. You look him directly in the eye. If you look down it means you are letting his criticism impact on your self-esteem. Even if his eyes are bugging out of his head and his neck muscles strained, look him sincerely in the eyes. Your objective is to focus on the issue or behavior about which he is being critical. You are in control of yourself. If you cave in to your emotions you will be rewarding him. You have the power. There is a protective shield around you. This level of self-mastery and disassociation may even cause you to smile inside. His once effective techniques have no effect on you. It's almost an out of body experience. Betty, it is as if you are a third party watching. You are an actress on stage. Sincerely look into his eyes searching for the message."

LISTEN!

"Truly listening and not reacting is difficult. There is a strong urge to want to explain, justify, or defend. Betty, this is where you 'zip your lip.' Don't apologize. Don't make excuses. Don't speak. Just gaze into his eyes and LISTEN.

"You are too young to remember the old style record players. Maybe you've seen one in an attic or a museum. They played records of different sizes. They would also play at different speeds, i.e., 45, 78, or 33 ⅓. The records of the same speed were placed in a stack on a metal center post. An automatic arm would extend from the side once the record was in place. A needle protruding from the arm fit perfectly into the record groves. At last! Music! It was quite primitive compared to the CDs of today. However, the old record players had an unusual characteristic. No matter where the record was playing, the beginning, the middle, or the end, if you bumped the record player, the automatic arm would stop and go all the way back to the beginning and start all over again. That is just like someone who is criticizing. If they are interrupted they go back all the way to the beginning and start over. Sometimes they increase the tone of their voice another octave because they believe you are not listening. So I want you to listen for the issue or behavior which is the object of his concern so he won't have to start all over again.

"Next, I'm going to ask you to write down his criticisms. This may sound like a contradiction. I've already asked you to look into his eyes and to listen to what Ed is saying."

"Won't writing it down distract me from looking and listening?"

"The answer is no, if you will only look down to write and look up into his eyes. Only look at his eyes and the paper. It works and I'll explain why."

STEP TWO: WRITE THE CRITICISMS DOWN WHERE THEY CAN BE EVALUATED.

"Years of experience have verified the importance of writing down criticisms. The difference between those who succeed in receiving criticism and learning from it and those who fail in this task is their willingness to follow this counsel. There are two important reasons why you should write down Ed's criticisms. The first is psychological. Writing down the criticisms will allow the criticism to enter your ears, flow through your brain, down your arm and hand to the paper. Otherwise the criticisms will stay in your brain. Maybe the greatest benefit is spiritual. By writing down the criticism as an issue or behavior you are protecting your 'worth, self esteem and value as a daughter of God.' You are focusing on the issues or behaviors in question. This is a legitimate process.

"The second important reason for writing down the criticism is to evaluate it at a later time. There are a myriad of secondary benefits. They include:

- *It alerts the critical person to just how often he is criticizing.*
- *It shows that you are willing to listen.*
- *It demonstrates a sincere attempt to improve.*
- *It increases your credibility.*
- *It helps you focus."*

"What if Ed objects to me writing down the criticisms?"

"Most critics are suspicious of your motivation. They wonder if you are preparing for divorce. They are fearful you are building a case against them. They hate being reminded of how frequently they criticize. Most will object. They will also mock your efforts. This is especially true of the insecure. Be prepared for Ed to object to your writing down his criticisms. He doesn't want a record kept. 'Nevertheless', 'in spite of,' and 'regardless' of his objections, write down the criticisms.

"When he asks you, 'What are you writing down, Betty?' say to Ed, 'I'm writing down your criticism of my behaviors and issues so that I can honestly evaluate them.'"

"Ed may say, 'Why do you have to write it down in order to remember it?'"

" I want you to say in your own words something like this, 'Ed, if it is important enough for you to say it, it is important enough for me to write it down. I'm sorry if it makes you uncomfortable, but this is my way of dealing with it.'"

"Obviously this will require courage on your part not to back down. If he fails to agree, offer him the alternative of writing you a letter expressing his criticisms where you can evaluate them. If Ed persists in being verbally critical, write it down.

"Now I am going to ask you to keep a writing pad and pencil within reach at all times. This may require writing pads in every room in your house especially the bathroom, bedroom, and glove box in the car. There will be at least two times when it will be difficult to do so. One is when you are in the shower or bath and the other is when you are driving. Even under these two conditions, I would like you to write down the criticisms on paper afterwards. Remember, from a psychological view, you are taking the criticisms from your mind and transporting them out of your body onto the paper."

Even as I spoke Betty was taking notes as rapidly as she could. "What you are now doing with me is what I want you to do with Ed. The difference is you feel safe here and not with Ed. But what you are doing now is perfect. You are looking, listening, and writing. Are you clear so far as to what to do? What are the first two steps in the art and skill of receiving criticism from Ed?"

"Protect my ego. Stop, look, and listen and then write down the criticisms."

"That's right. No one has the right to physically, emotionally, verbally, or spiritually abuse you. If you feel any of these are happening, excuse yourself. Simply announce you are leaving the room. You are not leaving the relationship. Tell Ed you will be back when he is in emotional control (or when you are in control) and can logically focus on the concerns.

"Just because Ed is upset or frustrated does not mean you are being abused. However, you be the judge as to whether or not you are prepared to receive it. We will assume you are and that Ed is on a critical binge, but it is not yet abusive. Let's review the steps so far. When verbally criticized do not defend yourself, do not make excuses, and do not justify your behavior. Just STOP, LOOK, LISTEN, AND WRITE. A defensive response or an excuse or a justification is perceived as 'NOT HEARING,' and usually results in the critical person repeating his verbal criticisms. Ed believes you are not focusing on the content of what he is saying to you. It's as if your ears fell off and he has to speak louder in order for you to properly get the message. Frequently ,your excuses only upset him and add fuel to his fiery words.

"There is another benefit to listening and writing it down. When you choose not to combat, you help create an atmosphere which can allow you to focus on the issue or behavior in question. If you choose to combat, the content will be lost in a war of words and a new issue will emerge—the self esteem of one or both of you. Soon a crisis of individual worth is created and the focus of the original criticism lost. It will not be long until a hurt feeling, the argument itself, or some threatened divorce becomes the diverted battleground. Unchallenged allegations given in the heat of frustration soon lose their fervor. Once challenged, however, adrenaline begets adrenaline, the heart beat speeds up, the bodily energy increases, and fatigue gives way to a new found power to combat."

STEP THREE: FEED BACK THE CRITICISM WITHOUT EMOTION.

"Betty, some people feel unless one is emotional one is not serious. This is a characteristic learned in the family. It's not healthy. About half of all men feel manipulated when women cry. They feel it is a diversion from facing facts. Almost always when someone is crying or yelling it is a plea for understanding and acceptance. However, it is a diversion to ego and away from the issue. Consciously or unconsciously, crying when criticized is a reaction to feeling rejected. Sometimes, unless a person is emotional, he doesn't give himself or herself permission to express feelings. There are appropriate times for tears. The art of receiving criticism is not one of them.

"Continue to write down the expectations or the frustrations of Ed. Be a court reporter. Eventually, he will finish. After he is through criticizing you, FEED IT BACK TO HIM WITHOUT EMOTION. Do it just as if you were reading a recipe from a cook book. For example, 'So what you are saying, Ed, is I spend too much time talking on the phone with my friends. If I spent less time on the phone, I would have more time to devote to cleaning the house and cooking.' This does not mean in any way that you agree with him or with his evaluation or criticism. It means you heard him. This acknowledges his concerns and gives him an opportunity to clarify or expand. It will have an end. Ed may launch into a repeat of the items. Just put a check mark by the criticism he has already mentioned."

Although Betty knew the things which were a source of frustration for Ed, she never let him fully express himself. Before he could complete a thought, they would be fully engaged in a verbal battle. Name-calling, swearing, yelling and another night on the couch by one or the other ensued. The pattern was well-established. The next day, no one talked. Eventually small talk would cautiously give way to a guarded peace. Neither was emotionally safe for their mate. At the slightest hint of any criticism, Betty would go into a tirade and harangue Ed on his lack of *appreciation, his insensitive nature, and attack his weaknesses. I asked Betty to hear him out, even if it involved repetition.*

"Keep track of his criticisms. Which ones are recurring? After awhile, you will be able to number them."

Ed was critical of five things:

1. Betty was overweight.
2. Betty allowed the kids to eat in the car.
3. Betty was a poor housekeeper.
4. Betty wasn't a good mother.
5. Betty was a poor money manager.

Betty wanted unconditional acceptance. She wanted Ed to overlook the fact that the doctors had told her she was borderline diabetic. Weight loss would help her. I asked Betty if she remembered why she originally came to me. She said, "I was concerned about how to stop my husband from criticizing me. I really wanted you to fix him through me."

"I know you are reaching your wits end. I sense you feel overwhelmed. What I am sharing with you is the answer to your question. You may not see it clearly. But by taking control of your ability to protect your ego, and committing to become your highest and best self you are on the way to changing the interaction between you and Ed."

STEP FOUR: EXCUSE YOURSELF FROM ANY IMMEDIATE RESPONSE AND SET A TIME AND PLACE TO GET BACK TOGETHER.

"Avoid the very, very, very, big temptation to verbally or emotionally respond at this time. This is not the time to cry, or to become angry, or to stomp out of the room and slam a door. After this great exercise of patience it would be a pity to lose all that effort. An immediate response shows no effort to honestly evaluate the content of the criticism. Ed may just want you to promise you will improve. However, when you do not keep your promise, he will use that to tear you down.

"This is what I want you to say to Ed. 'I've heard you, Ed. It wasn't easy but believe me I have heard you. I'm not prepared to respond now. I need some time to think about these things. I want to evaluate my ability, willingness, and energy to make the changes you've suggested. I'm not capable of anything now but an emotional reaction. Give me three days to evaluate. I propose we meet on Wednesday at 7: 00 p.m. at the park. I will be prepared to talk to you then.'"

"Do not allow him to draw you into a conflict. Excuse yourself and be civil and kind. This reaction will disarm him. He may not know how to respond except with a negative statement like 'Right! I'm sure you'll think about it and nothing will change.'"

STEP FIVE: EVALUATE THE CRITICISM

"It's time to be honest with yourself. It's time to pan for gold. Maybe you have never given yourself permission to be honest. Is there any truth whatsoever to these criticisms? Until you honestly evaluate the situation, , you will be an emotionally unhealthy person.

"I want to review with you quickly what an emotionally healthy person is.

- *An emotionally healthy person accepts responsibility for her own happiness, unhappiness, and behavior. She realizes that life is a gift. It is her responsibility to improve her life. She escapes denial by facing reality. She does not have to live with God or the Devil, nor with anyone else. She does have to live with herself, "eternally" with self. Self improvement is her job. This is why you are committed to become your highest and best self.*

- *An emotionally healthy person is able to forgive herself and others.*

- *An emotionally healthy person will make a plan to take herself from the reality of where she is to a higher and better self.*

"Betty, are you in agreement with these three basic characteristics of an emotionally, healthy person?"

"Yes," she said.

"Your willingness to accept personal accountability for your behavior and happiness, forgive self and Ed, and make a plan , means you can now look at the criticism. For now we are not talking about Ed. It is not Ed's meanness, insensitivity ,and improper criticism. Ed is not the focus. It is you, Betty. If you would like, I'll walk you through how to evaluate the criticism."

"Yes, I would like that. It's kind of scary. I'm not sure I'll like what I find."

"Do you remember where you put your 'Ego'?"

Betty and I met for six hours over the next two days. She was trying very hard to protect her self esteem around Ed. At the same time she worked on loving behaviors. Her mind-walk consisted of a fairy tale image of a woman whose aura was surrounded with a bright light that protected her from all harm. Her ego was safely guarded in the midst of the light. Like some powerful electronic field or bug-zapper, the criticisms would come towards her ego and be destroyed by the protective field. Betty was learning to take her frustrations to God and her love to Ed. Ed had managed to focus on five critical issues.

Betty was overweight. She was borderline diabetic. Independent of Ed, she needed to lose thirty pounds for health reasons. I asked Betty to evaluate her ability, her willingness, her time, and her energy in relationship to losing thirty pounds. It was obvious that she did not lack knowledge. What she lacked was commitment to the value of losing weight. She had the ability, the time, and the energy. What she lacked was willingness.

"Betty, independent of Ed's criticism, would it be in your mortal best interest to lose weight?"

"Yes," she said.

"Remember that an emotionally healthy person accepts responsibility for his or her behavior, happiness, and weight. They forgive self and they make a plan to become a better self. For our purposes a goal depends upon you and a wish is something that depends upon others."

I asked Betty to put together a realistic program wherein she could lose thirty pounds over the course of a year. "Make it a plan that does not depend upon Ed. It is your goal to eat more wisely and to lose .6 lbs per week over the entire year. Are you willing to build or join a support group on weight management and commit to stay with it for a year? This is not a commitment to me. This is a commitment to yourself to become your best self."

In like manner each of Ed's criticisms were evaluated. As Betty looked at "allowing the kids to eat in the car" she thought that what Ed really wanted was a clean car. She determined to ask Ed for a clarification. Regarding housekeeping she decided that she and Ed needed to agree on a common standard on what it meant to keep the house clean. She decided to ask Ed for a clear definition of "what he considered a good mother to be." She also made a commitment to establish a realistic budget and to stay with it. All of these decisions she believed would indeed help her to become a higher and better, self, wife, mother, and sister in the Church.

STEP SIX: RESPOND AT THE APPOINTED TIME AND PLACE.

"Betty, when you meet tomorrow night with Ed at 7:00 p.m. in the park, stay in emotional control. This is a time of great defensiveness for the both of you. If he loses control, excuse yourself. If you feel you are going to go off the emotional deep end, excuse yourself. Set up another appointment. DO NOT LET THIS TURN INTO AN ARGUMENT. There is a tendency to let that happen.

"Do not over commit. Remember actions speak louder than words. These last two days have been a good experience because you've changed your approach. Ed hasn't changed. He is reacting to you.

"Your responses will probably fall into one of these categories:
I will change.
I disagree and this is why . . .
I need more specific information before I can make an intelligent evaluation.
I am unwilling.
I am unable.

"Go prepared. Write down in black and white what you are willing to do. Also have a specific list of questions that will clarify his definition of "a clean house," "a good mother," "a reasonable budget."

Ed could see some positive efforts on Betty's part as a result of counseling. Ed finally agreed to come and see me as a counselor. When I visited with Ed and Betty, I explained there are always three issues in any relationship. First, there is Ed with Ed. Second, there is Betty with Betty. Third, there is Ed and Betty. Each of them have issues separate from the person they married. Ed agreed. I asked Ed if he felt he was critical.

"No," he said, "I am just honest."

"Do others perceive you as critical, other than your wife?"

He admitted they did.

"If you were killed in a traffic accident tomorrow, would all of Betty's challenges go away? Would she automatically lose weight? Would her skills as a mother and homemaker suddenly improve? If she were killed, would your ability to control your tongue go away as an issue?"

"I suppose not," admitted Ed.

"No. Your issues and hers are independent of each other. Ed, you have issues as a father whether or not Betty is around."

It was obvious that uninvited criticism had taken this relationship to an all-time low. Ground rules were established to which each agreed. Betty was to work on her issues, Ed would work on his issues, and the two of them together, with my guided help, would work on the relationship. Both agreed to follow the steps in the "Art of Giving and Receiving Criticism."

Giving respect took practice, as did asking for and receiving permission to criticize. After a few weeks, they were prepared to work on the art of receiving criticism. Betty was firmly entrenched in hypersensitivity. Ed was a "zealous" hyper-critic. It took a great effort and considerable hard work, tears, and diligence before she was able to separate her self worth from an issue or behavior. She learned to write down the criticism from her husband without comment. The miracle that took place was that Ed became aware of his hyper-criticism. How? Every time Betty picked up a pad and pencil and began to write, he was reminded of who was criticizing and how often. This awareness alone had the effect of decreasing the sheer volume of his negative comments.

The second miracle was his completing his thoughts and fully expressing himself. The third miracle was his confession of how silly he felt, listening to himself being out of control with body language and tone of voice, while his wife sat there writing it down. He became less intimidating and calmly related his concerns. Betty began to feel a sense of power in not letting his criticisms hurt her ego. She would feed back his criticism like a secretary reading the dictation of a letter to a boss. He would usually add a word or two and this part was over.

For example, Betty felt she was thirty pounds overweight, while her husband thought she was fifty pounds too heavy. For Betty, the kids eating in the car was a practical matter of feeding hungry children. For her husband, the permitting of children to eat in the car was a sign of disrespect to him, and irresponsibility for her. He wanted the car kept clean. He worked hard to provide for the family. Food on the floor or a greasy fingerprint on a window was considered an affront to his providership. He reasoned that if Betty cared, she could make the children wait until they were home, or go to a park to eat, but not allow them to eat in the car. For Betty, a budget was a guide; for her husband it was a divine decree. Clutter was acceptable to Betty; it represented a "pig pen" for her husband. Because she did not discipline the children the way her husband thought she should, he considered her a poor mother. In Ed's eyes Betty was a fat, uncaring, overspending, poor housekeeper, and lousy mother who did not appreciate him. Betty felt no motivation to change and had resigned herself to never being enough. Feeling totally unacceptable to him, she could not understand why he wanted to still be intimate with her. She hated him at times, and felt trapped in a marriage she could not escape. Without any professional or technical training, she was an economic prisoner. Each felt a love for the children and were looking for me to change their partner. The five issues were always the same, but gradually things began to change.

I suggested to Ed that what he was doing in criticizing Betty had not succeeded in changing her. I wanted him to let go of all five expectations. He wasn't sure he could. His moment of truth was about to happen. He was ready for the biggest "AHA" of his life.

"Is there any doubt, even the slightest, that your wife is unaware of your concerns about weight, the kids eating in the car, overspending the budget, her poor housekeeping skills, or her not being the kind of mother you would like her to be? Listen carefully to your own words."

"No. I know she knows. She just doesn't care."

"You are absolutely right, Ed. Betty does not lack knowledge of your concern. What she lacks is motivation to do anything about it. Betty is motivated by her dreams and her desire for acceptance , not by yours. She does not share your values. She is not convinced that your values should apply to her."

"Think about it," I said, *"of what value is your criticizing her? If she doesn't lack knowledge, why are you giving her knowledge ? You ought to work on motivation and encourage her. Your criticisms of her are counter-productive. They only frustrate the both of you and destroy any desire for her to want to change. She is filled with resentment for you."*

"You mean I need to work on building her up and not on tearing her down?"

Aha! Shazam! I wasn't about to let him off the hook!

"Why?" I said.

"Because what I'm doing isn't working, and my trying to punish her and intimidate her by yelling only causes her to withdraw from me."

*"What Betty lacks is a commitment to your values. She doesn't lack knowledge of what your values are. Currently, you are not her friend. You are not committed to help her become her highest and best self. Ed, do you even know what her values are, her hopes, her dreams? Remember all people are motivated by **their** goals, not by yours. Your agenda is to change her, to make her into your image of what you think she ought to be. The truth is, she is not acceptable to you and both of you know it. You, my friend, are at a crossroads. You can decide to focus on loving Betty as she is, or you can do nothing about it. Let things go on as they are until one of you has truly had enough and leaves the relationship.*

"If anything I have said makes any sense to you at all, then stop criticizing her today, and apologize to her for trying to make her into your image. Tell her you are not going to criticize her weight anymore. It is her body. It is her health. She has the responsibility to care for it. Negotiate with Betty on the budget. Be flexible, but also realistic. Let her see the true picture of your finances and give her the option of selling the house and moving to a less expensive one, where you will be able to spend more on other things, or enlist her support in making the sacrifices necessary to stay where you are.

"It's reasonable to expect hungry children to want to eat in the car. It's also reasonable to expect them to clean up after themselves. Give Betty some options. Prepare a way for her to be successful. For example, "Betty, it would mean a lot to me if you would teach the kids to clean up after themselves. However, if they don't, would you please just do it yourself or hire a neighbor boy or girl to do it? As far as the house cleaning is concerned, agree on a standard of cleaning that may be less than what you would wish and maybe a little more than Betty would want. If you are still not happy, then you need to either hire outside help to come in on a periodic basis and clean to your standard or do it yourself. After all, it is not her standard, it is yours. You must own it. If you want to spend time cleaning the house because you feel better about it, then do it with a good attitude and not attempt to put a guilt trip on her.

"Within the bounds of non-abuse, Betty is entitled to define for herself what kind of a mother she would like to be. She is also entitled to her own lousy relationship. She must also accept the consequences of her choices as they relate to the children and to you. She does not trust you. You are emotionally unsafe to her. It will take time and responsible behavior on your part. She can come to trust and love you again. My many, many years of experience have seen many couples grow in and grow out and grow back in love again, sometimes several times in the same marriage."

I asked Ed if he would be willing to try. With quiet determination he nodded his head, yes. Next, I asked him to commit to treat Betty with respect by never criticizing her again without her permission. Also, I asked Ed to focus on the Art of Giving Criticism. Again he nodded his head. This is a man who has been a "critiholic," all of his life, agreeing to reasonable behavior.

Betty, who was hypersensitive, was to specialize in the "Art of Receiving Criticism." What previously had been a weakness, was now becoming a strength. In order to finish her training in the art of receiving criticism, she was to evaluate the criticism. She was to see if doing or becoming whatever was criticized would help her in becoming her highest and best self. This was not according to her husband's standard, but according to her own. If losing weight was a healthy choice and consistent with being a better self, then she would have to accept the responsibility to join a support group or whatever was needed to make it happen. The next step in the "Art and Skill of Receiving Criticism" was to evaluate her resources. Did she have the time, the energy, or the will to accomplish the change? What choices could she make within the limits of her circumstances to make it happen?

Betty worked on her issue of hypersensitivity to criticism. Ed worked on his issue of being hypercritical. An amazing thing happened. Their relationship began to improve. As respect was gifted to each other, their mutually defensive attitudes were replaced with more loving dispositions. Each came to the awareness that true progress in a relationship is only made by common consent and by moving at a pace mutually agreeable to both. Everything isn't perfect in their relationship today, but they are emotionally bonded and walking a common path. Things are better than they have ever been and neither of them is willing to go back to the dysfunctional way it was before.

CHAPTER ELEVEN

DEALING WITH A TOXIC PERSONALITY

What I am writing involves an amazing coincidence. While writing on this chapter on a Sunday afternoon, I was interrupted by an emergency phone call in which I was asked if I could meet with a couple who said they desperately needed to meet with me as a Relationship and Communication Counselor. I consented, and in a matter of minutes they were in my den at my home.

This is a story of a ten-year marriage with four children. The parents of the wife had arrived from out of state at the wife's request with a U-Haul truck. They were to take their daughter and four grandchildren back to another state. The husband was frantic and willing to do anything to save this marriage. The mother and father of the wife were loading the truck while I was counseling with the couple. I met with them individually and then as a couple. "Tell me," I said to the wife, "what is so frustrating to you about your marriage that you are willing to pack up and leave?" What follows is as near as I can come to her exact statements which were interspersed with tears and soul-rending sobs
"He is so critical of everything I do, or wear, or cook. He yells at me for the stupidest things..., I can't even hold a map right..., he is so controlling..., he has to comment on everything I'm doing or not doing..., he is always mad at me for something..., he is so intense..., he snaps at me and I can never have an opinion of my own. He is always angry at me..., I can't take it anymore..., I called my parents and told them to come and get me. I've tried to talk to him, but he discounts everything I say..., he has to be right..., he is so dominating..., every time I attempt to express myself, he shuts me off with rude remarks..., Well, I'm not going to take it anymore. It's not just me, he does the same things with the kids..., I can't be criticized anymore..., I feel no love for him, only resentment. Well, I guess I do feel some love for him or I wouldn't be so hurt..., but not enough to stay in this marriage..." (Dr. John L. Lund, May 1997.)

After they left, I picked up my manuscript at this very point to continue my writing. What more could be said as a testimonial of the negative effects of a toxic personality?

WHAT IS A TOXIC PERSONALITY?

A toxic personality is a person one **cannot please**. He or she appears incapable of giving total acceptance. A toxic personality is one for whom the other party WILL NEVER BE GOOD ENOUGH. Frequently, the toxic person dangles acceptance like a "carrot on a string." The person who wants to be accepted and appreciated can never quite reach the carrot. Toxic people only give partial acceptance for pleasing them. The toxic person withholds love as a punishment. It is consistent with the toxic personality to be inconsistent. They promise a reward which is often denied. The earned privileges are never secure. Toxic personalities come in many varieties. Some are gruff. Some are pleasant. Some appear indifferent. They can be very affable but one still walks away emotionally empty. Most toxic people have a very difficult time accepting blame. They always have to be right. Another trait of many toxic personalities is to change the rules. Just when it appears that acceptance is within grasp, the toxic person pulls it away. Toxic people have long lists of expectations. But just as one appears to meet all of the requirements they change the items on the list. They tend to be controlling, very judgmental of others, highly critical, and manipulative. Toxic people create crisis. They feed on pitting people against each other.

It is not uncommon for the toxic person to pick out a "favored one." This keeps the hope alive in the hearts of others that some day they may be a "favored one." Some day they may be " enough." The devastating thing about toxic people is their ability, consciously or unconsciously, to keep hope for acceptance and love alive. Toxic people seem to be aware of their power. When someone stops trying to please the toxic, that person is treated with gross disdain. Why? Because the person who stopped trying "to please" took away the toxic person's power. This is frightening to those who are toxic. They crave control. Often, under the guise of perfectionism they justify their rejection of others. On one hand, the toxic person holds out acceptance as a bribe, while on the other hand he uses rejection as a method of control. This sends a message to others, "Beware or you could be the next person put on the 'black list' of rejection." Toxic people have a difficult time forgiving others. Why? Because withholding forgiveness is one more means of control.

Often, even when giving a compliment, there is some holding back of full acceptance, or some "trailing barb." A "trailing barb" is a statement added to a compliment which expresses that a "better job could have been done." Their creed is "Do more, for less, and a better job."

EXAMPLES OF TRAILING BARBS

"That's so nice your boy, Gary got a B+ in math. Did you know his cousin, Darrell got an A?"

"Dinner was great tonight. If we could have had a dessert, it would have been perfect!"

"The lawn looks really nice, thanks for mowing it. We need to do a little better job on the trim, however."

The toxic person does not seem to be able to give a complete compliment and let it stand alone. Even when someone else pays him or a loved one a compliment, he finds a critical thing to say in the name of balance or fairness or of being honest. **One cannot please a toxic person. One cannot make him happy. One cannot even keep him from being unhappy.**

In dealing with a toxic person, one must let go of the expectation to please. It is this very expectation that gives him power. If acceptance is what one wants, the toxic person cannot give acceptance. He fears if he gives acceptance, the other person will stop trying to please him. He fears he would lose his power. This is not always a conscious behavior, but it is a consistent one. He cannot let the other person please him or be "enough." Most toxic people believe they themselves are not enough, so how could anyone else be enough?

The "seeker of the acceptance" believes that with a little more effort, one could achieve acceptance. But no, the carrot is always pulled away. With a toxic person, the agenda is constantly changing in order to keep other people off balance. The focus is always on others. When the toxic person becomes the focus they will quickly move to a crisis in order to divert attention from himself. If a crisis does not exist the toxic person will create one. He or she always seems to be offended. The family or associates of the toxic person live in fear of offending him.

In addition to one's not being "enough," not rich enough, nor thin enough, nor good-looking enough, not a good enough provider, nor housekeeper, nor parent, nor human being— the toxic person feels the need, or divine call from God, to point out other people's flaws, shortcomings, weaknesses, errors, mistakes, and lack of perfection. If one wants acceptance, he gives non-acceptance. If one wants a compliment, he receives a "trailing barb." If one wants appreciation, he gets depreciation. By definition a toxic person is one who cannot or will not give what another wants. He may never be able to do it. What if the toxic person is one's parent, one's spouse, one's child, or all of the above?

AN EMOTIONALLY HEALTHY PERSON

For a relationship to be emotionally healthy, it takes two emotionally healthy individuals. Remember what constitutes an emotionally healthy person:

- An emotionally healthy person accepts responsibility for his own happiness and unhappiness and owns his expectations and behaviors. He is able to say "I was wrong," "It was my fault."
- An emotionally healthy person forgives self and others. He or she does not hold grudges nor withhold loving behaviors.
- An emotionally healthy person makes a plan to move ahead in becoming his or her highest and best self, in spite of difficult circumstances. He or she does not act the victim. He or she does not get easily offended.

TOXIC PEOPLE ARE EMOTIONALLY UNHEALTHY

Toxic people are constantly blaming others for their unhappiness. The world they live in is an "if only," and "it could have been" world. Most toxic people are experts in transferring blame. If they are wrong it is because someone else gave them false information or they will define their behavior in such a way as to justify it. They weren't really wrong. It only appeared that way.

Toxic people want freedom to criticize anyone, anywhere because of their unique circumstances. They may assume a role of superior position, wisdom, knowledge, or insight. Another favorite role of toxic people is that of victim or martyr. However, whichever role they choose, they are easily offended and hypersensitive to being criticized themselves. The very reasons they give in criticizing others, they cannot apply to themselves. There is a big-time double standard. They have high expectations of others but resist those same expectations being applied to them.

Frequently a gruff exterior hides toxic people's vulnerability. They are incredibly insecure. They mask their insecurities by claiming to be a "Perfectionist," a "Control Freak," or a "Giver of Constructive Criticism." The victim or martyr uses his status to control others. He does this by defeating all solutions to his problems. A common phrase is "I've tried that and it didn't work."

Most toxic people cannot make a personal progress plan for their own individual lives. In order for them to be happy, everyone in their circle of influence must live according to the toxic person's expectations.

Toxicity comes in degrees. Everyone may recognize a toxic characteristic in themselves. However, when several of these characteristics exist, one may come to the sudden awareness that he or she is a toxic person. Here are some of the common toxic personalties:

AMY, THE PERFECTIONIST

Amy is the mother of five children, two from a previous marriage and three with Phil, her current husband. Amy is a perfectionist. She takes a great deal of pride in being a person of high expectations. Her first two children were girls. They never came to accept Phil. The relationship between Phil and the girls was strained at best, and not close. Amy blamed Phil and resented him for not connecting with her daughters. However, every time Phil attempted to assert himself as a father, Amy would rush to the defense of her daughters. Phil quit trying. This was one more reason Amy was frustrated with Phil. He wasn't involved enough in their lives and when he did involve himself he over-reacted, according to Amy.

The first daughter ran away from home at sixteen and never returned. The second daughter married at seventeen. The premature exodus of these two daughters was blamed on Phil. When the third child, a boy, also left home at sixteen, Amy was perplexed. She wanted to blame Phil but could not quite settle on a reason. When the fourth daughter ran away at sixteen, they wound up in a counselor's office.

Amy came to the realization that although Phil had his problems, she did too. It was a revelation to her that she was the major reason for her children leaving. Her perfectionism had translated into constant criticism. Phil, with all of his shortcomings, had not driven off her oldest two daughters. She had. Her smug attitude about her perfectionism was shattered. Amy worked hard to keep her house looking good. In her mind it was her job to criticize others into helping. The more she criticized, the less they did. When they became lazy, rebellious, and unwilling her criticisms were backed by punishments. The privileges they enjoyed, such as having their friends over for a night, driving the car, going out on weekends, etc., etc., etc., were restricted. All of their freedoms were being curtailed. Being grounded was the norm.

Some of Amy's children were verbally abusive to her. They were "in her face." Two of her children were passively aggressive. They dragged around. They were always late. They left most jobs incomplete. Even when the children did what they thought was a good job, Amy's perfectionism would find something that could have been done better. They were never quite good enough. The result of Amy's constant carping was hopeless alienation. She was emotionally unsafe. Her true feelings of love were never able to break through her aura of negativism. Her habit of criticizing had become a self defeating behavior. In her mind she was right. They were wrong. It was her duty to point out the flaws. She had the truth on her side. Amy was toxic.

There is an axiom in psychology which says the more insecure one is on the inside, the greater the need to control the outside. In order for the control freak to feel good about his or her world, he or she must stay in control of it. This means controlling others. Being a control freak is a form of criticism. The message it sends is, "I must control you because you are not smart enough to control yourself. You are incompetent. You must do as I say because you are not capable on your own."

THE KINGDOM OF LESTER, THE CONTROL FREAK
Lester was an accountant. He was of one religious faith and his wife belonged to another church. They had four daughters. There was no television in their home and only classical music was allowed. There was a very strict dress code enforced. Each of the daughters had a serious list of chores to perform each day. Music lessons were mandatory. One half hour of free time was granted if the day's homework from school had been completed. School let out at 2:20 p.m. and the girls were expected to be home by 2:45. The daily vacuuming, yard work, cleaning and laundry would take an hour and fifteen minutes. At 4:00 p.m. all five women would begin to prepare for the evening meal. Dinner was always formal. There were always cloth napkins and fresh flowers except for a couple of months during the winter when an appropriate potted plant, like a poinsettia, would do. A display of poor manners or laughter at the dinner table would result in one or more of the girls being sent to their rooms without dinner. A mandatory apology was required first. After dinner the girls were sure to be quiet while they cleaned up after the meal. Excessive noise was forbidden. Shoes were not worn in the house but neither was one allowed to go barefoot. Slippers were the preferred standard and stockings were tolerated.

The remainder of the evening was spent practicing the musical instrument chosen by the parents. They were adamant that each daughter learn the piano and one stringed instrument. Guitars were not an option. After music practice it was time for homework. The parents met regularly with the teachers and knew precisely how each girl was doing. At 8:30 p.m. the girls prepared for bed. They were expected to be in their rooms by 9:00 p.m. All lights were out at 9:15 p.m. The father made a personal bed check on each daughter. Each girl had her own room. However, it was made clear that the room was on loan to them. The beds had to be made immediately after arising.

This routine was followed religiously from Monday to Friday. A music lesson after school or a pre-approved school activity would be the only exception. Friends were not permitted in the house except on Saturday afternoons between 12:00 and 4:00 p.m. The girls were not permitted to sleep over at someone else's house and of course, they were not allowed to have friends sleep at their place. The truth is the girls were afraid to have their friends over. They were embarrassed by the strictness of their life style. Even minimum exposure to others at school made them aware of their limited freedom.

When the girls began to be teenagers trouble started. Ironically the oldest was outwardly conforming. However, behind her parent's back she was living a double life. She smoked. She sneaked out of her window at night and was immoral. She had earphones and listened to acid rock when her parents thought she was listening to classical music. She had cleverly exchanged the inside of her personal classical cassettes by opening up the plastic and super-gluing it back. On the outside it read Mozart; on the inside was the obscene music of the "Black Sabbath." Much like her own life, on the outside she was the perfect daughter, on the inside she was "wild thing."

It all came to a point of crisis when the father heard a noise in the house about midnight. He opened the daughter's bedroom door. There he found his daughter and a young man. He went into a rage and ran for his 45 caliber gun. The youth fled from the house. The house was in an exclusive wooded area with a long serpentine driveway. The police report stated as the youth fled, the father pursued, firing his gun as he ran. Large pieces of bark flew as bullets ripped through them. I was the court appointed counselor. The oldest daughter ran away from her parents and lived in a foster home until she was eighteen. The second daughter had an abortion at fifteen and was sent away by the father to live with one of his sisters.

The father, Lester, was a CPA and operated his own business. He had a rigid schedule and few employees would work for him for any extended period of time. He experienced a high turnover. Everything was black or white for Lester. There were few grey areas. Things were right or wrong. Anything that was different from what Lester thought, was wrong! Life was absolute. Everything needed to be done a certain way. It was wrong to paint with simple up and down brush strokes. Lester's way was the right way. It wasn't just a "different" way, but the "right way." "King" Lester could control his world. He had power at home and at work. It was "His way" or "the highway."

People like Lester have a hard time learning that the art of parenting is not the art of hanging on, but the art of letting go. When a baby is born it is helpless. Abandoned, it will die. A parent or caring adult must assume full responsibility for the life of the infant. True parenting involves gradually transferring the responsibility for life to the shoulders of the child. Lester could never let go. His need to control everything extended to the lives of those around him. His control style of parenting did not allow for personal growth. Obedience, conformity and outward performance replaced individual value judgements. The girls had no personal values. They were not allowed to have their own opinions. Therefore, they rebelled. Even in rebellion they had not yet come to their own values. They were only reacting to their father's control of their world.

Tragically, the father died in his mid-forties. The mother immediately changed her hairstyle. Lester liked it only one way. She redecorated the house and started to discover who she was. She loosened up considerably and found out she had a sense of humor. Her marriage to Lester was an exercise in fear. She was constantly afraid of his disappointment or disapproval. She enabled him as a "control freak" out of her own fear. She was equally responsible for supporting this unhealthy environment which tried to force change from the outside.

This was the principle that Lester and his wife did not understand. Criticism is external. Change is internal. Remember the example of the sponge. One can force it to conform by external pressure. The question is, "Has the sponge changed?" No. It has only temporarily altered its shape. As soon as the hands which hold it let go, it will return to its natural state. Threat, intimidation, and criticism are external forces. They may alter behavior in the presence of the critic. However, in the absence of the critic they will find their own way. What most critics fail to recognize is the real issue. The criticized seldom lack knowledge of their weaknesses and flaws. What they lack is a commitment to the value of the critic. No one can change a person who is unwilling to change. Not even fear of death by cancer will stop the smoker who is unwilling to change. **People don't change people. People change themselves or are changed by the Holy Ghost.**

The term "education" comes from the word "educe," meaning to draw forth. True education is that which is drawn from within the person. Change can be encouraged. It can be brought forth by enticing, by inspiring, by rewarding, and by loving. Remember most people do not lack knowledge of their need to change, they lack inspiration to change.

Continued criticism leads to rebellion and stubbornness. It breeds contempt for the critic. Defiance, justification, excuses will abound, but behavior will not change. It engages the giver and receiver of criticism into an adversarial relationship with no winner and two losers. Only when the alcoholic decides for himself on the inside that change is worthwhile, will change take place. All of the external criticism, job loss, or family humiliation will not substitute for a decision which can only be made on the inside.

BELINDA, THE CRITIHOLIC

Belinda was a very hard worker. She gave one hundred and ten percent all the time. She had high expectations of herself and others. She had no time for soap operas or anything unproductive. Her whole value system revolved around the work ethic. Few could match her stride for stride. She was generous and dependable. She received great praise at work from her employers. She had been advanced several times on merit alone. On two of the advancements her replacements were not able to accomplish as much work as she accomplished. Extra workers were hired. Belinda took her work home and would come in nights, work weekends or whatever the job would require. She was a workaholic. From her perspective she was a hard worker, dependable, and reliable. To her family, husband, and friends, she was out of balance.

Belinda gave much of herself and expected others to do the same. All of her relationships were strained. Few wanted her help if it obligated them to her high expectations to return in kind. She was not sought out and yet she worked hard to please.

The problem with Belinda was her tongue. She had no tolerance for the lazy. The slow were only endured. Belinda honestly felt she was entitled to be critical of others. Her hard working efforts gave her the right to be judgmental of others less committed. She felt she did not need their permission to be critical. As a mother and as a wife and as a sister in her own family she found herself alienated and isolated. Not one wanted to be around her. She was devastated and deeply hurt. Not only was she frustrated by their lack of commitment to the work ethic, their rejection of her seemed unwarranted. She felt unappreciated. After all she had done and continued to do, why would she be treated with such aversion?

The issue is not about being a workaholic. It is about being a "critiholic." People who ignore the permission of others before they criticize them are violating the fundamental tenet of relationships, which says, "Common consent is the basis of all healthy relationships." Mutual agreement is a key principle. Parents, employers, and those in authority can get away with criticizing those they command for awhile. However, if common consent is not achieved at some point their relationship will fall apart. Usually, the one criticized will exit first. Children will leave home, desperate to get away from the critical parent. Employees will change jobs or quit. Spouses flee. The commanded avoid the commander.

The "Perfectionist," the "Control Freak," the "Critiholic" who give themselves permission to criticize without receiving the permission of the one criticized are a law unto themselves. Eventually they will be left alone. They will be frustrated. They will live a life of regret and complaint, a life of what should have been. They will feel unappreciated and not valued. Mostly they will be perplexed and puzzled. Do they change? Maybe. Mostly they continue to give themselves permission to be "Constructively Critical."

THE TOXIC'S CREED

Give me your emotionally poor, your hyper-criticized hungry for acceptance, your fearful low self-esteemed huddled masses yearning to breathe free and be loved. I will constructively criticize them into being emotionally rich, self actualized, filled to the eyelids with self confidence. They will brim with love for self and others. No longer will they be huddled masses yearning to breathe free. This I will do. I will point out their areas of needed improvement. I will focus on their weaknesses. I will shine the light of truth on the unacceptable. I will concentrate on the flaw and remove their blemishes. All I need are willing subjects who can see the wisdom of my counsel.

SHARON WANTED TO BE LOVED

Sharon wanted to be loved. She wanted her husband, Aaron, to be happy. One of her dearly held values was a peaceful home where everyone was kind and people "got along" with each other. To Sharon, this meant one sacrificed what one wanted for the greater good. No matter how hard Sharon tried, however, she was unable to accomplish her dream.

Aaron was constantly criticizing Sharon. She couldn't try hard enough. Not matter what she did it didn't quite measure up to Aaron's expectations. Sharon was convinced that if she tried harder, then her efforts would be enough for Aaron. Sharon was a co-dependent who felt responsible to make Aaron happy. She could not do it, but she kept going back. She just wanted affection, acceptance, and appreciation for trying and for accomplishing what she did. She wanted no more nor less. Sharon, however, kept coming for her approval to a "toxic source"—her unhappy and "never-pleased," husband, Aaron.

When I talked to Sharon, we started immediately on a program where she accepted responsibility only for her own happiness and for her own unhappiness. I explained to Sharon, "You are not responsible for Aaron's happiness, nor his unhappiness, Sharon. That is his choice. You are hereby released from trying to make him happy. If he is unhappy, that also is his choice.

"Sharon, for the purpose of our discussion, I want you to think about a 'goal' as something over which you have control. It depends solely upon you. A 'wish,' Sharon, is an expectation that depends upon others for its fulfillment. According to this definition, is making Aaron happy a goal or a wish?"

"It's a wish," she said.

"Is making yourself happy a goal or a wish?"

"It's a goal, because it depends upon me," she responded.

"Is getting acceptance, affection, appreciation, and love from Aaron a goal or a wish?"

"It's a wish," she said dejectedly.

"Sharon, it is your own expectations that are setting you up for failure. They are based on a false premise that if you are good enough you will receive acceptance. Remember how all frustration comes from unmet expectations? You are going to a dry well for water and no matter how many trips you take to the well, your expectation for water is never going to be met. Aaron is a dry well. You have one hundred per cent control over being a loving person. That's a worthy goal. You have no control of being loved by others. That's a wish.

"If you choose to stay in this relationship with Aaron, you will have to change the rules of engagement. You will need to establish a new set of goals which truly depend upon your doing what **you** can. It is up to you, Sharon, to take control of your happiness and commit to one objective— to become your highest and best self. You have your own natural resources, your own gifts, talents and abilities to accomplish this task. Your expectations must be reasonable and within your sphere of control. Do not depend upon Aaron for your acceptance.

"Sharon, let's go over some ground rules which will allow you to stay married to Aaron and to survive a 'Toxic Personality':

"*Become emotionally healthy yourself*. This means you accept responsibility for being a happy person, an unhappy person, and for your behavior. You own it. You do not need to make Aaron happy. You cannot, even if he agreed. He alone is responsible for his happiness and unhappiness. It's his choice. It's your choice to take control of your life and to forgive yourself for your past. You must also make your own plan to become a higher and better self, independent of Aaron, or of anyone else. Regardless of the past, you have positive choices in the present. Do not trade happiness for pity nor sympathy. It's a poor trade. Many do it everyday. It is a copout. Give yourself permission to be emotionally healthy.

"*Define your own standard of excellence*. In other words, define what is enough for **you**. Do not let everyone else set the parameters of what a good mother is, what a good wife is, what a good person is. Let go of the expectation of measuring up to their definition, their wants, their needs, their expectations. The way to release yourself is to stop trying to PLEASE them in order to be loved by them. Co-dependents find it hard to let go of wanting to please others and frequently wind up becoming enablers.

"*Let others accept responsibility for their own happiness*. As long as you act in such a way that gives them the impression that you have the power to make them happy or unhappy, why should they accept responsibility for their life? When things go wrong, they will blame you. It's your fault. 'You should have...,' or 'shouldn't have...,' 'you need to...,' or 'didn't need to...,' 'you ought to have...,' or 'ought not to have....' They will transfer to you the responsibility for their unhappiness if you let them. It's so easy for others to blame you for their lack of happiness. That is what 'Toxic People' do.

*"Live to your **own definition** of enough. You can at least please yourself. If your expectation is 'pleasing others' you have no control over doing so, because the toxic personality will keep redefining the standard in such a way that you can never measure up. The thing to keep in mind about a toxic person is that you are 'darned if you do' or 'darned if you don't.' They are going to be frustrated with you, regardless of your behavior. You cannot be governed by their frustration. Most toxic people use their frustration with others as one of their tools of manipulation, of control, of intimidation. Toxic people have endless lists of expectations. Just as you get close to doing everything on the list, Aaron will change the list. He can never let you 'be enough.'*

"Sharon, when you see the insanity of this treadmill, you will come to realize that toxic people are 'crazy makers.' They drive you crazy trying to please them. The crazier your life becomes, the more in control they become, and because you are going crazy, the focus can be on your aberrant behavior. 'You' are the one out of your mind, and 'they' are the ones who are justified. Most toxic people were raised that way in their families. They were never enough as individuals, as children, as siblings, so, 'what's the big deal'? Not measuring up, not being enough, trailing barbs, constant criticism, blame-fixing, this is normal."

If Sharon chooses to stay in this relationship with toxic Aaron, she will have ample opportunity to practice the "art of receiving his criticisms." In addition she will need to set up her own goals for improvement wherein the judge and jury of her performance is herself. She already knows what the verdict will be for anything she does as judged by Aaron. It won't be enough for him! But it will be enough for Sharon. At last, Sharon can succeed. The rules of the game cannot be changed arbitrarily. The boundaries cannot be shifted. There will be a chance for success if Sharon takes control of her own mental health and sets her own standards of excellence.

The solution for Sharon is to commit to become her highest and best self and to embark upon a solo course to becoming emotionally healthy. Sharon committed to apply the rules she learned for surviving a toxic personality. Armed with new determination and a "fresh writing pad," she was ready to deal with Aaron's complaints.

One of Aaron's main complaints was about Sharon's housekeeping. Aaron's standard of housekeeping as stated to the counselor was, "I'm reasonable. I just want a clean house." The unstated, unrealistic expectation by Aaron was, "Anything less than perfection will be criticized."

Sharon's standard of housekeeping was "I'm reasonable. The house is clean, but not clutter-free. I like to keep some of my projects out where I can see them. It reminds me of what I need and want to do with them."

Sharon reviewed the criticism of Aaron and set her ego aside and determined it was not reasonable to have several projects out in the open all the time. After thinking about it and talking it over with one of her friends she came up with a plan to obtain some orange boxes, label them, and place her different projects in them. She decided she would only keep one project out at a time. The other undertakings would have to be stored and rotated. This now became Sharon's personal standard of excellence.

Aaron's actual words when he found out about Sharon's plans to put her projects in orange boxes and store them were, "That's great. I'm really proud of you, but why don't you put all the projects in boxes and only take out the one you want while you are working on it, and then put it away also?" [Notice the "trailing barb"].

If Sharon's expectation was to please Aaron, she would be disappointed by his response. In Aaron's mind, Sharon's solution was a step in the right direction, but it wasn't "quite good enough."

As a counselor I told her, "It will take time and practice to free yourself from feeling disappointed with Aaron's responses,"

Sharon asked me, "How am I supposed to respond to a trailing barb?"

"Why don't you smile when he gives you a trailing barb and say in your heart, "That's Aaron."

"Your verbal reaction to Aaron could choose to focus on the positive part of his statement. "I'm glad you were proud of me. Frankly, I"m proud of myself and I feel good about it."

"Don't respond to the negative trailing barb. Ignore it, when you choose to comment on it, you are reinforcing its worth. If he won't let it go and continues to fuss and fume over the one project you have out at a time, acknowledge his frustration and continued criticism by saying, 'I'm sorry you're still frustrated over my one project being out, but it's just the price you pay for being married to a wonderful person like me!' Your resolve must be firm and consistent. If you waffle or give in, you will only encourage his criticism."

Another area of expectation for Aaron was about Sharon's level of education. Aaron had expressed, "I think Sharon needs to get a Bachelor's Degree. It will make her more marketable if something happens to me. Also, women who are college educated are more interesting to talk to."

Sharon's response was, "I don't want to take the time to go back to college right now. I want to be a wife and a mother. I'd rather increase your insurance or look at some other options."

Sharon reviewed the criticism of Aaron and set her ego aside to evaluate his concern. "Education is important and it would make me a better self if I were to expand my mind. I have time to do something, but I don't have the time or the will to be a full-time student." Sharon pondered her options. She visited with some friends and family. She bounced some ideas off them to see if she was being reasonable. Finally she explored her proposal with Aaron, the toxic, who she knew in advance would not find her solution "good enough." This time it was not his acceptance she sought, but to inform him of the options she could support.

Sharon set her own standard, her own goal. She decided she would like to be a trained real estate agent and was committed to go to school to do so. This would give her a career which she could rely upon if needed. Also, she could work at her own pace.

Aaron's actual statement was, "You never do what I want yo to do. Why can't you just once do it my way?"

*The answer to Aaron's question was this, "Because you are toxic, Aaron. Even if I were to sacrifice my total identity to what you think I should, need, and ought to be, I would still not be enough. You would still be dissatisfied with me and both of us would be miserable. I can't be responsible for your happiness nor your unhappiness, Aaron. I'm trying really hard to be responsible for my own happiness. **That's why I can't do it your way. I can only do what I can do.**"*

I shared with Sharon the story found in the Gospels, about a woman who knelt at Jesus' feet. She washed his feet with her tears and dried them with the hairs of her head. She had a very costly alabaster box of ointment. Judas Iscariot upbraided her for wasting this resource worth more than a man's wages for three hundred days. The Savior rebuked Judas with the following words:

> *Let her alone; why trouble ye her . . , **She hath done what she could**. (Mark 14:6, 8.)*

The Lord's standard of excellence is not perfection. It is to do what one can. I read these verses to Sharon and she seemed to derive hope in them. This particular relationship improved because Sharon set her own standard. In doing so, she defined enough for herself and measured up to her own expectations of what a good person would do in her circumstances.

WHAT IS THE LOVING THING TO DO?

Toxic people need love too. They may not deserve one's love based upon their conduct. Being a loving person is a choice one makes to live life as a caring person. One must evaluate the level of trust one can invest in each relationship. Remember, trust and love are two separate issues. Trust is the "fruit" of responsible behavior. Trust is a conditional investment. Loving can be an unconditional investment. The loving thing to do with toxic people may be to stay as far away from them as one can. Being a loving person does not require one to be stupid or unguarded. It does not require one to trust those who have demonstrated they are not worthy of that trust.

Being a loving person and doing the "loving thing" will depend upon one's ability to protect himself from toxic people. They are toxic because one cannot get from them what he wants. They are a dry well from which one cannot extract water. They are what they are. It does no good to become angry with them or to hate them. It will not change them. One must let go of the expectation one possesses for them to be different than they are. Once one accepts this reality, he or she can make a choice to love them. It is appropriate to mourn the loss of the relationship which "should have been." It is emotionally unhealthy to pretend the relationship is something it is not and may never be. Wisdom dictates that once people accept the way things are, have been, and will yet be, they have accepted the truth of his or her relationship with the toxic person. Let God be responsible to change the toxic heart.

A WAY TO EVALUATE

Sometimes, people are so close to the problem, or are so emotionally involved, they lose all sense of perspective. Here is a helpful tool in evaluating what one should do when one is confused.

Imagine you are counseling your own child, who comes to you with the identical problem you face. Your child explains to you in precise detail the nature of his or her concerns, which mirrors exactly what you face. Next, your child asks, "What would you counsel me to do? I will not hold you accountable because the decision is mine alone. I just want your honest opinion. Should I leave or should I stay and work on it?"

Knowing what you know, how would you counsel your own child? My experience tells me people will counsel their children with more objectivity than they will allow themselves in the same situation. Sometimes one tolerates an intolerable situation that one would never ask one of his children to endure.

CHECKLIST FOR
PREPARING ONE'S SELF
TO DEAL WITH TOXIC PERSONALITIES

- ☐ Affirm one's desire to become his or her highest and best self.
- ☐ Let go of the expectation that the toxic person will give what one wants, i.e., acceptance, love, approval.
- ☐ Define one's own standard of excellence.
- ☐ Define "enough" in specific terms.
- ☐ Ask oneself, "What would a good and loving person do?"
- ☐ Ask oneself, "How would I counsel my child in this exact circumstance?"Follow your own counsel.

The toxic person may be a father or mother, brother or sister, a son or a daughter, a spouse, or an in-law. One will have to devise a plan which will keep him emotionally safe during the interactions that normal living will thrust upon him. Remove any expectations to ever be enough in that person's eyes.

SANDY AND HER MOTHER-IN-LAW

Carol is a classic mother-in-law who feels no one is good enough for her Jeff. She truly believes that Sandy seduced Jeff into marrying him and that Jeff married below his potential. Sandy has never felt accepted by Carol. They can make small talk with each other, but they both feel a cautious reserve. Carol is openly critical behind Sandy's back about her skills as a wife, mother. Sandy tolerates her mother-in-law, but is deeply hurt by her statements which find their way back to Sandy's ears via a sister-in-law and other family and mutual friends.

Jeff is aware of both his mother's disapproval and of Sandy's hostilities because of it. He feels constantly torn between them. He feels everything is a test of his loyalties between being a son and a husband. He is always hearing his mother dropping hints about how he should insist that Sandy do a better job. Sandy is equally open in telling Jeff about his mother's weaknesses of being critical, overbearing, and interfering. Sandy also expects Jeff to defend her by standing up to his mother and telling her to "butt out" of their lives.

Carol, the mother-in-law, is always buying gifts for Jeff and her grandchildren and her favorite daughters-in-law who bow to her wishes. Sandy feels she can't compete and purposely discourages any relationship with Carol and her grandchildren as a form of punishment for Carol's inappropriate conduct.

WHAT IS THE LOVING THING FOR SANDY TO DO WITH CAROL, THE TOXIC MOTHER-IN-LAW?

First, Sandy would have to be willing to commit to be her highest and best self in this situation. She needed to let go of the expectation that she would ever be enough for Carol. Next, Sandy would need to set her own standard of excellence and acceptance as a wife and mother and daughter-in-law. Sandy decided she would invite Carol over for dinner once a month with the family. She felt it would be a good idea to organize, with the other daughters-in-law, a surprise birthday party for Carol. Sandy agreed to a number of things that were reasonable, not because Carol deserved it or because she was looking for any approval from Carol, but because Sandy was a good person. She imagined how she would counsel her own daughter in an identical situation and then followed her own counsel. But what else would be the loving thing to do?

Sandy was counseled to let Carol have her own "lousy" or "good" relationship with her son, Jeff, and with her grandchildren. She was advised to ignore Carol's critical comments by saying to herself and others, "That's Carol" and nothing more. The catty thing to do would have been to criticize her mother-in-law and speak ill of her to Jeff and others, constantly pointing out her flaws and short comings. The loving thing to do would be to ignore the mother-in-law's caustic comments and behavior and to encourage a healthy relationship with Jeff and the grandchildren.

"Sandy, do not force Jeff to choose between yourself and his mother. You would only be resented for doing so. Rise above ever speaking ill of Carol to Jeff. His mother will not change and Jeff cannot change her. Don't expect Jeff to defend you or to stand up to his mother. Let him define for himself his relationship as a son."

Sandy hated going over to Carol's home because Carol would spend the whole time doting on Jeff. She would wait on him hand and foot. No wonder Jeff enjoyed going over to his mothers. She did the same with the grandchildren, but expected Sandy to work in the kitchen or join with her in waiting upon the rest of the family. Sandy would complain all the way there and back in the car, and while they were in Carol's home, Sandy would bristle with quiet frustration. Jeff and the kids had a better time when Sandy did not go along.

I suggested the loving thing for Sandy to do was to go and have a good attitude, BUT if she could not, then to stay home and do something she would like to do. "Send them off to Carol's with a smile and receive them back with gladness. Don't sulk, nor pout, nor play the role of a martyr. In this way you remain in control of your life and avoid setting up unnecessary competition with Carol."

"Sandy, focus on being your own person and meet your own standard of a good wife and mother and even a good daughter-in-law. This is the loving thing to do. All human relationships are composed of two people. One can only be one half of any relationship to which he or she is a party. In a non-toxic relationship one can enjoy emotional closeness and both give and receive loving behavior. In a toxic relationship one can still be a loving person, but one must protect him or herself by drawing boundaries with which they are comfortable.

"Sandy, define for yourself a one-sided program where you are willing to gift unconditional acts of kindness. Do this, not because Carol "deserves" it, but because you are a loving person. To act in this manner fulfills the Lord's invitation."

Everyone wants to love and be loved. It has already been established that being loved by others is a wish, a worthwhile wish, but out of one's control. Being a loving person is a goal within one's grasp. **Loving** depends upon self but **being loved** depends upon others. Putting one's focus on being a loving person gives internal peace and the power of self-mastery.

JESUS TAUGHT

Ye have heard that it hath been said, Thou shalt love thy neighbour, and hate thine enemy.

But I say unto you, Love your enemies, bless them that curse you, do good to them that hate you, and pray for them which despitefully use you, and persecute you;

That ye may be the children of your Father which is in heaven: for he maketh his sun to rise on the evil and on the good, and sendeth rain on the just and on the unjust.

For if ye love them which love you, what reward have ye? Do not even the publicans the same?

And if ye salute your brethren only, what do ye more than other? do not even the publicans so?

Be ye there perfect, even as your Father which is in heaven is perfect (Matthew 5:43-48).

This particular scripture requires the disciple of Christ to live a higher law. It is the "Law of Love." It is consistent with "The Greatest Revelation That God Has Ever Given To Man." Toxic people are wonderful guinea pigs upon which the Christian ideal can be practiced. They are "your enemy." They do "curse you," "hate you," and "despitefully use you." This wonderful scripture concludes by saying, "Be ye therefore perfect, even as your Father, which is in Heaven, is perfect." In this context, being perfect is not about being obedient. It is about being loving. The entire paragraph, starting with verse 43 to verse 48 is talking about becoming a loving person (Matthew 5:43-48). The intent of the scripture is to say, "Be ye therefore perfect [in loving], even as your Father which is in Heaven is perfect [in loving]." This brings the discussion about "Giving and Receiving Criticism in The Lord's Own Way" full circle. It is not about finding fault. It is about loving! It is about surviving as a Disciple of Christ in a telestial world. It's about living in the world, but not being a part of the world. It is not an "eye for an eye" and a "tooth for a tooth." It's about living in the real world and applying the principles of righteousness. It's about calling upon the powers of Heaven. It's finding out there is power in living the Gospel of Jesus Christ.

CHAPTER TWELVE

THE END AND A NEW BEGINNING

Frequently, people will ask, "Where was this information when I needed it thirty years ago?"

My answer is, "It's never too late for a new beginning." Jesus Christ demonstrated the power of loving words. There are children and grandchildren, friends and neighbors, who are starving for the want of kind words. This work closes with the words of modern prophets.

President Thomas S. Monson bore a fervent testimony to the importance of giving loving words and of having a positive outlook towards life.

PRESIDENT THOMAS S. MONSON
There are hearts to gladden. There are kind words to say.
(General Conference Report, October 1965, p. 143.)

LET US OFT SPEAK KIND WORDS
Let us oft speak kind words to each to other
At home or where e'er we may be;
Like the warblings of birds on the heather,
The tones will be welcome and free.
They'll gladden the heart that's repining,
Give courage and hope from above,
And where the dark clouds hide the shining,
Let in the bright sunlight of love.

Like the sunbeams of morn on the mountains,
The soul they awake to good cheer;
Like the murmur of cool, pleasant fountains,
They fall in sweet cadences near.
Let's oft, then, in kindly toned voices,
Our mutual friendship renew,
Till heart meets with heart and rejoices
In friendship that ever is true.

Oh, the kind words we give
Shall in memory live
And sunshine forever impart.
Let us oft speak kind words to each other;
Kind words are sweet tones of the heart.
(Joseph L. Townsend, text; LDS Hymn Book, # 232, 1985.)

PRESIDENT GORDON B. HINCKLEY

What a wonderful time to be alive. How enthusiastic I feel . . . I hope you are enthusiastic, because there is a terrible ailment of pessimism in the land. It's almost endemic. We're constantly fed a steady and sour diet of character assassination, fault finding, evil speaking one of another. . . The tragedy is that this spirit of negativism seems to prevail throughout the country. . .

This spirit has infected the atmosphere on university campuses and the workplace, even this campus. The snide remark, the sarcastic jibe, the cutting down of associates—these too often are the essence of our conversation. In our home, wives weep and children finally give up under the barrage of criticism leveled by husbands and fathers. Criticism is the forerunner of divorce, the cultivator of rebellion, sometimes a catalyst that leads to failure. Even in the church it sows the seed of inactivity and, finally, in many cases, apostasy.

I come this evening with a plea that we stop seeking out the storms and enjoy more fully the sunlight. I'm suggesting that we accentuate the positive. I'm asking that we look a little deeper for the good, that we still our voices of insult and sarcasm, that we more generously compliment virtue and effort.

I'm not asking that all criticism be silent . . . I am not suggesting that our conversation be all honey . . . What I am suggesting and asking is that we turn from the negativism that so permeates our society and look for the remarkable good in the land and times in which we live: that we speak of one another's virtues more than we speak of one another's faults; that optimism replaces pessimism.

Let our faith replace our fears. When I was a boy, my father often said to us, "Cynics do not contribute, skeptics do not create, doubters do not achieve."

There is too much fruitless, carping criticism . . .

In our individual circumstances, let us look for and cultivate the wonders of our opportunities. . . . It is so easy, under the pressure of the daily grind, to become negative and critical, to be shortsighted and go down in defeat. . . .

On one occasion when the Savior was walking among a crowd, a woman who had been long sick touched his garment. He perceived that strength had gone out of him. The strength that was his had strengthened her. So it may be with each of us. Let me urge you to desist from making cutting remarks one to another. Rather, cultivate the art of complimenting, of strengthening, of encouraging. . . .

It is a responsibility divinely laid upon each of us to bear one another's burdens, to strengthen one another, to encourage one another, to lift one another, to look for the good in one another, and to emphasize that good. There is not a man or woman in this vast assembly who cannot be depressed on the one hand, or lifted on the other, by the remarks of his or her associates. . . .

All of this seems to say to me . . . every one of whom later became great, might have done much better . . . had he received less of criticism and more of encouragement.

My dear young friends, don't partake of the spirit of our times. Look for the good and build on it. There is so much of the sweet and the decent and the good to build upon.

You are partakers of the gospel of Jesus Christ. The gospel means "good news." The message of the Lord is one of hope and salvation. The voice of the Lord is a voice of gladness. The work of the Lord is a work of glorious and certain reward. I do not suggest that you simply put on rose-colored glasses to make the world look rosy. I ask, rather, that you look above and beyond the negative, the critical, the cynical, the doubtful, to the positive (President Gordon B. Hinckley, Fireside, BYU Marriott Center, Sunday, March 6, 1994, underlining mine).

About The Author

Dr. John Lewis Lund is a native of Olympia, Washington. After his mission to Mexico, he returned to complete a B.A. degree in Sociology at Brigham Young University, where he also completed a Master's degree in education. A second Master's degree was pursued at the University of Washington in Seattle. It was there he determined to study Interpersonal Relationships. His doctoral work at the University of Washington in "Interaction Analysis" produced a book entitled Avoiding Emotional Divorce. In 1972, Brigham Young University awarded him the degree of Doctor of Education.

Brother Lund has been employed as an educator for the Church Education System since 1965. His assignments have taken him on a thirty year journey throughout Washington, Idaho, California, and Utah. He has served as an Institute of Religion Director adjacent to Utah State University, The University of Idaho, and the University of Washington. Currently he is an instructor at the University Institute adjacent to the University of Utah.

Because of his special work in "Interaction Analysis and Transactional Analysis" he has served throughout the last thirty years as a marriage and family counselor in Washington, California, and Idaho. In Utah, Dr. Lund also holds three certifications as an arbitrator, a mediator, and a negotiator. He was asked to serve for five years in the State of Washington as a Family Court Commissioner.

His Church service includes being a Bishop in Olympia, Washington, a Bishop in Moscow, Idaho, and a member of a Stake Presidency in Logan, Utah. After several High Councils, he presently teaches a Sunday School class, in Murray, Utah.

Brother Lund and his wife, Bonnie Gertsch of Midway, Utah, are the parents of eight children, i.e., John Jay, Robert Earl, Heidi Savage, Kaari Smith, David Eric, Kristi, Chariti, and Joseph Ammon. They range in age from thirty-two to eighteen. The five married children have blessed them with eleven grandchildren and wonderful spouses.

INFORMATION ABOUT OTHER BOOKS AND AUDIO CASSETTE TAPES BY DR. JOHN L. LUND

Write to:
The Communications Company
P.O. Box 57008
Salt Lake City, Utah 84123

Phone Orders
1-888-DrJ-Lund
(1-888-375-5863)

BOOKS:

The Art of Giving And Receiving Criticism $14.95

The Parables of Jesus $14.95

Avoiding Emotional Divorce . . . . $ 9.95

AUDIO CASSETTE TAPES:

Human Intimacy (1 cassette) . . . . $ 9.95

The Art of Giving and Receiving Criticism (4 cassettes) $24.95

The Art of Parenting Teens and Other Miracles (4 cassettes) $24.95

Relationships and Communications (4 cassettes) $24.95

True Disciples of Christ (4 cassettes) $24.95

Parables of Jesus (4 cassettes) $24.95

The Faces of Eve (4 cassettes) $24.95

Utah residents add sales tax (6.25%)

Shipping and handling . . . . $ 4.00